IN
QUEST
OF
JESUS

IN
QUEST
OF
JESUS

Revised and Enlarged Edition

W. BARNES TATUM

ABINGDON PRESS
NASHVILLE

IN QUEST OF JESUS

Library of Congress Cataloging-in-Publication Data

Tatum, W. Barnes.
  In quest of Jesus / W. Barnes Tatum. — Rev. and enl. ed.
     p. cm.
  Includes bibliographical references and index.
  ISBN 0-687-05633-0 (alk. paper)
  1. Jesus Christ—Historicity. 2. Bible. N.T. Gospels—Criticism, interpretation, etc. I. Title.
BT303.2.T35   1999
232.9—dc21   99-12264
                                                                        CIP

Quotations of Eusebius on pages 27 and 29 are reprinted by permission of the publishers and the Loeb Classical Library from EUSEBIUS: THE ECCLESIASTICAL HISTORY translated by Kirsopp Lake and J. E. L. Oulton, 2 volumes, Cambridge, Mass.: Harvard University Press, 1926, 1932.

Passages on pages 100-101 from Ernst Käsemann, *Essays on New Testament Themes*, SCM Press, 1964, are quoted by permission of SCM Press, London, England.

The map on page 22 is from Mitchell G. Reddish, *An Introduction to the Gospels*, copyright © 1997 by Abingdon Press.

Quotations on pages 93-94 reprinted from REIMARUS: FRAGMENTS, edited by Charles H. Talbert, are copyright © 1970 Fortress Press. Used by permission of Augsburg Fortress.

Scripture quotations, unless otherwise indicated, are from the New Revised Standard Version Bible, copyright © 1989, by the Division of Christian Education of the National Council of the Churches of Christ in the United States of America.

Scripture quotations noted NEB are from *The New English Bible.* © The Delegates of the Oxford University Press and The Syndics of the Cambridge University Press 1961, 1970. Reprinted by permission.

99 00 01 02 03 04 05 06 07 08 — 10 9 8 7 6 5 4 3 2 1

MANUFACTURED IN THE UNITED STATES OF AMERICA

To My Mentors

at

The University of St. Andrews, Duke University,

and Yeshiva University

Robert McL. Wilson

Matthew Black

Hugh Anderson

Kenneth W. Clark

John Strugnell

W. D. Davies

Louis H. Feldman

Preface to
Revised Edition

"But there are also many other things that Jesus did; if every one of them were written down, I suppose that the world itself could not contain the books that would be written" (John 21:25). I quoted these concluding words from the Gospel of John as the opening lines of the preface to the first edition of this book.

On that occasion, in 1982, I observed how the author of these concluding words from John could not have imagined the myriad upon myriad of books to be produced over the centuries in response to what Jesus did. Now, in 1999, I must admit that neither could I imagine the renewed interest in Jesus research that would produce another myriad of Jesus books over the next decade and result in my *In Quest of Jesus: A Guidebook* remaining in print for fifteen years.

Many books about Jesus focus their attention primarily on the Gospels that testify to his life. Other books about Jesus survey the different ways historians have reconstructed the events in his life. This volume embraces both approaches and considers, throughout, the interrelationship between literary study of the Gospels and historical research into the career of Jesus.

This book is written for the general reader, although it communicates the diverse findings of professional scholarship. It is designed to be an introduction to a serious study of the Gospels and intensive research into the life of

Jesus. No one who writes about the Gospels and Jesus, of course, can completely escape one's own scholarly and confessional commitments. But I have tried, so far as possible, to keep my predilections in the background. Thus this book is designed to function as a guide that will encourage in its readers the development and refinement of their own viewpoints, in academic and church settings or through solitary perusal.

Personal acknowledgments are in order. I continue to be indebted to those undergraduate students at Greensboro College who have often become the teachers as I have become their student. Students in my New Testament courses should find themselves familiar with much of this material, including the expansions of the book beyond the first edition.

Special mention should be made of Chris Frilingos, who has offered a number of helpful suggestions during the rewriting process. He became acquainted with the first edition in my Jesus course at Greensboro College. Subsequently he used the book, in its British edition, as a graduate student at the University of St. Andrews, Scotland. More recently, as a doctoral student at the University of North Carolina at Chapel Hill, he adopted it as a textbook for the Jesus course he was teaching.

Colleagues who used the book on other campuses have made helpful comments along the way. These include Dennis C. Duling of Canisius College, Marcus J. Borg of Oregon State University, Daryl Schmidt of Texas Christian University, John L. White of Loyola University of Chicago, and Mahlon Smith of Rutgers University.

My participation in the Jesus Seminar for more than a decade has enabled me to engage in regular, ongoing, formal conversations about the many issues in Gospel scholarship and Jesus research discussed herein. The good humor of these conversations has not belied their seriousness. I am grateful to Robert W. Funk for having nurtured this working forum and for other friendships developed with fellow scholars as well as with nonacademics who have associated themselves with the seminar.

Members of St. Timothy's United Methodist Church in Greensboro, since its inception under the pastoral leadership of Kenneth H. Carter, have given further expression of the widespread interest in Jesus scholarship and the relationship of this scholarship to their own spiritual journeys. These members include Linda W. Tatum, who has contributed hours of discussion and technical recommendations at many points during my rewriting and writing.

Support of various kinds for this volume has also come from Greensboro College. Philip A. Rolnick and Rhonda Burnette-Bletsch, faculty colleagues, have given encouragement by telling me to get on with it and then facilitating that process. Stephen Ford, Tony Wyatt, Patricia Humburg, and Elizabeth Bernhardt have done what librarians do best, a lot of everything. Pam McKirdy, who oversees the library, and Brian O'Connell have provided computer assistance at crucial moments in the production process. Daniel N. Keck, Dean of the Faculty, has extended tangible affirmation by facilitating a grant from The Royce and Jane Reynolds Endowment Fund for Faculty Development to underwrite expenses related to preparation of the manuscript.

I have chosen to dedicate the book to my own professional mentors who, through their scholarly careers, passed on to me a life of teaching, research, and writing.

W. Barnes Tatum
Greensboro College
Greensboro, North Carolina

Contents

PART THREE: CONTINUING ISSUES IN THE LIFE AND MINISTRY OF JESUS

CHARTS AND DIAGRAMS

Introduction
Who Is Jesus?

To come of age in the United States is to have some familiarity with Jesus and his story. This remains true for persons without church affiliation as well as those with church membership, even though this nation has become increasingly diverse culturally since the outwardly conformist 1950s.

Christian churches and Jewish synagogues, which have long dotted the American religious landscape, have been joined—particularly in metropolitan areas—by Muslim mosques, Hindu and Buddhist temples, and Sikh gurdwaras. Nonetheless, this nation continues to be culturally very much a "Christian" country. Perhaps only the non-Christian in the United States or an American who has invested time in a non-Christian society—such as Saudi Arabia or village India—can fully appreciate how Christian is this "one nation under God."

The public calendar divides time and history into two periods. Although the designations B.C.E. (Before the Common Era) and C.E. (Common Era) are now often used in place of the explicitly Christian B.C. and A.D., the coming of Jesus some two thousand years ago still marks the transition from the earlier to the later periods. And the new millennium, 2001 and all of that, has triggered in some sectors of Christianity the eager expectation of the second coming of Jesus. Sunday, the Christian day of worship, still constitutes the traditional day of rest and anchors two-, three-, or four-day weekends. Other church "holy days," Christmas and Easter, continue to serve as focal points for two of the more important holiday seasons.

The mass media serve to keep the Jesus story before the public. The evangelistic appeals and worship programs on radio and television have multiplied as cablevision has expanded. The electronic church of the 1980s has been complemented by religious web sites and chat rooms in the 1990s. Over the past half-century, the name of Billy Graham has taken its place alongside those of Fulton J. Sheen, Billy Sunday, and Dwight L. Moody in the galaxy of American religious stars. Newspapers regularly provide information about church services and activities. Saturday editions throughout the country devote sizable sections to religious news. Weekly magazines often feature those "hot" topics that deal with Jesus-related issues. Even occasions of seem-

15

ingly inexplicable tragedy, in their own disturbing ways, serve as reminders of this country's religious heritage. For example, the fate of the Branch Davidians in Waco in 1993 and of the Heaven's Gate cult in California in 1997 received front page coverage in the press and prime-time reporting on television.

The variety of pointers to Jesus has no limit in a commercially oriented society that perceives profit as well as salvation in the Jesus story. Billboards shout: "Jesus is Lord—accept him as your Savior today." Bumper stickers read: "I ♥ Jesus." Magnets more modestly announce: "Jesus is coming soon! Look busy!" Then there are the T-shirts, some from "God's Gym" showing Jesus bench-pressing the cross, and the fashionable jewelry in the shape of a Christian cross, something the Romans probably did not anticipate.

Jesus has also done Broadway and Hollywood; or Hollywood and Broadway have done Jesus.[1] The cinematic spectacles of the 1960s, Samuel Bronston's *King of Kings* (1961) and George Stevens's *Greatest Story Ever Told* (1965) gave way to more contemporary musicals of the 1970s. Both the Tim Rice/Andrew Lloyd Webber rock opera *Jesus Christ Superstar* and the John-Michael Tebelak/Stephen Schwartz musical *Godspell* made it to the screen after various stagings. Then on successive Sunday evenings during the Easter season of 1977, a large American television audience experienced the premier showing of Franco Zeffirelli's made-for-television film *Jesus of Nazareth*. Zeffirelli's visual adaptation of the Jesus story continues its run during appropriate holiday seasons. The musical *Godspell* remains a favorite offering by local stage companies and school drama troupes. The rock opera *Jesus Christ Superstar* was revived for a twenty-fifth anniversary tour and even starred members from the initial stage and screen productions.

Rare is the person, therefore, who does not possess some understanding of Jesus or hold some opinion about him. You, the reader, bring to this book a prior perspective on him. You, too, are already able to respond to the question "Who is Jesus?"

To sit down with pen and paper, or before a computer screen, and to respond in writing to the Jesus question, drawing exclusively on your existing understanding, represents one way of reminding yourself of your mental portrayal of Jesus. Or to examine the statements of others about Jesus is a way of discovering their mental portrayals. But whether the statement about Jesus belongs to you or to someone else, one thing is quite certain: that expression will reveal as much about the author as it will about Jesus. To write or to speak about Jesus inescapably involves laying bare our own knowledge and commitments as well as the understandings and values of our generation. What we say, or what we refrain from saying, is self-revealing. People do tend to make Jesus over in their own images. In our day and in ages past, persons have approached Jesus and his story from various angles.

In his monumental volume *Jesus Through the Centuries: His Place in the History of Culture* (1985), Jaroslav Pelikan presents, roughly in chronological order, a series of eighteen different ways Jesus has been viewed in the history of culture.[2] He draws on a vast array of cultural evidence—literary and visual. Although not reproducing Pelikan's categories or his evidence, we will briefly review four angles from which people have approached Jesus and the resulting characterizations of him. Each characterization highlights a particular dimension of his life and ministry.

Jesus the Dying Savior. Some people reduce Jesus' significance to his atoning death on the cross. "Jesus came to die for my sins," they say. They express little interest in his ethical teachings or his miraculous deeds. This view of Jesus, a dominant tendency across the years, underlies the influential treatise on the atonement by Anselm the Archbishop of Canterbury (died 1109), *Cur Deus Homo*. He explained why God became human in Jesus. But no one celebrated Jesus as dying Savior with any greater verve than did Charles Wesley.

The poet laureate of the eighteenth-century Methodist revival in England, Charles Wesley wrote the words for over six thousand hymns. His hymns disclose him to be a person of both classical Christian learning and vital Christian experience. Like his brother John, Charles Wesley was educated at Oxford University. Also like his brother, he had a conversion experience that he could date: in May 1738.

The hymns of the younger Wesley move within the framework of trinitarian theology and incarnational christology. The texts contain many references to early Christian literature. They make frequent allusions to the Bible, from Genesis to Revelation. They also refer to various aspects of Jesus' ministry. Neither Jesus' birth nor his resurrection, neither his teaching in parables nor his association with outcasts, is ignored. But at the center of this breadth and depth stands the cross of Jesus with a sometimes graphic emphasis on his blood atonement. "O for a Thousand Tongues to Sing" was written by Wesley to commemorate the first anniversary of his conversion experience. The tenth stanza (of what were originally eighteen stanzas) proclaims:

> He breaks the power of canceled sin, He sets the prisoner free;
> His blood can make the foulest clean; His blood availed for me.

Atonement applied, probably with another allusion to his conversion experience, is the overriding theme of this stanza from "O How Happy Are They":

> That sweet comfort was mine,
> When the favor divine
> I first found in the blood of the lamb;
> When my heart first believed,
> What a joy I received,
> What a heaven in Jesus's name!

17

There was within certain Christian circles in Wesley's day an adoration for the "blood and wounds" of Jesus. A stanza from the hymn "Arise, My Soul, Arise" reflects this kind of language:

> Five bleeding wounds he bears, Received on Calvary;
> They pour effectual prayers; they strongly plead for me:
> "Forgive him, O forgive," they cry,
> "Forgive him, O forgive," they cry, "Nor let that ransomed sinner die!"

One of the earliest collections of Wesleyan hymns was a slim volume entitled *Hymns for Those That Seek and Those That Have Redemption in the Blood of Jesus* (1747). Here also appears a rather singular focus on the cross and the death of Jesus.

Jesus the Example. Other persons place the greatest emphasis on the life of Jesus. "Jesus set an example to be followed," they say. They understand Jesus' death on the cross to be more of a martyrdom, resulting from his total obedience to the will of God in the midst of a hostile society. This view of Jesus is reflected in the wandering ministry of Francis of Assisi (died 1226). He lived in poverty among the poor in imitation of Jesus. But interest in Jesus as example was especially characteristic of the turn-of-the-century movement that left as its enduring legacy to American Christianity an enlarged gospel, a social gospel.

Walter Rauschenbusch, whose name became synonymous with that of the social gospel, acquired a firsthand acquaintance with the problems of industrial urban society while pastor of Second German Baptist Church, New York City. In his systematic *Theology for the Social Gospel* (1917),[3] Rauschenbusch spoke of Jesus as the "Initiator of the Kingdom of God." He challenged Christians to follow Jesus' call and to bring all society, all institutions, under the will of God.

Jesus as a model to be emulated is also the premise of Charles M. Sheldon's popular novel *In His Steps*, first published in the 1890s.[4] The plot involves the Reverend Mr. Henry Maxwell, who repeatedly exhorts his parishioners to conduct their lives in accordance with the question "What would Jesus do?" Sheldon originally wrote the book to be read aloud to his own congregation in Topeka, Kansas. He based the book on an episode in his own life when he had walked the streets of the city in disguise and suffered rejection by persons failing to walk in the steps of Jesus.

Jesus the Monk. Some persons stress another aspect of Jesus' life—his inner struggle to serve God and not human desires. "Jesus experienced the ongoing struggle between flesh and spirit," they say. They consider his death on the cross to be his final act of mortification of the flesh and the ultimate triumph of the spirit. This view of Jesus as monk certainly typified the monastic movement that began in the deserts of Egypt with Anthony (died ca. 356) and Pachomius (died ca. 346). This characterization of Jesus also appears in the writings of Crete-born Greek novelist Nikos Kazantzakis. His novel *The Last Temptation of Christ* (1951, English trans. 1960) became the basis for the Martin Scorsese film of the same name that caused a public uproar in 1988.[5]

The last temptation of Christ as he hangs on the cross is the temptation that has hounded him throughout his life. He has been tempted to abandon his spiritual calling for the sensual pleasures of home and wife, of sex and children. But Jesus yields not, not on the cross, not earlier. Throughout his life he has persistently rejected his former fiancée Mary Magdalene even though his rejection drove her to harlotry. The story of Jesus, therefore, becomes the literary vehicle for Kazantzakis' own conventional, yet not so conventional, philosophy of life. His outlook has much in common with Greek Orthodox Christian spirituality. But his outlook also shows indebtedness to various mentors, especially the French philosopher Henri Bergson. Echoing the thoughts of Bergson, Kazantzakis elsewhere writes: "It is not God who will save us—it is we who will save God, by battling, by creating, and by transmuting matter into spirit."[6] In life, Kazantzakis was threatened with excommunication; but in death, he was finally granted a Christian burial on Crete.

Jesus the Troublemaker. Still other persons emphasize another aspect of Jesus' life—not his inner struggle but his outer conflict. "Jesus violated the law and disturbed the peace," they say. Or, "He sided with the oppressed in opposition to the oppressor." Or again, "He spent too much time eating and drinking, often with the wrong crowd." Or still further, "He treated women as persons and not as things." People who make these kinds of comments often consider the cross to be a stark reminder that Jesus constituted a threat to those in positions of influence and power.

This view of Jesus as troublemaker is the dominant understanding reflected in those ancient non-Christian writings that make at least passing reference to him. These writings include the *Annals* by the Roman historian Tacitus, who wrote early in the second century. These writings also include the Jewish Talmud, that massive collection of materials from the rabbis finalized in two versions by the fifth and sixth centuries C.E.

In recent decades, an appreciation of Jesus as troublemaker has come not from persons hostile to him but from Christians who thought that he had been unduly domesticated by church and society. These nonconformists frequently spoke and wrote about Jesus against the backdrop of social movements that burst upon the American scene in the 1960s and 1970s.

The present-day recognition of multiculturalism as a social value first began to emerge during those crucial years as a result of social forces not from without but from within American life. The black power movement, as an extension of the earlier civil rights movement, protested the oppression of blacks within a predominantly white society. The so-called hippie movement protested the materialistic values of middle-class America. The feminist movement protested the subordination and exploitation of women within male-dominated social structures.

Varying presentations of Jesus as troublemaker appeared in the lectures of Clarence Jordan, the sermons of Albert B. Cleage Jr., the occasional writings of Harvey Cox, and a provocative article by Leonard Swidler.

Clarence Jordan, scientific farmer and Greek scholar, founded Koinonia Farm in rural Georgia in 1942 on the gospel-based ideals of pacifism, economic stewardship, and racial harmony. The Farm was ostracized, shot at, and bombed in the 1950s and 1960s because of its witness to racial unity. But it survived. Jordan often lectured around the country in support of the Farm's ideals and products. He rejected the effeminate Jesus of illustrated Bibles in a stirring but humorous talk, "Jesus the Rebel." Jesus therein appeared as "a man among men . . . a rebel," a nonviolent rebel in contrast to Barabbas the violent revolutionary.[7]

Albert B. Cleage Jr. served as pastor of the Shrine of the Black Madonna in urban Detroit during the tumultuous years of ghetto riots and assassinations in the late 1960s. The sermons preached in that sanctuary with its mural of a black madonna and child have received considerable notice in their published form, *The Black Messiah* (1968).[8] Cleage dismissed the Pauline-supported, white understanding of Jesus as too individualized and spiritualized. He viewed Jesus as a revolutionary black leader, a "zealot" who was striving to build the Black Nation of Israel in opposition to the white Roman Gentiles. This Jesus did not reject violence as a means to that end.

Harvey Cox, Harvard theologian with a varied list of publications, commemorated Jesus' birthday many years ago with a playful essay in *Playboy* magazine (January 1970) entitled "For Christ's Sake." The article was accompanied by a striking page-size picture, in sepia and black, of a laughing Jesus. Calling into question any understanding of Jesus as a safe, moralizing ascetic, Cox presented Jesus—according to the caption above Jesus' Falstaffian face—as a "joyous revolutionary," as one whose eating and drinking led to the accusation that he was a glutton and a drunkard. This portrayal was in keeping with Cox's professional interest in festivity and his personal fascination with the "hippie" movement at that stage in his career and life.[9] His presentation was also, quite obviously, in keeping with the editorial stance of the magazine in which it appeared.

Leonard Swidler, a professor of religion with ecumenical concerns at Temple University, focused attention on Jesus' relationship with women. His essay appeared in the periodical *Catholic World* (January 1971). The central thesis of this essay appeared as its title, "Jesus Was a Feminist." In developing this thesis, Swidler explored the role of women in the ministry and teaching of

Jesus. His reflections coincided with the emergence of the feminist movement as a powerful force in American life.

Jesus, therefore, has been characterized in a variety of ways. In ages past, and more recently, he has appeared as dying Savior, example, monk, and troublemaker. Like us, the creators of these portrayals tend to make Jesus over in their own images. Like us, they highlight those dimensions of his ministry that speak most directly to them. But who is Jesus? Or, to phrase the question in the past tense, who was Jesus—really?

This study is an invitation for you, whatever your present viewpoint, to undertake a more disciplined quest for an answer to this question. As your guides along the way, you will be accompanied by others who have blazed the trail before you—church people and scholars, both ancient and contemporary. Your quest coincides with the rebirth of Jesus scholarship in academic circles. Recent scholarly discussions, however, have become public events and engendered popular debate. The dimension of current interest in what scholars are saying about Jesus was vividly dramatized during a recent Easter season. All three weekly newsmagazines, *Time*, *Newsweek*, and *U.S. News & World Report*, simultaneously featured Jesus on the covers of their April 8, 1996, issues.

Your search will proceed in three stages. At stage one, you move from your own understanding of Jesus to a consideration of those literary sources on which all understandings ultimately depend—including the four Gospels of Matthew, Mark, Luke, and John. At stage two, you move from the Gospels, with their own distinctive portrayals of Jesus, to the level of historical reconstruction of Jesus' life and ministry within the setting of first-century Roman Palestine. Finally, at stage three, you examine continuing issues in the study of Jesus' life and ministry by drawing on insights from the previous two stages. Your personal quest will have succeeded if your understanding of Jesus has been broadened and sharpened and if you develop a conceptual framework for evaluating the many cultural and scholarly expressions of the Jesus story.

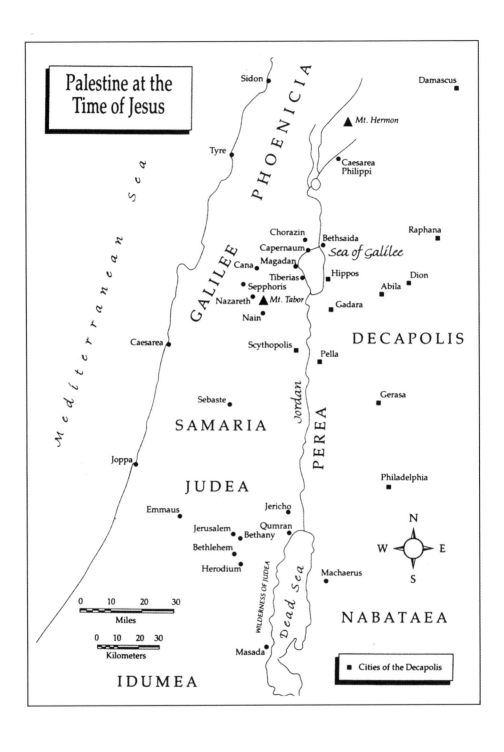

Palestine at the
Time of Jesus

Mediterranean Sea

Sidon

PHOENICIA

Damascus

▲ Mt. Hermon

Tyre

Caesarea
Philippi

Chorazin
Bethsaida
Capernaum
Cana   Magadan
Sea of Galilee
Raphana

GALILEE
Tiberias   Hippos
Sepphoris
Nazareth   ▲ Mt. Tabor
Nain

Dion
Abila

Gadara

DECAPOLIS

Caesarea

Scythopolis
Pella

Sebaste

SAMARIA

Jordan

PEREA

Gerasa

Joppa

JUDEA

Philadelphia

Emmaus

Jericho

Jerusalem   Qumran
Bethany
Bethlehem

Herodium

WILDERNESS OF JUDEA

Dead Sea

Machaerus

N

W   E

S

Masada

NABATAEA

0   10   20   30
Miles

0   10   20   30
Kilometers

IDUMEA

■ Cities of the Decapolis

PART ONE

Literary Sources for the Life
and Ministry of Jesus

1

Gospel Origins

The four Gospels of Matthew, Mark, Luke, and John constitute the first books of that collection of twenty-seven writings known to us as the New Testament. The four Gospels, therefore, represent canonical literature—Christian Scripture. But they are literature. Each Gospel was written at a specific time and in a particular place. Each was written for an ancient audience and in response to concerns shared by that audience and the Gospel writer. What can be known about the literary origins of these four Gospels?

This exploration of Gospel origins involves a consideration of three main points. First, the four Gospels themselves contain little explicit information about their origins. Second, Christian writers from the second century onward often comment about the origins of the four Gospels, usually associating them with apostles. *Apostle* became a technical term within the church for first generation Christians closely associated with Jesus himself. Third, modern scholars have come to recognize a more complicated process of literary origins for the four Gospels than simply authorship by individual apostles.

The Gospel Writers and Gospel Origins

In the editions of the New Testament familiar to us, we find the four Gospels introduced by uniform headings: "According to Matthew," "According to Mark," "According to Luke," and "According to John." We assume that these explanatory words are integral parts of the Gospels themselves. But these headings were probably second-century additions and did not appear in the original manuscripts of the Gospels. Only as the four Gospels were collected and used together would there have been a need for distinguishing among them in this fashion. Without these personalized headings, all four Gospels are anonymous documents.

The authors of Luke and John, however, include in their Gospels brief statements explaining their reasons for writing. The author of Luke introduces his work with a formal preface commonplace in writings of antiquity (Luke 1:1-4; cf. Acts 1:l). The author of John reserves his statement of purpose for the very end of his work (John 20:30-31). Most modern scholars agree that the Gospel of John originally ended with chapter 20. Chapter 21 represents a later addition either by the author or, as is more likely, by someone else (cf. vv. 24-25). This is not the place to consider all the issues of interpretation raised by these passages from the Gospels of Luke and John. But in anticipation of our investigation of Gospel origins, several observations are in order.

Even the authors of Luke and John, who offer some explanation for what they are doing, *maintain silence about their identities.* Only the secondary chapter added to the Gospel of John identifies the author as a disciple—the enigmatic "beloved disciple" (John 13:23; 19:26; 20:2; 21:7, 20; also 18:15; 19:35). But neither the secondary chapter nor the body of the Gospel declares the "beloved disciple" to be John, son of Zebedee.

Both authors allow for their having *received information from others orally.* Although both emphasize that their accounts rest on the testimony of eyewitnesses, neither claims to be an eyewitness. In fact, the author of Luke explicitly acknowledges dependence on others, whom he calls "eyewitnesses and servants of the word." Again, it is the secondary chapter at the end of the Gospel of John that confers eyewitness status on the author by identifying the author as the "beloved disciple."

The author of Luke even acknowledges dependence on *written sources.* The author not only refers back to "eyewitnesses and servants of the word" but also notes that many others had already written "an orderly account" of the events to be narrated anew.

Furthermore, both authors admit their own editorial roles in formulating the *portrayals of Jesus* in their Gospels. The author of Luke writes "an orderly account" to an otherwise unidentified "Theophilus" in order that he "may know the truth." The author of John writes a selective account, observing how "Jesus did many other signs in the presence of his disciples, which are not written in this book." The author writes so that the readers of the Gospel may "come to believe that Jesus is the Messiah, the Son of God."

Ancient Perspectives on Gospel Origins

Although the four Gospels themselves are anonymous documents, Christian writers during the earliest centuries of the church refer to these Gospels and report what is being said about them in their day. The words attributed to Papias, Bishop of Hierapolis (who wrote early in the second century) are significant because they are generally recognized to be the earliest references to the origins of the Gospels of Mark and Matthew. Reporting what had been passed on to him, Papias says:

> Mark became Peter's interpreter and wrote accurately all that he remembered, not, indeed, in order, of the things said or done by the Lord. For he had not heard the Lord, nor had he followed him, but later on, as I said, followed Peter, who used to give teaching as necessity demanded but not making, as it were, an arrangement of the Lord's oracles, so that Mark did nothing wrong in thus writing down single points as he remembered them. For to one thing he gave attention, to leave out nothing of what he had heard and to make no false statements in them.[1]

> Matthew collected the oracles in the Hebrew language, and each interpreted them as best he could.[2]

Some modern scholars doubt that Papias' reference to "the oracles in the Hebrew [Aramaic?] language" was intended by him as a reference to the Gospel of Matthew. But if he was referring to the Gospel of Matthew, he has reported what was being said about the writing of two Gospels—Mark and Matthew. These words of Papias are recorded in *The Ecclesiastical History* of Eusebius, Bishop of Caesarea (died 339). This monumental work constitutes an invaluable source for understanding the church in its infancy. Elsewhere in his history, Eusebius has also recorded a statement by Papias that indicates Papias' preference for the unwritten word about Jesus:

> I inquired into the words of the presbyters, what Andrew or Peter or Philip or Thomas or James or John or Matthew, or any other of the Lord's disciples, had said, and what Aristion and the presbyter John, the Lord's disciples, were saying. For I did not suppose that information from books would help me so much as the word of a living and surviving voice.[3]

The so-called Muratorian Canon contains some of the earliest references to the writing of the Gospels of Luke and John. This annotated catalog of the books of the New Testament may have originated in Rome as early as the closing years of the second century, although a fourth-century dating with Syria as the place of origin has also been proposed. The list evidently began with statements about the Gospels of Matthew and Mark. But now, having survived in Latin only in fragmentary form, it opens with complete commentary on the Gospels of Luke and John:

> . . . at which however he was present and so he has set it down.
> The third Gospel book, that according to Luke.
> The physician Luke after Christ's ascension (resurrection?),

since Paul had taken him with him as an expert in the way (of the teaching),
composed it in his own name
according to (his) thinking. Yet neither did he himself see
the Lord in the flesh; and therefore, as he was able to ascertain it, so he begins
to tell the story from the birth of John.
The fourth of the Gospels, that of John, (one) of the disciples.
When his fellow-disciples and bishops urged him,
he said: Fast with me from today for three days, and what
will be revealed to each one
let us relate to one another. In the same night it was
revealed to Andrew, one of the apostles, that,
while all were to go over (it), John in his own name
should write everything down....[4]

There had begun to appear, therefore, agreement within the church that the
New Testament should include the four Gospels said to have been written by
Matthew, Mark, Luke, and John. Irenaeus, Bishop of Lyons (died 202),
expresses this emerging viewpoint in his writing *Against Heresies*. His comments on the four Gospels include references to possible places of origin for
the Gospels of Mark and John. His comments are also accompanied by an
interesting theological argument in support of specifically four Gospels—no
more, no less. Irenaeus says:

> So Matthew among the Hebrews issued a Writing of the gospel in their own
> tongue, while Peter and Paul were preaching the gospel at Rome and founding
> the Church. After their decease Mark, the disciple and interpreter of Peter, also
> handed down to us in writing what Peter had preached. Then Luke, the follower
> of Paul, recorded in a book the gospel as it was preached by him. Finally John,
> the disciple of the Lord, who had also lain on his breast, himself published the
> Gospel, while he was residing at Ephesus in Asia.[5]

> The Gospels could not possibly be either more or less in number than they are.
> Since there are four zones of the world in which we live, and four principal winds,
> while the Church is spread over all the earth, and the pillar and foundation of the
> Church is the gospel, and the Spirit of life, it fittingly has four pillars.... From this
> it is clear that the Word...gave us the gospel, fourfold in form but held together
> by one Spirit.[6]

However, within the early church, there is not unanimous agreement about
the authority of the four Gospels of Matthew, Mark, Luke, and John.
Considerably more than four Gospels were written and accepted as authoritative among different groups of Christians. The texts of these other Gospels, in
recent years, have been made readily available in English translation.[7] Among
them are Gospels attributed to such apostles as Peter, Thomas, and Philip.

Also, during the formative years of the church, the Gospel of John itself presents a special problem. This Gospel was quite popular among Gnostic Christians. The name "Gnostic" (derived from the Greek word for "knowledge") commonly designates those Christians who held a dualistic worldview that contrasted the realm of spirit over against the realm of matter. These believers often denied that God the Father had created the material world, which they considered to be evil. They also denied that Jesus the Son was truly human. They believed in salvation by "knowledge"—a knowledge that enabled the individual soul to remember and to return to its home in the heavens. One of the first commentaries on any Gospel was the gnostic Heracleon's commentary on the Gospel of John. Furthermore, there were non-Gnostic Christians who rejected the authority of this Gospel and attributed its authorship to a well-known gnostic teacher named Cerinthus.

Even Christian writers who defend the authority of the Gospel of John as the work of the apostle John, however, must admit its distinctiveness in comparison with the Gospels of Matthew, Mark, and Luke. Both Clement of Alexandria (died 215) and Augustine, Bishop of Hippo (died 430), describe the peculiarity of John in memorable phrases. Their reflections on all four Gospels include important statements about the chronological order in which the Gospels were allegedly written.

The ancient historian Eusebius reports the view of Clement of Alexandria in these words:

> And again in the same books Clement has inserted a tradition of the primitive elders with regard to the order of the Gospels, as follows. He said that those Gospels were first written which include the genealogies, but that the Gospel according to Mark came into being in this manner: When Peter had publicly preached the word at Rome, and by the Spirit had proclaimed the Gospel, that those present, who were many, exhorted Mark, as one who had followed him for a long time and remembered what had been spoken, to make a record of what was said; and that he did this, and distributed the Gospel among those that asked him. And that when the matter came to Peter's knowledge he neither strongly forbade it nor urged it forward. But that John, last of all, conscious that the outward facts had been set forth in the Gospels, was urged on by his disciples, and, divinely moved by the Spirit, composed a spiritual Gospel.[8]

Augustine was destined to become one of the most influential thinkers in Western theology. More than a century after Clement, he wrote a meticulous work on *The Harmony of the Gospels*. He sought to explain the basic agreement among the four Gospels in spite of their differences. He also spoke at length about the origins of the Gospels and the chronological order in which they were written:

Now, those four evangelists whose names have gained the most remarkable circulation over the whole world, and whose number has been fixed as four...are believed to have written in the order which follows: first Matthew, then Mark, thirdly Luke, lastly John....

Of these four, it is true, only Matthew is reckoned to have written in the Hebrew language; the others in Greek. And however they may appear to have kept each of them a certain order of narration proper to himself, this certainly is not to be taken as if each individual writer chose to write in ignorance of what his predecessor had done, or left out as matters about which there was no information things which another nevertheless is discovered to have recorded. But the fact is, that just as they received each of them the gift of inspiration, they abstained from adding to their several labours any superfluous conjoint compositions. For Matthew is understood to have taken it in hand to construct the record of the incarnation of the Lord according to the royal lineage, and to give an account of most part of His deeds and words as they stood in relation to this present life of men. Mark follows him closely, and looks like his attendant and epitomizer. For in his narrative he gives nothing in concert with John apart from the others; by himself separately, he has little to record; in conjunction with Luke, as distinguished from the rest, he has still less; but in concord with Matthew, he has a very large number of passages. Much, too, he narrates in words almost numerically and identically the same as those used by Matthew, where the agreement is either with that evangelist alone, or with him in connection with the rest. On the other hand, Luke appears to have occupied himself rather with the priestly lineage and character of the Lord. For although in his own way he carries the descent back to David, what he has followed is not the royal pedigree, but the line of those who were not kings. . . .

These three evangelists, however, were for the most part engaged with those things which Christ did through the vehicle of the flesh of man, and after the temporal fashion. But John, on the other hand, had in view that true divinity of the Lord in which He is the Father's equal, and directed his efforts above all to the setting forth of the divine nature in his Gospel in such a way as he believed to be adequate to men's needs and notions. . . . For he is like one who has drunk in the secret of His divinity more richly and somehow more familiarly than others, as if he drew it from the very bosom of his Lord on which it was his wont to recline when he sat at meat.[9]

This survey of ancient perspectives on Gospel origins is representative rather than exhaustive. Others who spoke for emerging Christianity also published their opinions. But by the time of Augustine, four Gospels had firmly established themselves as the cornerstone of the New Testament. A consensus viewpoint had crystallized about their origins. Several observations about this viewpoint can be made on the basis of the statements we have surveyed.

These ancient writers affirm the *apostolic authorship* of the four Gospels, in spite of the controversy surrounding the Gospel of John. They claim that the apostles Matthew and John wrote the first and fourth Gospels. They say that

Mark and Luke, as companions of the apostles Peter and Paul, composed the second and third Gospels.

These writers, therefore, do attribute Gospels to Matthew and John as eyewitnesses of Jesus' earthly ministry. But they still recognize the *role of oral tradition* as the stories and sayings of Jesus were passed down by word of mouth. They acknowledge that Mark and Luke had relied on Peter and Paul for their information about Jesus. And Papias, at the outset of the second century, still expresses his preference for oral instead of written communication.

Augustine carries forward the belief expressed earlier by Irenaeus and Papias that the Gospel of Matthew had been written originally in Hebrew. There are, however, two—possibly three—conflicting opinions about the *chronological order and literary relationship among the four Gospels.* Augustine himself advanced the position that the Gospels were written in their New Testament order with each evangelist aware of the labors of his predecessors: Matthew, Mark, Luke, and John. Earlier, Clement of Alexandria cited a primitive tradition that the Gospels with genealogies, Matthew and Luke, were written before Mark and John. Still earlier, the words by Papias about the writing of Mark imply that Mark had been the first Gospel to be written.

These early scholars readily acknowledge, ingeniously defend, and variously describe the diversity of the *portrayals of Jesus* in the four Gospels. Irenaeus argues that the plurality of Gospels is transcended by a unity of Spirit. Clement of Alexandria and Augustine characterize the Gospel of John as distinctive over against the other three Gospels. Augustine also pays careful attention to the special emphases in each Gospel, although he describes Mark as essentially an "epitomizer" of Matthew.

A Contemporary View of Gospel Origins

Modern scholars of the past two centuries have subjected the four Gospels to detailed analysis. Out of these investigations has emerged an understanding of Gospel origins considerably more complex than indicated by the scholars of old. This sketch of the process leading to the writing of the Gospels takes into account the claims and conclusions of modern scholarship. While others might describe the process differently, a contemporary view of Gospel origins can be stated as follows.

The life of Jesus spanned roughly the *first third of the first century.* Born at a time when Rome ruled, Jesus was a Jew reared in Galilee, within a social setting that experienced both attraction toward and resistance to Greek culture. His Jewish contemporaries used the Aramaic language in conversation. They read the Scriptures written in Hebrew and translated them into Aramaic. This was an age when persons were accustomed to remembering the spoken word. Such an emphasis on memory may seem strange to us. In our day of electronic

31

gadgetry more than one teacher has been asked by an enterprising student, "May I tape the lecture?" The teacher-student relationship in Palestine, however, was based not on taping, nor even on writing, but on speaking and hearing, on recitation and memory. Within this environment, and whatever their own levels of literacy, Jesus and his disciples understandably wrote nothing about him during their public activity together.

Even if Jesus' disciples had kept notes during his ministry, they still could not have written a Gospel. They lacked the faith-perception required for the writing. Indeed, all four Gospels depict the disciples as confused about Jesus' goals and ambivalent in their loyalty. In Jerusalem itself, Judas betrayed him, Peter denied him, and all the men deserted him (but cf. John 19:26). The four Gospels also suggest that the resurrection experiences of the disciples triggered for them the faith-perception that made a written Gospel a possibility. The church was seemingly begotten out of the appearances of the resurrected Jesus to his own—to Mary, to Peter, and to others (1 Cor. 15:3-8; Mark 16; Matt. 28; Luke 24; John 20, 21). Henceforth Jesus' disciples began to proclaim the "gospel" (literally, "good news") of what God had done through the life, death, and resurrection of Jesus.

Jesus' followers, however, still did not immediately write a Gospel. Since within certain Jewish circles a general resurrection was expected at the end of history, the resurrection of Jesus signaled for his earliest advocates—Jews all—the beginning of the end. They lived with the fervent expectation of Jesus' return in glory on the clouds of heaven. Thirty or forty years passed, therefore, before the gospel message became a Gospel book.

The *middle third of the first century* was a time for the infant church's expansion from Jerusalem through Palestine into the wider Graeco-Roman world. The book of Acts affords a glimpse into this momentous development. This was also a time when Jesus' followers began to share with one another and with others the stories and sayings they remembered from his earthly ministry. What mattered to these early believers was neither every detail nor exact wording. What mattered was the meaning of these past words and deeds for their present lives as they proclaimed, taught, and defended the gospel message. As they passed on this oral tradition about Jesus, they began to collect individual stories and sayings into larger groupings—and even to write them down. The hypothetical Q document and the *Gospel of Thomas*, which we will discuss later, may have been among these early collections of Jesus' words. The account of Jesus' suffering in Jerusalem was possibly the first portion of his story to be told consecutively as a sequence of events (Mark 14–15; Matt. 26–27; Luke 22–23; John 18–19; also *Gospel of Peter*).

The spread of the church into the wider Graeco-Roman world required that the tradition of Jesus' words, deeds, and passion be translated from Aramaic into Greek, the international language of the eastern Mediterranean basin. A key person in the missionary outreach of the church to Gentiles was Paul. He was a Jew, but not from Palestine. He was from Tarsus in Asia Minor, which is now Turkey. Speaking and writing Greek fluently, Paul established communities of believers in many towns in Asia Minor and Greece—including the city of Corinth. He wrote letters to his young churches, not Gospels. But his letters indicate that he was familiar with a tradition of Jesus' sayings. Occasionally he quotes or refers to these sayings in support of his arguments (cf. 1 Cor. 7:10; 9:14; 11:23-26; et al.). Paul probably died a martyr's death, as did Peter, in Rome in the 60s. The gospel message became a Gospel book within a decade of their deaths, possibly even in Rome.

The *last third of the first century* was a time when the church prepared itself for its historical pilgrimage across the centuries. This was also the time of the writing of the four Gospels. Several factors within the life of the church contributed to the writing of the Gospels toward the end of the first century. These factors are also attested in the non-Gospel writings of the New Testament. One factor was that people who had known Jesus personally were growing old. Some were already dead (Acts 12:2). Another factor was the failure of Jesus to return in glory as soon as expected by the earliest believers (2 Pet. 3:1-13). This has often been referred to as the "delay of the parousia." The Greek word *parousia* (literally, "coming") became a standard term to designate the second coming of Jesus Christ (cf. 1 Thess. 4:15; 2 Thess. 2:1; et al.). Still another factor was the tendency among some converts to interpret the Jesus story in unacceptable ways. There were those who denied the true humanity of Jesus (1 John 4:2-3; 2 John 7). An additional factor was the growing separation between church and synagogue. The church, which was Jewish in origin, became increasingly Gentile in membership (Rom. 9–11; also Rev. 2:9; 3:9). These factors, among others, led to the need for more permanent accounts of the Jesus story. The gospel message became a Gospel book, specifically four Gospel books.

As written, the four canonical Gospels purport to record sayings spoken by Jesus during his earthly ministry in Palestine. But within the early church, Jesus was not just a figure of the past. To his own he was alive and in their midst. Within some Christian communities, the exalted Jesus was understood to be speaking to his followers then and there through Spirit-inspired prophets. The book of Revelation with its visions of the end-time represents a writing by such a prophet named John (Rev. 1:1, 4, 9; 22:8). John wrote down his revelation of the exalted Jesus near the end of the first century. But evidence of this kind of charismatic activity raises the possibility that "heavenly sayings" spoken by the exalted Jesus through believing prophets may have found their way into the tradition of "earthly sayings" that originated with Jesus during his Palestinian ministry. The four Gospels themselves may preserve "heavenly" as well as "earthly sayings" of Jesus.

The person initially responsible for transforming the gospel message into a Gospel book, with a sequential account of Jesus' ministry, was evidently the author of the Gospel of Mark. Ironically, we can see that he still understood the word *gospel* to designate not a book but a message—the "good news" of what God had done through the life, death, and resurrection of Jesus (Mark 1:1; 13:10; et al.). This Gospel was soon joined in circulation by the Gospels of Matthew, Luke, and John.

The *Gospel of Mark* was probably written around the year 70, possibly in Rome. The author may have been John Mark, the Jewish-Christian from Palestine associated with Paul and Peter. The author portrays Jesus as the Crucified Christ in writing to comfort and to encourage his readers who have experienced persecution. For him and his audience, the sufferings of the present time represent the sufferings of the end-time. They expect the exalted Jesus to return soon in glory for final judgment and salvation. The word *apocalyptic* commonly designates those ideas and images related to an expectation of the end of the world. The author of Mark, therefore, writes his Gospel as an apocalyptic preacher. He preaches the "good news" of what God has done and will do through Jesus Christ, the Son of God, and has created his Gospel out of diverse oral and possibly written sources.

The *Gospel of Matthew* was probably written in the 80s somewhere in Syria. The Gospel bears the name of one of the twelve disciples, but the author is unknown. He appears to have been a Jewish-Christian scribe writing for a predominantly Jewish-Christian community. With Jesus portrayed as the Teaching Christ, the Gospel represents a churchbook or manual designed to guide the community in matters of faith and practice. The author used the Gospel of Mark as his main written source. Although he followed the outline of Mark rather closely, he added other traditions—including infancy and resurrection stories. He also had access to a sizable body of teaching materials.

The *Gospel of Luke* was probably written in the 80s as well. The exact place of origin is unknown; but it was most certainly written outside of Palestine. The author may have been Luke the Gentile Christian physician who sometimes traveled with Paul. Writing to a Gentile named Theophilus, he appropriately portrays Jesus as the Universal Christ. The Gospel of Mark was among his written sources. The infancy and resurrection stories added by him differ considerably from the infancy and resurrection stories of Matthew. A learned man and somewhat self-consciously a historian, the author wrote his Gospel as the first volume of a two-volume work. The second volume is the book of Acts, which has been separated from the Gospel of Luke in our New Testament by the Gospel of John. Luke and Acts together constitute a history of Christian beginnings—Jesus' life and the church's growth.

The *Gospel of John* was written before the end of the century, before the year 100. The author probably does not use any of the other three Gospels as a written source for his information about Jesus. The Gospel of John, therefore, would be literarily independent of Matthew, Mark, and Luke. The Gospel also differs from these Gospels in significant ways. Not the least of the differences is the way Jesus talks about himself in long discourses containing sayings that begin with the words "I am." These discourses probably owe a great deal to the creativity of the evangelist and the evangelist's community. Since the "I am" sayings in the Gospel are similar in form to sayings by the exalted Jesus in the book of Revelation, they may even represent "heavenly sayings" spoken by Jesus through the Spirit to the evangelist. The Gospel was once thought to be the most Hellenistic or Greek of the four, but it probably grew out of the life of a Jewish-Christian community. The central issue confronting the evangelist and his community seems to have been that of belief in Jesus as the Messiah, the Christ, the Son of God. This issue may have involved nonbelieving Jews who denied Jesus' messiahship and divine sonship. The issue may also have involved Christian believers who in "Gnostic" fashion overemphasized Jesus' divine sonship at the expense of his humanity. That the Gospel was written by John, son of Zebedee, in Ephesus appears doubtful. But whoever wrote it portrays Jesus as the Eternal Christ become flesh. The inspired, creative character of the Gospel identifies the author as something of a prophet-theologian.

The preceding sketch of Gospel origins takes into account modern scholarly opinion but offers a rather conventional outline of those origins. However, in recent years a very different understanding has been set forth for what transpired between the life of Jesus and the writing of the Gospel of Mark.[10] According to this alternative understanding, in response to Jesus in rural Galilee in the 30s there appeared diverse movements whose participants recognized the authority of Jesus' words and viewed him as their founder-teacher. Only later, in the Hellenistic cities beyond Galilee, were these Jesus movements transformed into a cult that venerated Jesus as a God. The letters of Paul presuppose this development. The locus of Jesus' authority had shifted from his words to his crucifixion and resurrection. This alternative understanding of Christian origins, as we shall see, throws into relief the importance of the Gospel of Mark in the emergence of Christianity. But for the moment our more conventional descriptions of how the Gospels came to be should be clarified by several observations.

Our overview suggests that the Gospels of Mark and Luke may have been written by their namesakes, but that the Gospels of Matthew and John were probably not written by theirs. The *apostolic authorship* of each Gospel is thereby questioned or denied. This represents a middle course between the alternatives often expressed in contemporary biblical scholarship. A few modern scholars still defend the ancient claims that all four Gospels were written by Matthew, Mark, Luke, and John. These scholars often stress that two of the

Gospel writers rest their cases on the authority of eyewitnesses. They also surmise that the early church would surely have remembered the authors of all four. Other modern interpreters, however, declare that the authors of all four Gospels remain unknown. These interpreters observe that the Gospels are anonymous documents. They also emphasize that the early church associated the Gospels with apostles in order to secure their authority.

Our overview describes at length the process by which the *oral tradition* about Jesus was passed down and applied to new situations before the writing of the Gospels. The dynamic but faithful character of this process is recognized. This also represents a middle course between the alternatives sometimes expressed in contemporary biblical scholarship. Some scholars have asserted that the primitive church freely created and attributed to Jesus sayings and stories he never said or did. Other interpreters, however, have suggested that the early Christian community slavishly transmitted a tradition of words by Jesus memorized at his feet during his ministry. Nonetheless, as contemporary scholars generally affirm, the Gospel of John does appear to be the product of a creative process different from that reflected in the other three Gospels. Those ancient churchmen who commented on the Gospels anticipated but did not fully appreciate the emphasis in modern scholarship on the period of oral transmission of tradition about Jesus.

Our overview presents Mark as the first Gospel to be written and as the principal written source underlying both Matthew and Luke. The Gospel of John stands apart from the others as a literarily independent work. The priority of Mark and the independence of John remain the dominant, but not the only, viewpoints in contemporary biblical scholarship. Furthermore, these viewpoints clearly contradict at points the ancient views about the *chronological order and literary relationship among the four Gospels.* The priority of Mark contradicts the positions of Augustine and Clement that Mark was written after Matthew. The independence of John contradicts their statements that John was familiar with the other Gospels. Also, the modern view that all four Gospels were originally written in Greek contradicts the ancient belief that Matthew was initially composed in Hebrew.

Finally, our overview of Gospel origins highlights the theological focus peculiar to each Gospel. There appears an appropriate correspondence between the *portrayal of Jesus* in each Gospel and the social setting of that Gospel. Each writer, therefore, has edited information about Jesus so that the story of Jesus addresses the concerns of the intended readers. The story of Jesus as the Universal Christ in the Gospel of Luke, for example, was appropriate for Theophilus in a way that the story of Jesus as the Teaching Christ in the Gospel of Matthew would not have been. Like us, the Gospel writers tended to make Jesus over in their own likenesses. Those ancient churchmen who commented on the Gospels also recognized the theological diversity among the four Gospels. But they, such as Augustine, were more interested in harmonizing the differences rather than exploring how those differences grew out of specific sets of historical circumstances.

This chapter on Gospel origins has outlined a contemporary view of how the four canonical Gospels came to be, taking into account certain ancient perspectives. This view is based on insights derived from two hundred years of rigorous analysis of these Gospels. Chapter 2 surveys in more detail the particular methods of interpretation that have been refined over this period of time. It will become evident that biblical scholarship has moved well beyond the ancient question of who wrote the Gospels. Chapter 3 goes further into the theologies of the Gospels and the Gospel writers by delineating more sharply how they have individually portrayed Jesus.

2

Gospel Criticism

In our everyday usage, the word *criticism* often has negative connotations. To criticize another person means to speak about that individual in an uncomplimentary manner. But the root meaning of the term has to do with "passing judgment" or "making evaluation," positive or negative. Gospel critics evaluate the Gospels. They approach the Gospels with certain questions. Who wrote them? When? Where? To whom? Why? What sources did the author use? Written sources? Oral? What did the author's editing of these sources reveal about this theological perspective? About this view of Jesus? What is the story of Jesus in this Gospel? How does the Gospel writer tell this story? What is the social world presented in the narrative? The social world presupposed by the narrative?

These questions, and others, share a common feature. They involve the study of the biblical documents within the first-century setting out of which they originated. They are not questions about the beliefs and theology of the persons who ask them in the twentieth century. They are questions about the documents and those who wrote them. These questions, therefore, represent expressions of the general method used by Gospel critics—the historical-critical method.

We have adopted the phrase *historical-critical method* as a comprehensive name for a whole body of specialized methods developed in recent years and applied to the biblical writings, especially to the four Gospels. The assumption underlying the application of the historical-critical method to the Gospels is that writings are documents composed by persons out of, and for, specific historical situations. The use of this method for interpreting the biblical writings has become commonplace in the contemporary church. The use of the

38

historical-critical method in the service of Christian faith rests upon the additional assumption that an adequate appreciation of the biblical message for our lives today requires an understanding of that message in its original setting. To fully appreciate, for example, the proclamation of the "good news" of Jesus Christ by the author of Mark, we should come to terms with the varied historical dimensions of that Gospel.

Our discussion of Gospel origins in the preceding chapter already depended upon the questions, and some of the answers, of historical criticism, or Gospel criticism. This chapter surveys the history of Gospel criticism. This history falls into five main periods.

Period 1: Pre-Criticism (Before the Nineteenth Century)

The church during its earliest years faced the issue of which Gospels were to be considered as authoritative alongside the Scriptures, or Old Testament, inherited from Judaism. Each of the four Gospels incorporated into the New Testament was associated with a past figure of the first Christian generation: Matthew, Mark, Luke, and John.

Questions about the reliability of the Gospels as historical documents, therefore, have always been asked. But, as is generally recognized, a rigorous historical-critical approach to the Gospels constitutes a relatively new development. After the four Gospels had been established as Scripture, the tendency prevailed to view them in the light of and in support of the church's doctrine. The Gospels were not studied as literary and historical documents with their own theological integrity apart from official teaching and personal belief. We have seen, for example, how Augustine explained the differences between the Gospels of Matthew, Mark, and Luke, on the one hand, and the Gospel of John, on the other. He said that the three earlier Gospels focused on "those things which Christ did through the vehicle of the flesh of man" and that John presented the "true divinity" and "divine nature" of Jesus Christ. Augustine here does not take into account those first-century historical and theological factors that may have influenced the evangelist's distinctive portrayal of Jesus. Rather he describes those differences in terms of a fifth-century theology that affirmed Jesus Christ to be one person with two natures, a human nature and a divine nature.

By elevating Scripture as the central authority in matters of faith and practice, the Protestant Reformation prepared the way for historical criticism. The Reformers appealed to the "plain sense" of Scripture and rejected as unscriptural many beliefs and customs of the medieval church. But they, too, continued to view the Gospels in the light of and in support of their emerging Protestant theologies. No less a person than Martin Luther offered this theological assessment of the Four Gospels in his "Preface to the New Testament" (1546): "John's Gospel is the one, fine, true, and chief gospel, and is far, far to be preferred over the other three and placed high above them. So, too, the epistles of St. Paul and St. Peter far surpass the other three gospels, Matthew, Mark, and Luke."[1] Luther, like Augustine before him, failed to appreciate fully the Gospels as writings produced out of and for specific situations in the life of the early church. But to say this is not to reproach them. They simply reflect the times in which they lived.

The intellectual revolution of the seventeenth and eighteenth centuries, represented by the rise of Deism in England and the Enlightenment on the European continent, finally led to the appearance of a consistently historical approach to the biblical writings. This was the age when philosophy and reason struggled to become independent of theology and faith. Historical analysis of the four Gospels became a possibility apart from prescribed church teaching. Such traditional church teaching as the apostolic authorship of the four Gospels, for example, would be called into question and even rejected.

The first of the specialized historical-critical methods to appear was source criticism. This particular discipline seeks answers to questions that confront even the most casual reader of the four Gospels.

Period 2: Source Criticism (Nineteenth Century)

A comparison of the four Gospels reveals that three—Matthew, Mark, and Luke—are remarkably similar. They have much in common that sets them apart from the Gospel of John. They present a similar outline of Jesus' ministry. They offer a similar characterization of Jesus and his message. They also contain many of the same stories. More than this, the commonality of the three Gospels extends to exact wording. Compare, for example, the three accounts of Jesus' debate with the religious leaders over his authority (Matt. 21:23-27; Mark 11:27-33; Luke 20:1-8).

There is still another pattern of similarities involving only two of the Gospels, Matthew and Luke. These Gospels share a sizable amount of teaching material. At many points the wording itself is identical. Compare, for example, Jesus' words on serving God and wealth (Matt. 6:24 and Luke 16:13).

Consequently, various points of agreement exist among Matthew, Mark, and Luke. But there are also striking peculiarities. Accounts of Jesus' infancy appear in Matthew and Luke but are absent from Mark. These two accounts of Jesus' infancy, however, differ considerably from each other. Furthermore, each of these Gospels contains material peculiar to it. For example, the parable of the sheep and the goats is found only in Matthew (Matt. 25:31-46), the parable of the prodigal son (Luke 15:11-32) only in Luke.

Out of these similarities and differences an obvious question presents itself: *What is the literary relationship among the Gospels of Matthew, Mark, and Luke?* Are all three dependent upon some now nonexistent common source? Are the authors copying one another? Who is copying whom?

This issue appeared shortly after the Gospels were gathered together. It was raised in the earliest years of the church's life. In the fifth century, it was given its most definitive answer for that period by Augustine. The question was reopened, however, at the close of the eighteenth century. The discipline of source criticism had emerged. *Source criticism can be defined as the discipline that seeks to identify the sources, especially the written sources, behind the Gospels.* Scholars spent much of the nineteenth century setting forth hypotheses that, in their judgment, would best explain the literary evidence. As we shall see, a consensus emerged, but the debate continues.

An important figure in reopening the question of literary relationships, and hence the issue of sources, was the German textual scholar J. J. Griesbach. Prior to the 1770s various "harmonies" of all four Gospels had been devised in an attempt to reconcile the differences among them. In the middle of the decade, Griesbach published what he called a "synopsis" of the Gospels of Matthew, Mark, and Luke. He arranged the texts of these Gospels in parallel columns to the virtual exclusion of John. These three Gospels became known as the "synoptic" Gospels because they together ("syn-") view ("optic") the Jesus story. Griesbach was not satisfied with creating a useful instrument for comparing these Gospels. In 1783 he published his own solution to the so-called synoptic problem. Like Augustine, Griesbach affirmed the written priority of Matthew and the familiarity of each Gospel writer with the labors of his predecessors. Instead of the Augustinian order of Matthew » Mark » Luke, however, he proposed the order of Matthew » Luke » Mark. This "Griesbach hypothesis" has in recent decades been advocated anew by American scholar William R. Farmer[2] and others. In the nineteenth century, however, this view was not to be the wave of the future. It crashed upon scholarly shores, made headway, and then receded.

The future belonged to a view initially popularized by a German scholar of a later generation. H. J. Holtzmann, in an 1863 study of the synoptic Gospels, set forth a "two-document hypothesis" to explain the literary relationship among Matthew, Mark, and Luke.[3] As it has developed, this view can be succinctly stated in two propositions: (1) Mark was the earliest Gospel to be written and was used independently by the authors of Matthew and Luke as their main written source; and (2) Matthew and Luke also possessed another written document, now lost, that consisted primarily of Jesus' teachings. This hypothetical document received the designation "Q" (for *Quelle*, or "source," in German). We referred to the Q document as an early collection of Jesus' teachings in our discussion of how the Gospels came to be.

Therefore, the two main written sources underlying the synoptic Gospels, according to the two-document hypothesis, are Mark and Q. This solution and some of the arguments on its behalf can be summarized as follows:

Mark was the earliest Gospel to be written and was used as the principal written source for Matthew and Luke. The time-honored reasons for the priority of Mark continue to be presented in our day.

First, content. Mark is brief. If Mark is the earliest Gospel, it is relatively easy to understand why and how the authors of Matthew and Luke used Mark in the composition of their Gospels. Basically, they added to Mark: infancy stories at the beginning, teachings throughout, and resurrection stories at the end. But if Matthew is the earliest followed by Luke and then Mark, it is more difficult to understand why and how Luke and Mark used their predecessors. Why did Luke totally replace the infancy and resurrection accounts in Matthew with accounts of his own instead of harmonizing them? Or why did Mark omit entirely the infancy stories, most of the resurrection material, and so many of the sayings found in Matthew and Luke?

Second, order. The synoptic Gospels usually contain shared stories in the same sequence in each Gospel. If Mark is the earliest Gospel, it makes intelligible why Matthew and Luke never agree in sequence over against Mark. When either Matthew or Luke deviates from the Markan sequence, the other keeps that sequence as though both are following Mark independent of one another. Mark, for example, reports in sequence the list of the twelve disciples (Mark 3:13-19), the raising of Jairus' daughter (Mark 5:21-43), and Jesus' rejection at Nazareth (Mark 6:1-6). When Matthew places the raising of Jairus' daughter (Matt. 9:18-26) before the list of the twelve disciples (Matt. 10:1-4), Luke follows the Markan sequence with the list of the twelve disciples (Luke 6:12-16) before the raising of Jairus' daughter (Luke 8:40-56). But when Luke places Jesus' rejection at Nazareth (Luke 4:16-30) before the list of the twelve disciples (Luke 6:12-16), Matthew follows the Markan sequence by reporting Jesus' rejection at Nazareth (Matt. 13:53-58) after the list of the twelve disciples (Matt. 10:1-4).

Third, style. Matthew and Luke are written in a more polished form of Greek than Mark. If Mark is the earliest Gospel, the tendency toward grammatical improvement and clarification is easily understood. Whereas Mark, for example, occasionally reports Aramaic expressions on the lips of Jesus (Mark 5:41; 7:34; 14:36) these words are missing in Matthew and Luke.

Fourth, theology. Matthew and Luke reflect more of a reluctance to present Jesus and his disciples in what might be considered an unfavorable light than Mark. If Mark is the earliest Gospel, there is understandably apparent a tendency toward greater theological sensitivity. Compare, for example, Mark 4:38 with Matthew 8:25 and Luke 8:24; Mark 6:4 with Matthew 13:58; Mark 10:18 with Matthew 19:17 and Luke 18:19; and Mark 10:35 with Matthew 20:20.

(Hereafter in our study, the abbreviation "par." will be used to identify passages in Mark that have parallels in either Matthew or Luke or both. "Mark 11:27-33 par.," for example, indicates that the Markan story of Jesus' debate over his authority also appears in one or both of the other synoptic Gospels.)

If Matthew and Luke did not copy from one another, then the presence of a similar passage in these Gospels—but not in Mark—must be explained. In addition to Mark, Matthew and Luke must have had access to another main source. The hypothetical Q document provides such an explanation.

Some scholars who accept the priority of Mark have preferred to explain the similarities between Matthew and Luke by their having drawn upon common oral tradition. In recent years, other scholars have labored, both collectively and individually, to reconstruct the text of Q based on a meticulous analysis of the sayings material common to Matthew and Luke. Today many favor the view that Q was a written document.

Whether a document or not, Q *serves as a useful symbol for passages shared by Matthew and Luke but absent from Mark.* (Hereafter in our study, Q passages will be identified with an equals sign. "Matthew 6:24 = Luke 16:13," for example, means that Jesus' saying on serving God and wealth appears in both Matthew and Luke.)

The Gospel of Mark and Q, however, still do not account for all the contents of the Synoptics. There remains considerable material peculiar to Matthew, on the one hand, and Luke, on the other. B. H. Streeter, a British scholar, expanded the "two-document hypothesis" into a "four-document hypothesis." His volume on *The Four Gospels* (1924)[4] represents something of a monument to the entire era of source criticism. He argued that four main documents form the basis for the synoptic Gospels: Mark, Q, M, and L. The sources symbolized by the letters M and L were allegedly documents containing for the most part the teachings of Jesus preserved exclusively in either Matthew or Luke. Streeter attracted only a few supporters for his "four-document hypothesis" with M and L as symbols for written sources, and he did not use these letters to designate much of the narrative material peculiar to either Matthew or Luke. *But the letters M and L can be retained to identify any and all material peculiar to the Gospels of Matthew and Luke respectively.* Therefore, this equation presents itself: synoptic Gospels = Mark, Q, M, and L. So modified, the two-document, or two-source, hypothesis can be diagrammed as follows:

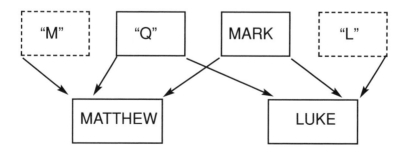

Around the turn of the nineteenth century, further observations were made about the synoptic Gospels that resulted in the emergence of another critical discipline alongside source criticism.

Period 3: Form Criticism (Early Twentieth Century)

A reading of the synoptic Gospels discloses that the stories and sayings of Jesus are loosely connected by brief notations about where and when these events occurred in his ministry. The stories and sayings are strung together like so many beads on a string. The reader can easily detect the narrative thread that runs through the early chapters of Mark, the earliest Gospel:

> Now after John was arrested, Jesus came to Galilee...As Jesus passed along...They went to Capernaum...As soon as they left...That evening...In the morning...And he went throughout all Galilee... When he returned to Capernaum . . . Jesus went out again beside the sea ...One sabbath...Again he entered the synagogue...Jesus departed with his disciples to the sea...And he went up the mountain...Then he went home....(Mark 1:14ff.)

The stories and sayings of Jesus that are linked together by phrases such as these sometimes appear at very different places in his ministry in the individual Gospels. Notice, for example, the different narrative settings for the beatitudes and the Lord's Prayer. Jesus pronounces the beatitudes on a mountain in Matthew but on a plain in Luke (Matt. 5:3-12 = Luke 6:20-23). He teaches the Lord's Prayer in Galilee in Matthew but on the road to Jerusalem in Luke (Matt. 6:9-13 = Luke 11:2-4).

There is still another interesting characteristic of the stories about Jesus. They are self-contained dramas with their own plots and supporting casts. Usually they do not depend upon what occurs before or after them in the overall sequence of events. Jesus heals a leper (Mark 1:40-45 par.). He appoints twelve disciples (Mark 3:13-19 par.). He debates with Pharisees and Herodians about paying taxes to Caesar (Mark 12:13-17 par.). These incidents could have happened anywhere and any time during the ministry of Jesus.

These features of the Gospels point the way to a leading question: *In what form, or forms, was the Jesus story passed down orally before it was written down?* Was that story told in a sequence beginning, for example, with the baptism of Jesus and concluding with his crucifixion? Or was each story and saying passed on individually apart from any general outline of Jesus' ministry? And what about the words and deeds? How were they used in the early church before they were written in the Gospels? Within worship? As preaching? For teaching?

Persons during the beginning years of the church candidly admitted that the story of Jesus was not immediately written in books. But the question of this oral process was raised and addressed in new ways in the opening decades of the twentieth century. With the written priority of Mark established to the satisfaction of most scholars, attention shifted to the process behind the written sources. The discipline of form criticism had appeared. *Form criticism can be defined as the discipline that seeks to understand the Gospel tradition as it was transmitted orally, before it was written down.* Form critics gave answers that were varied, sometimes unconvincing, and often controversial. But their proposals could not be ignored.

Three German scholars produced the foundational works in form criticism shortly after World War I. The term *Formgeschichte* (literally, "form history") became the name of this approach to the Gospels.

K. L. Schmidt concentrated his attention on the narrative framework of the Gospels, especially the outline of Jesus' ministry in Mark. In a study published in 1919, he declared the sequence of events in Mark to be primarily the creation of the Gospel writer.[5] The reader of Mark, therefore, could not rely on the outline of Jesus' ministry as being historically accurate even though Mark was the oldest Gospel.

Martin Dibelius and Rudolf Bultmann directed their efforts at a detailed analysis of the individual sayings and stories in the synoptic Gospels. The work of Dibelius appeared in 1919, *From Tradition to Gospel* (English trans., 1935).[6] The work of Bultmann appeared shortly thereafter in 1921, *History of the Synoptic Tradition* (English trans., 1963).[7] Both scholars classified the stories and sayings of Jesus according to certain types or forms. They also identified certain "laws" that had governed the oral telling and retelling of these stories and sayings. One such "law" was this: details tend to be added in the repetition of a story. Consider, for example, the addition of details in the story of Jesus' arrest when someone cuts off the ear of the high priest's servant (Mark 14:43-52 par. and John 18:1-11). The most controversial aspect of the work of Dibelius and Bultmann was the claim, especially by Bultmann, that many of the stories and sayings of Jesus had not only been passed on by the church but had been created within the church. Whereas K. L. Schmidt questioned the historical accuracy of the outline of Jesus' ministry in Mark, Dibelius and Bultmann seemed to be denying the historical faithfulness of many of Jesus' stories and sayings.

As might be expected, the proposals of these founding form critics met with less than universal approval. British scholars, in particular, issued reasoned dissenting opinions. C. H. Dodd would later become the unofficial dean of British biblical scholarship as the general chairman of the translation committee of the New English Bible (1970). He often challenged Schmidt's view that the outline of Jesus' ministry was largely the fabrication of the Gospel writer. Dodd perceived similarity between the outline of Jesus' ministry in the Gospel of Mark and the outline of Jesus' ministry in the sermons of Peter and Paul in the book of Acts (especially Acts 10:37-41; 13:23-31).[8] Dodd claimed, therefore, that Mark preserved an older, generally accurate understanding of the shape of Jesus' ministry. Another British scholar, Vincent Taylor, entered into dialogue with the proposals of Dibelius and Bultmann. He strongly disagreed with the implication that many of the stories and sayings of Jesus had been created within the early church. But in *The Formation of the Gospel Tradition* (1935),[9] Taylor accepted to a large extent the way these critics had classified the stories and sayings of Jesus into types.

Debate continues in our day about the exact role of the primitive church in the oral transmission of the Jesus story before the Gospels. Widespread agreement has been reached, however, concerning the classification of the Gospel material into three broad categories: stories, sayings, and passion narratives. These three kinds of material can be further described as follows.

The *Gospel stories* report what Jesus did, his deeds. The stories themselves can be subdivided into three groups with each having a different aspect of Jesus' activity as its focal point.

First, miracle stories. These narratives have at their center some miraculous act by Jesus himself. This act may involve the casting out of a demon, the healing of a physical malady, the resuscitation of a dead person, or some control over nature.

Second, pronouncement stories. These narratives have at their center a pronouncement, or saying, of Jesus himself. The situations prompting Jesus to make a pronouncement vary. Sometimes they involve debate between Jesus and his opponents over such issues as the payment of taxes to Caesar. But they may involve discussion with an interested inquirer or the instruction of the disciples.

Third, simple stories. This grouping represents something of a catchall category. Terms such as *legends* and *myths* have been used for many of these narratives. But these words popularly convey the notion that these stories are "pure fiction." The expressions *historical stories* and *biographical stories* have also been used. But these phrases seem to claim that the stories are "pure fact." A more neutral designation is desirable, such as *simple stories*. These narratives have at their center neither a miraculous act of Jesus nor a pronouncement by Jesus. Jesus himself appears as the focal point of these stories as he submits to the baptism of John or rides into Jerusalem on an ass amidst shouting crowds of people.

The *Gospel sayings* represent what Jesus said, his words. The sayings of Jesus can be subdivided into two broad groups.

First, parables. A large number of parables have been preserved in the synoptic Gospels. The Gospel of Mark possibly contains a small collection that probably had been assembled even before the writing of this Gospel, including the parables of the sower, the seed growing secretly, and the mustard seed (Mark 4:1-34). Parables may be short or long, but Jesus' parables can be defined as figures of speech that make comparisons between commonplace objects, events, and persons, and that transcendent reality symbolized by the phrase *kingdom of God*.

Second, simple sayings. This grouping represents a broad category for non-parabolic sayings. Included here are the many short statements that appear on Jesus' lips. These sayings are diverse in literary structure and content. Among them are proverbs, brief statements of conventional wisdom, such as the so-called golden rule (Matt. 7:12 = Luke 6:31), and aphorisms, terse statements that run counter to accepted wisdom, such as the command to hate father and mother (Matt. 10:37 = Luke 14:26). Other examples of simple sayings are: beatitudes, or blessings (Matt. 5:9); woes, or curses (Luke 6:24); legal commentaries (Matt. 5:21-22); warnings (Matt. 7:15); laments (Matt. 23:37 = Luke 13:34); and apocalyptic pronouncements (Mark 13:24-27 par.).

The *Gospel passion narratives* consist of a series of stories that report the events of Jesus' final hours from his final meal through his crucifixion (Mark 14–15 par.; John 18–19; and *Gospel of Peter*). A couple of interesting features distinguish these narratives. On the one hand, the stories in these narratives must occupy the positions they do in relation to one another. Each story depends upon what occurs before and after it in the unfolding sequence of events. The Last Supper, for example, must be narrated before the arrest in Gethsemane, and the arrest in Gethsemane before the legal proceedings before the high priest and the Roman governor. On the other hand, in the passion narratives there exists the greatest similarity between the story of Jesus in the Synoptics and the story in John. Because of these features, the opinion has often been expressed that the passion narratives represent the first portion of the Jesus story to be told as a consecutive story. The passion narratives, therefore, constitute one of the three main kinds of oral tradition preserved in our written Gospels. This threefold classification can be diagrammed as follows:

STORIES

1) miracle stories
2) pronouncement stories
3) simple stories

SAYINGS

1) parables
2) simple sayings

PASSION NARRATIVES

Midway through the twentieth century, a third discipline joined source criticism and form criticism as methods for understanding more fully the synoptic Gospels. Like its parent disciplines, this newer method grew out of an examination and comparison of the Gospels themselves.

Period 4: Redaction Criticism (Mid-Twentieth Century)

Form critics explored the oral process by which the stories and sayings of Jesus were passed down before the writing of the Gospels. Source criticism established that Matthew and Luke used Mark as their main written source. When the authors of Matthew and Luke retold a story borrowed from Mark, however, they made editorial changes in the story. Sometimes they added words. At other times they omitted words. Oftentimes they altered the exact wording and phrasing. On occasion they placed the particular episode in their versions of the Jesus story at points quite different from the position it occupied in the Markan version.

Carefully compare, for example, the miracle story of the stilling of the storm in Matthew 8:23-27 with the same story in Mark 4:35-41. In Mark the story appears immediately after Jesus had finished teaching his disciples in parables. The story includes the statement that Jesus' followers "took him with them." During the storm, Jesus' companions in the boat reproach him: "Teacher, do you not care that we are perishing?" Jesus then stills the storm and accuses them of having "no faith." But the author of Matthew has placed this same story immediately after Jesus' command to a disciple: "Follow me." And the story itself opens with the observation that "his disciples followed him." During the storm, Jesus' companions in the boat cry out for help: "Lord, save us! We are perishing!" Jesus calls them people of "little faith" and then stills the storm. Are these differences between the Matthean and the Markan versions incidental or insignificant? Or has the author of Matthew introduced these subtle changes quite intentionally in order to make a particular point or points for his reading audience?

Each of the Gospel writers, in addition to the editorial changes within a particular story, also had to make decisions about the overall shape of his Gospel. Each had to decide how he was going to begin and end his version of the Jesus story.

Notice, for example, how the author of Mark ended the Gospel rather abruptly. At least the oldest manuscripts of the Gospel conclude with this verse about the women who visited the tomb in order to anoint the body of Jesus: "So they went out and fled from the tomb, for terror and amazement had seized them; and they said nothing to anyone, for they were afraid" (Mark 16:8). Some scholars have suggested that the original conclusion of the Gospel was lost, by accident or by mutilation. Most scholars agree that the longer ending represented in our New Testaments by Mark 16:9-20 was added to the Gospel by someone other than the original author. But if the departure of the women from the tomb constituted the intended conclusion, why did the evangelist end the Jesus story so suddenly? Why did the evangelist not report any appearances of the resurrected Jesus to his disciples in Galilee?

Or, to take another example, the author of Luke does not cut short the telling of the Jesus story. Instead, the author extends it. The Gospel of Luke has as its sequel the book of Acts. Why has this evangelist supplemented an account of Jesus' ministry with a history of the church's expansion?

These questions about the way each Gospel writer has edited or redacted his information about Jesus come together into one central question: *What does a Gospel writer's editorial work indicate about that writer's theology and, by implication, the situation for which the Gospel was written?* Augustine of old anticipated this question about the theology of each Gospel writer, but he was interested in harmonizing the differences among the Gospels. At mid-twentieth century, however, scholars began to accentuate these differences. They concerned themselves not with the unity beneath the differences but the varying theological perspectives indicated by them. The discipline of redaction criticism had been born. *Redaction criticism can be defined as the discipline that seeks to discover the theology of each Gospel writer and the social situation of the writer by studying the ways the sources have been edited and the final work composed.*[10] Sustained redactional study of the Synoptic Gospels began shortly after World War II. This approach had its forerunners in English-language scholarship. But again the main impetus came from German scholars. The English name for the discipline relates to the German expression *Redaktionsgeschichte* (literally, "redaction history").

Günther Bornkamm, in a brief 1948 analysis of the story of the stilling of the storm, demonstrated that the author of Matthew had creatively interpreted that story in adapting it from Mark.[11] The evangelist edited the episode to highlight the theme of discipleship, or following Jesus, for his own tempest-tossed community. When those people of "little faith" cry out, "Lord save us!" Jesus then calms the winds and the waves.

Whereas Bornkamm initiated redactional study of the Gospel of Matthew, two other scholars pioneered the analysis of the Gospels of Mark and Luke.

In 1956 Willi Marxsen published a collection of essays, the very title of which suggests his interest in the Gospel writer: *Mark the Evangelist* (English trans., 1969).[12] Central to the theology of Mark, according to Marxsen, was the evangelist's belief that the second coming of Jesus would soon occur specifically in Galilee. Marxsen derives his conclusions from a careful study of the Gospel text, but he finds support in the way the author has concluded his Gospel. The evangelist does not report any postresurrection appearances of Jesus, thereby leaving the reader with the expectation of Jesus' appearing in Galilee, as announced by Jesus himself (Mark 14:28) and the angel in the tomb (Mark

16:7). The appearance of Jesus expected by the evangelist and the original readers, however, was not simply a postresurrection appearance but the coming of Jesus at the end of history for final judgment.

Hans Conzelmann produced the most thorough of the first redactional studies. His 1954 publication examined the thought of the author of Luke-Acts. Thus the English translation was entitled *The Theology of St. Luke* (1960).[13] Conzelmann also identified the second coming of Jesus as central to the theology of Luke. But the evangelist's major concern was not the nearness of the second coming but its delay, its failure to happen as soon as expected by first-generation Christians. Conzelmann based his conclusions on a careful study of the Gospel text, but support also came from the evangelist's having supplemented his Gospel with the book of Acts, a history of the church. Faced with the failure of Jesus to return, the evangelist viewed the church as occupying a more permanent place in history apart from the ministry of Jesus. Thus, according to Conzelmann, the author of Luke-Acts viewed God's dealing with the world in terms of three distinct periods: (1) period of Israel; (2) period of Jesus' ministry; and (3) period of the church. The ministry of Jesus, therefore, was the "middle of time."

Redaction criticism occupied a position near the center stage of Gospel study through the 1970s. Bornkamm, Marxsen, and Conzelmann were joined on stage by countless others. Out of these varied labors emerged the general recognition that each synoptic writer was not just a transmitter of tradition but a theologian. Each evangelist edited, or redacted, written and oral sources to enable the Jesus story to speak afresh for a particular time and place.

Redaction criticism functions best where a comparison can be made between the phrasing of a story in Mark, the earliest Gospel, and the phrasing of that same story in the later Gospels of Matthew and Luke. Then we can with some certainty see the way the Gospel writer has edited his material. Even where this comparison exists, however, some scholars have questioned whether every omission, addition, and alteration of a word or sentence has intentional theological meaning. A more obvious guide to the theology of an evangelist is the overall structure and the basic content of his Gospel.

In the next chapter we will pay special attention to the way each evangelist organizes his information about Jesus and to the kind of information the evangelist chooses to include. In at least a general sense, we will be taking our cue from redaction criticism.

Over the past two decades, however, the period of Gospel research dominated by redaction criticism has been superseded by a period characterized by two other approaches to the synoptic Gospels. Both approaches appropriate theories, methods, and techniques from secular disciplines. American scholars have been among the pioneers and leading advocates of both narrative criticism and social-scientific criticism.[14]

Period 5: Narrative Criticism and Social-Scientific Criticism (Late Twentieth Century)

As we have seen, redaction criticism presupposed the results of source criticism and form criticism. Redaction critics sought to identify the theology of the Gospel writers by analyzing how they edited written sources and oral tradition. By so identifying the theology of each Gospel writer, redaction critics also—by implication—gained insight into the historical circumstances to which the writer was responding.

Eventually, however, some Gospel scholars began to recognize the obvious about the Gospels and responded accordingly. They began to view the Gospels as more than pieced-together sources and collected forms. They appropriated the theory and methods of secular literary criticism and focused on the final form and the function of the Gospels. That is, the Gospels represent narrative literature. As narrative literature, the Gospels tell stories and possess the formal dimensions of stories including plot, characters, and setting.

Collectively, the Gospels tell the story of Jesus of Nazareth. The Gospels have a plot: a sequence of events connected by causality. Jesus appears. He speaks and acts. Some follow him but abandon him. Others dislike him and kill him. He dies on a cross. He is resurrected from the dead. The Gospels have characters: persons who interact with one another. These include Jesus, his male disciples and sympathetic women, the religious and political authorities, and the crowds. The Gospels also have settings: notations about place and time. Action occurs in Galilee and Jerusalem, by the lake and on the road, in a synagogue and in the Temple. Action occurs on a Sabbath and at Passover. Thus the Gospels collectively and individually have narrative worlds.

The recognition that the Gospels are stories leads to related questions: *What is the story of Jesus in this Gospel? How does the Gospel writer tell this story?* With the emergence of narrative criticism, the critical focus shifted from the theology of the Gospel writer to the story of Jesus as narrated in each Gospel. *Narrative criticism can be defined as the discipline that studies the formal literary dimensions of the individual Gospels.*[15] The Gospel writer has become more than a redactor and a theologian. The writer has become a storyteller—a narrator. The narrator presides over the literarily created narrative world. The interpreter can now speak about the "implied author" and the "implied readers" of the text. These are imaginative constructs. They refer not to the actual author but to the perspective from which the Gospel seems to have been written; not to the actual readers but to those who seem to be invited to respond to the Gospel.

The shift in Gospel study from redaction criticism to narrative criticism was signaled in the late 1970s and early 1980s in a series of nontechnical studies entitled *Stories of Jesus,* each of which centered on a particular Gospel. The first volume to appear was Werner Kelber's *Mark's Story of Jesus* (1979).[16] Although

51

Kelber focuses on the story of Jesus by providing a running commentary on the Gospel narrative, he concludes by suggesting what Mark's story implies about Mark's community in the aftermath of the destruction of Jerusalem in 70 C.E. Mark's negative critique of Jesus' own family, the twelve disciples, and the Galilean women provides an explanation for why Mark's own community had survived the destruction but the early Jerusalem church itself had disappeared. Those leaders of the Jerusalem church had not returned to Galilee after the crucifixion and resurrection to await the kingdom as Jesus himself had commanded them.

Significant narrative studies of the Gospels have appeared in recent years. The names of the monographs themselves suggest their narrative critical concerns: *Mark as Story* (1982); *Matthew as Story* (2nd ed.; 1988); *Narrative Unity in Luke-Acts,* (2 vols.; 1986, 1990); and *Anatomy of the Fourth Gospel: A Study in Literary Design* (1983).[17]

Narrative studies often confine themselves to the narrative world of the text with little or no interest in the social world behind and beyond the text. Some scholars have understandably questioned the value of approaching the Gospels with questions and techniques refined by secular literary critics in the study of works of fiction. And admittedly, narrative criticism—like redaction criticism—has limited possibilities for moving from text to history, from text to the community presupposed by the text, from text to the life of Jesus. However, the second recent turn in Gospel criticism offers greater historical promise; alongside narrative criticism has emerged social-scientific criticism.

While some Gospel scholars were analyzing the literary dimensions of the Gospels, others were turning their attention to the broader cultural and social setting within which the Gospels had been written. They appropriated the theories and models of the social sciences, especially cultural anthropology. They emphasized not only that the Gospels were written in a historical period far removed from ours, but that the Gospels presuppose a social system quite different from ours.

Gospel scholars taking a social-scientific approach ask two related questions: *What is the social world presupposed by the narrative world of the Gospels? How does the narrative world of the Gospels reflect that social world?*[18] History as an academic discipline focuses on the particular. But with the emergence of social-scientific criticism, Gospel criticism has been enlarged beyond the study of particular individuals, events, and institutions mentioned in the Gospels to the identification of those values and processes common to the complex social system presupposed by the Gospels. *Social-scientific criticism can be defined as the discipline, or family of disciplines, that studies the Gospels within the context of their social world.*

The so-called Chicago School of American biblical scholarship anticipated this phase of Gospel criticism early in the twentieth century.[19] The work of

German scholar Gerd Theissen, more recently, prepared the way for a socio-logical analysis of the early Jesus movement and the world of Jesus.[20] Among the strongest advocates for the use of social-science models in understanding specifically the Gospels has been American scholar Bruce J. Malina. Among his publications are *The New Testament World: Insights from Cultural Anthropology* (1981), *Christian Origins and Cultural Anthropology* (1986), *Windows on the World of Jesus* (1993),[21] and—with Richard L. Rohrbaugh—*Social-Science Commentary on the Gospels* (1992).[22]

For Malina and Rohrbaugh, the Mediterranean region constituted (and still constitutes) a "culture-continent." The Mediterranean world of the first centu-ry represents an agrarian society, not meaning agricultural, but preindustrial—although 90 percent of the population was rural. Like all social systems, the Mediterranean world was characterized by certain social norms and values that would have been shared by the authors and the readers of the Gospels. But the norms and values may not be apparent to the modern reader. The conceptual models constructed by the social sciences assist the modern reader in under-standing the social dynamics reflected in and presupposed by the text.

In their social-science commentary, Malina and Rohrbaugh juxtapose pas-sages from the synoptic Gospels with brief notes and scenarios that describe relevant dimensions of the ancient Mediterranean social system. An under-standing of the patron-client nature of that social system, in which persons of higher status and persons of lower status become reciprocally obligated to one another through favors and paybacks, casts light on the story of the centuri-on's son (Matt. 8:5-13 = Luke 7:1-10). An appreciation of the honor/shame nature of that social system, in which sensitivity to social status was of para-mount value, has implications for interpreting the story of Jesus' rejection at his hometown of Nazareth (Mark 6:1-6 par.). Knowing about life in a society characterized by dyadic personality, where people do not think of themselves as individuals independent from a group, such as the family, raises interesting questions about Jesus' own question in the story of Peter's confession at Caesarea Philippi (Mark 8:27-30 par.).

By the end of the twentieth century, therefore, the Gospels have come to be analyzed and read from a variety of angles. Before we turn to consider in more detail how they portray Jesus, their central character, we must return briefly to the Gospel that has remained on the sidelines throughout most of our review of Gospel criticism, namely, the Gospel of John.

Retrospective: Criticism and the Gospel of John

Within the early church, the view prevailed that John was written last in conscious contrast to the three earlier Gospels of Matthew, Mark, and Luke. The view that John was familiar with one or more of the other Gospels found supporters well into the era of modern biblical criticism. B. H. Streeter's monumental work on source criticism, to which we referred earlier, was entitled *The Four Gospels* (1924) — not *The Three Gospels*. Streeter argued that the fourth evangelist was familiar with Mark and Luke, but not Matthew.

However, another British scholar, P. Gardner-Smith, systematically reviewed the evidence in his *Saint John and the Synoptic Gospels* (1938)[23] and set forth the case for John's literary independence from the Synoptics. This gradually became the dominant scholarly view. One of the reasons for this shift in opinion about the relationship between John and the Synoptics was the renewed appreciation of oral tradition, introduced into the study of the Gospels by form criticism. Similarities between John and the Synoptics could be explained based on common tradition instead of literary dependence. Now, at the end of the twentieth century, this view itself has been seriously eroded.[24]

Other interesting proposals about sources underlying John have come to the fore. These include the claim that the fourth evangelist had access to a "signs source" — a written document consisting of a series of miracle stories that became the narrative foundation for chapters 1–12. Evidence for this source appears in the Gospel itself where the first two miracles are explicitly numbered as the "first" and the "second" signs that Jesus performed in Galilee (2:11 and 4:54). Some advocates of this view have even referred to this source as the Signs Gospel. The Signs Gospel may have been formulated within the setting of a Hellenistic synagogue. Those Jews who believed that Jesus was indeed the Messiah collected stories about Jesus' miracles to serve a missionary purpose in relation to their fellow Jews who disputed such a claim.[25]

3

Gospel Portrayals

We regularly read various kinds of literature. This variety may include newspapers and textbooks, novels and telephone directories. We have already reviewed the basic forms of the Gospel tradition as classified by form criticism, the stories and sayings that collectively make up a Gospel. We have also noted how narrative criticism approaches the Gospels not in terms of their parts but as literary compositions. But what kind of literature are the Gospels?

The claim has sometimes been made that the four Gospels represent a unique literary genre. The letters of Paul and the other New Testament letters reflect a structure common to other letters in the Graeco-Roman world. The book of Revelation has counterparts among different Jewish apocalypses that concern themselves with the end of the world. As a chronicle of the early church, the book of Acts possesses characteristics of Graeco-Roman and Jewish history writings. But the four canonical Gospels, according to the view popularized by Rudolf Bultmann, constitute a literary type peculiar to Christianity. A strong claim has been set forth, however, for the position that the four Gospels of the New Testament literarily represent examples of Graeco-Roman biography. In conscious opposition to Bultmann, American scholar Charles Talbert, followed by others, has argued that "the canonical gospels belong to the biographical genre of antiquity."[1]

Whether a unique genre or a form of ancient biography, the four canonical Gospels can collectively be described as confessions of faith in Jesus as the Christ of God. Like the other New Testament writings, therefore, these Gospels presuppose the faith of their authors. But their authors confess their faith, or share their faith perspectives, through narratives about the life of Jesus.

Recent years have witnessed the expansion of the category of gospel to encompass a variety of writings and literary types. Helmut Koester has proposed that "the corpus of gospel literature . . . should include all those writings which are constituted by the transmission, use, and interpretation of materials and traditions from and about Jesus of Nazareth."[2] Certainly the word "gospel" was used within the early church to designate writings about Jesus not included in the New Testament. Many of these came to be called apocryphal Gospels to distinguish them from the four canonical Gospels. The word "apocryphal," meaning "hidden," may have been used to explain why these gospels were not more widely known or to suggest that they had been hidden from the general public because their content was too advanced or too heretical.

In what follows, we are interested in how the individual Gospel writers have portrayed Jesus. We focus primarily on the four canonical Gospels; and recognize that even among these four appear two very different characterizations of Jesus: the Synoptic portrayal in Matthew, Mark, and Luke; and then the Johannine portrayal in John. We will also consider how Jesus has been portrayed in other Gospels, including the *Gospel of Peter*, the *Gospel of Thomas*, and what has become known as Sayings Gospel Q.

The Synoptic Portrayal

The Gospels of Matthew, Mark, and Luke offer similar portrayals of Jesus and his story since Mark was used by the other two as their main written source. The portrayal they share can be summarized as follows.

The synoptic Gospels present a similar outline of Jesus' ministry and many of the same stories. Jesus' baptism by John and his testing by Satan, or the devil, immediately precede the inauguration of his public ministry of words and deeds (Mark 1:9-13 par.). Only after the imprisonment of John does Jesus begin that ministry (Mark 1:14 par.). Most of his early activity takes place in his home territory of Galilee. Jesus goes to Jerusalem only once (Mark 10:1-52 par.). On that occasion his disruptive actions in the Temple constitute a decisive event (Mark 11:15-19 par.). Arrested and tried, he suffers crucifixion. At the concluding supper with his disciples, however, he prepares them for his death with words of explanation over the bread and the wine (Mark 14:22-25 par.). The Last Supper is a Passover meal and Jesus dies on Passover day. Insofar as only this Passover is mentioned in the course of his ministry, his ministry could have lasted less than a year.

The synoptic Gospels also present a similar characterization of Jesus and his message. The central theme of his message is that of "the kingdom of God" (Mark 1:14-15 par.). Jesus in his preaching uses the parable form with great frequency (Mark 4:1-34 par.). He also anticipates the end with apocalyptic teaching (Mark 13:1-37 par.). Generally, Jesus' activity is marked by what has been called a "messianic secret." He commands evil spirits, healed persons, and even his disciples to remain silent about his identity and his power. Jesus seems to prefer the name "Son of Man" for himself—not such designations as "Messiah" or "Son of God" (Mark 8:27–9:1 par.).

Along with their similarities, the synoptic Gospels also differ in their portrayals of Jesus. Each writer emphasizes dimensions of the Jesus story appropriate for the intended readers. Scholars have discovered that the presentation of Jesus in each Gospel, particularly within the context of the first-century social world, may tell us more about the origin of the individual Gospels than comments by such ancient interpreters as Papias, Irenaeus, Clement, and Augustine. To appreciate the distinctiveness of each Gospel, we will briefly review the Gospel in terms of its literary structure, its portrayal of Jesus, and, finally, its possible historical origin.

The Gospel of Mark

Mark, the earliest Gospel, is also the shortest. The Gospel begins with the ministry of John and his baptism of Jesus. It concludes with the departure of Mary Magdalene and her companions from the empty tomb. Thus the Gospel contains neither infancy stories nor resurrection appearance stories. Within the Gospel itself, emphasis falls on Jesus' actions instead of his teachings. There are only two main groups of sayings—the collection of parables (chap. 4) and the lecture on the coming end (chap. 13). Scholars offer different suggestions about the precise manner in which the evangelist has organized his material. But geography plays a foundational role. Accordingly, the Gospel presents an hour-glass shape with a narrow journey section (10:1-52) constituting the neck through which Jesus passes on his way from Galilee in the north (1:14–9:50) to Jerusalem in the south (11:1–16:8). (See diagram on page 58.)

Jesus the Crucified Christ. The Gospel of Mark has been called a passion account with an extended introduction. But, to be more precise, the entire Gospel is a passion narrative. Within the broadly conceived geographical scheme, the evangelist deliberately moves Jesus from his baptism to his crucifixion. The Markan author and the Markan story portray Jesus preeminently as the Crucified Christ.

An ominous reference to the arrest of John introduces Jesus' ministry of preaching and healing (1:14-15). Straightaway Jesus finds himself embroiled in controversy. As the "Son of Man," he forgives the sins of a paralytic and heals on the Sabbath a man with a withered hand (2:10, 27-28). Within the context of these disputes occurs the first allusion to Jesus' own fate—on his own lips (2:20). Out of these disputes grows a plot against his life by Pharisees

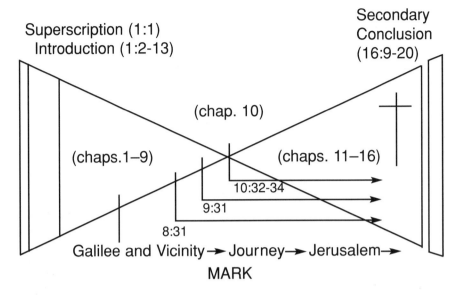

Superscription (1:1)
Introduction (1:2-13)

Secondary
Conclusion
(16:9-20)

(chap. 10)

(chaps.1–9)

(chaps. 11–16)

10:32-34

9:31

8:31

Galilee and Vicinity ➤ Journey ➤ Jerusalem ➤

MARK

and Herodians (3:6). The Pharisees were the Jewish religious sect devoted to applying the law of Moses, the Torah, to all of life. The Herodians were the political supporters of the family of Herod the Great, one of whose sons— Herod Antipas—ruled Galilee throughout the life of Jesus. Having alienated both the religious and the political authorities, Jesus also baffles his own relatives (3:31-35) and offends his own townsfolk (6:1-6). Then he withdraws from Galilee and confounds his own disciples (8:14-21).

The evangelist reports the turning point in the ministry of Jesus against this backdrop of growing hostility and increasing isolation. The setting lies northward of Galilee in the regions around Caesarea Philippi. The characters include Jesus and his twelve disciples. The plot involves a question, an answer, and an editorial comment. Jesus asks: "Who do people say that I am? . . . Who do you say that I am?" Peter replies: "You are the Messiah." The evangelist observes about Jesus: "And he sternly ordered them not to tell anyone about him" (8:27-30).

Now, and only now, does the Gospel writer have Jesus share with his followers what was implied earlier: he must die! Between Peter's confession near Caesarea Philippi and the arrival in Jerusalem, Jesus makes three so-called passion predictions, again referring to himself as "Son of Man": "the Son of Man must undergo much suffering, and be rejected by the elders, the chief priests, and the scribes, and be killed, and after three days rise again" (8:31; 9:31; 10:32-34). In Jerusalem Jesus does experience suffering, rejection, and death. His only words from the cross in this extended passion narrative are the words of lament from Psalm 22: "My God, my God, why have you forsaken me?" (15:34).

To better understand Mark's portrayal of Jesus as the Crucified Christ, we should note several related themes in the Gospel that have occasioned frequent comment.

The designation of Jesus as Son of God appears infrequently in Mark. Its careful placement, however, indicates its importance for the Gospel writer. The writer introduces Jesus as "Son of God" (1:1). Both God through the heavenly voice at baptism and transfiguration (1:11; 9:7) and the unclean spirits (3:11) recognize Jesus in this way. But the climactic confession occurs when Jesus dies and the Roman centurion beneath the cross declares: "Truly this man was God's Son" (15:39). Thus in Mark, Jesus' divine sonship expresses itself preeminently through his obedient suffering unto death. For the cross, Jesus made his way to Jerusalem. By the cross, he is revealed to be Son of God.

The theme of the "messianic secret" pervades Mark. The Gospel writer repeatedly points out how Jesus tried to keep his work and his identity a secret. Jesus orders demons, witnesses to his healings, and even his own disciples not to make him known (1:34; 3:12; 5:43; 7:24, 36; 8:30; 9:9, 30). In Mark, the evangelist appears to be using the secrecy motif to show that Jesus has de-emphasized the more spectacular aspects of his ministry in favor of his vocation as the suffering "Son of Man" (8:31; 9:31; 10:32-34) and suffering "Son of God" (15:39).

In Mark, as in the four Gospels, the cross of Jesus is not final. The predictions about his death are also predictions about his resurrection: "...and after three days rise again" (8:31; 9:31; 10:32-34; also 9:9). Redaction critic Willi Marxsen observed that the abbreviated resurrection account of women leaving the empty tomb leaves the reader with the expectation of Jesus' appearing. In the abrupt ending and the refusal of the women to tell anyone that Jesus will appear in Galilee, narrative critic Werner Kelber has seen a condemnation of the Jerusalem church. Whatever the precise implications of this conclusion, there is evidence elsewhere in the Gospel that the evangelist did expect the appearance of Jesus and the kingdom in the near future. Crucial in this regard is the so-called apocalyptic discourse of Jesus (chap. 13).

Here in Jerusalem on the eve of Jesus' crucifixion, he speaks to a group of disciples. He shares with them what events will take place between his resurrection and his return, his parousia. From the evangelist's reporting of this apocalyptic discourse, it seems likely that he views the time in which he and his readers are living as the suffering, or tribulation, just before the end (vv. 7, 14, 19, 24). A note of urgency runs through the speech with a repeated use of the imperative mode: "Beware" (vv. 5, 9); "But be alert" (v. 23); "Beware, keep alert" (v. 33); "Keep awake" (vv. 35, 37). The words of Jesus to his disciples at the conclusion of the discourse are obviously addressed to Mark and his contemporaries: "And what I say to you I say to all: Keep awake" (v. 37). The evangelist, therefore, alerts his readers to the fact that Jesus the "Son of Man" who acted with authority during his public ministry (2:10, 28), and who obediently went to the cross (8:31; 9:31; 10:32-34), will soon come with power and glory (13:26; also 8:38; 14:62). Final victory will then belong to Jesus the Crucified Christ.

A Persecuted Community. Early Christian writers attributed authorship of this Gospel to a certain Mark. They said that he had been associated with Peter in Rome before Peter's martyrdom during the persecution of Nero in the 60s. Presumably this Mark is the John Mark who had also traveled with Paul (Acts 12:25–13:13; Philem. 24; Col. 4:10; 2 Tim. 4:11) and whose mother had hosted the infant church in her Jerusalem home (Acts 12:12). This Mark was a Jewish Christian from Palestine.

Several features of the Gospel itself give plausibility to this ancient understanding of its origin. The rough-hewn Greek language of the Gospel preserves both Aramaic expressions (3:17-18; 5:41; 7:11, 34; 11:9-10; 14:36; 15:22, 34) and Latin loanwords (5:9, 15; 6:37; 15:16, 39). Jewish customs are explained for a presumably Gentile audience (7:3-4, 19). Also a number of stories highlight the role of Peter (1:16-20, 29-31; 9:2-8; 14:26-31, 32-42, 66-72; 16:7). Then there is the intriguing reference to the "naked boy" who was present in Gethsemane at the very moment of Jesus' arrest (14:51-52). Could this be an autobiographical aside by the author of the Gospel—by John Mark? Some interpreters have reasoned that the Last Supper was held in the Jerusalem home of John Mark and that John Mark as a young lad in his bed clothes followed Jesus to Gethsemane after the meal. Others have dismissed this suggestion as imagination run amuck.

The ancient view about the authorship and origin of the Gospel, therefore, is by no means certain. The material about Jesus in the Gospel appears more diverse than simply the preaching of Peter. The findings of form criticism indicate an involved process of oral transmission behind the stories and sayings of Jesus in this, the earliest Gospel. The emphasis in the Gospel on the sufferings of Jesus and his disciples (especially 8:27–9:1) in anticipation of his coming in glory (13:1-37) is appropriate for a document addressed to a persecuted community as had been the church in Rome in the 60s. But suffering for the sake of Jesus was not confined exclusively to that congregation. Syria and even Palestine, specifically Galilee, have been among other sites proposed as places of possible origin. With regard to dating, a clue may be found in the apocalyptic discourse. The desecration of the Jerusalem Temple and the destruction of Jerusalem seem to be either in the immediate future or in the immediate past (13:14). This desecration and destruction did occur as the climactic event in the Jewish War against Rome, in 70 C.E. A date for the writing of the Gospel around the year 70 seems likely.

The most significant interpretation of the Gospel of Mark in recent years has come from Burton Mack.[3] His view of Mark is integral to the alternative understanding of Christian origins that we touched on in our description of how the Gospels came to be.

For Mack, in many respects, the founder of Christianity is not Jesus, nor even Paul, but rather the author of Mark. Mack locates the writing of Mark in southern Syria, in the immediate postwar period, after the fall of Jerusalem to the Romans in 70 C.E. The Gospel grows out of the life of a community of Jesus people trying to establish their identity apart from the Hellenistic synagogues, by which they had been rejected, and over against other groups in the Graeco-Roman world claiming various kinds of loyalty to Jesus. The author, therefore, melded diverse Jesus traditions into the portrayal of Jesus we see in Mark. So the Gospel constitutes a "myth of origin" for the Markan community.

Furthermore, through its adaptation by Matthew and Luke and its subsequent inclusion in the Christian Bible as one of the four Gospels, Mark contributed to what was emerging as the "myth of origin" for the church universal that established itself after the conversion of Constantine in 313 C.E. and the actions of the Council of Nicaea in 325 C.E.

But whatever the particulars of Mack's view of Christian and Markan origins, this narrative account of Jesus' earthly ministry does represent preaching of the gospel message about what God has done and will do through him (1:1; 13:10; et al.). More specifically, the Gospel represents apocalyptic preaching because the parousia of Jesus is proclaimed as imminent (13:1-37). Mack himself underscores the apocalyptic dimensions of Mark. The author of the Gospel is an apocalyptic preacher. He writes to comfort and to encourage his readers whose own sufferings and the dramatic events involving Jerusalem constitute the tribulation of the last days. The author of Mark appropriately portrays Jesus as the Crucified Christ.

The Gospel of Matthew

The author of Matthew has incorporated into his Gospel as much as 90 percent of the material in the Gospel of Mark. Understandably, the Gospel of Matthew has been called a revised edition of Mark. But if Matthew is a revision of Mark, it is nonetheless a significant revision. The author of Matthew has prefaced his Markan material with a genealogy and certain infancy traditions. He has supplemented his Markan material with traditions related to the resurrection. Throughout the body of his Gospel he has introduced a considerable amount of material recounting Jesus' teachings.

In its overall design, the Gospel of Matthew reflects a geographical pattern similar to the one in Mark. As in Mark, Jesus' early activity in Galilee is connected to his later activity in Jerusalem by a brief travel section (chaps. 19–20).

The author of Matthew, however, has superimposed onto his inherited geographical pattern a scheme more *literary* in character and arranged Jesus' teachings into five groupings (chaps. 5–7; 10; 13; 18; 24–25). There is evidence that he intentionally organized this teaching material precisely into five groupings. The stereotyped phrase *kai egeneto* (literally, "and it happened") appears at the conclusion of each grouping: "Now when *[kai egeneto]* Jesus had finished . . ." (7:28; 11:1; 13:53; 19:1; 26:1). This fivefold arrangement of Jesus' teachings long ago prompted American scholar B. W. Bacon to propose an outline of the Gospel consisting of alternating narrative and discourse (chaps. 3–25) with a prologue (chaps. 1–2) and an epilogue (chaps. 26–28).[4] He perceived in this fivefold division a conscious imitation of the Jewish Torah, or law, and an intended presentation of Jesus as a second Moses.

Jack Dean Kingsbury, another American scholar, later proposed an outline of the Gospel consisting of three main sections: the person of Jesus Messiah (1:1–4:16); the proclamation of Jesus Messiah (4:17–16:20); and the suffering, death, and resurrection of Jesus Messiah (16:21–28:20).[5] Kingsbury also finds grammatical support in the Gospel for this threefold division. The phrase *apo tote* ("from that time") occurs at the points of transition between the three sections and nowhere else (4:17; 16:21). Such a threefold division in the Gospel, according to Kingsbury, derives neither from geographical nor literary but theological considerations. At decisive moments in each of the three sections, the evangelist emphasizes that Jesus is above all else "Son of God" (3:17; 16:16; 28:19).

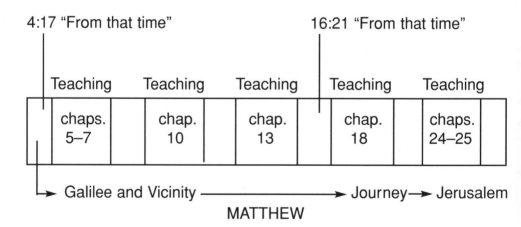

Jesus the Teaching Christ. Matthew gives special prominence to the teachings of Jesus. Like the author of Mark, the author of Matthew moves Jesus from baptism to crucifixion. But unlike the author of Mark, he interrupts the narrative movement by having Jesus deliver lengthy speeches. Matthew portrays Jesus preeminently as the Teaching Christ.

The author of Matthew does not confine his teaching emphasis to the five great collections of Jesus' sayings that appear in the Gospel. This emphasis also appears at the very end of the Gospel, where the evangelist reports how Jesus after his resurrection met his disciples on a mountain in Galilee. The evangelist concludes his Gospel with words spoken by the risen Jesus to his disciples on that occasion (28:16-20). Jesus' words constitute a farewell statement to the disciples about their responsibility between the time of his earthly ministry and the "end of the age."

For the author of Matthew, therefore, the end of the age seems more distant than it was for the writer of Mark. For Matthew and his readers, the present is a time of Jesus' promised presence in their midst (cf. 28:20; 25:31-46; 18:20; 1:23). The present is also a time for missionary work among the Gentiles as new disciples are baptized and taught. Those who become disciples within the church in later generations are to be taught to observe what Jesus commanded during his earthly ministry. The conclusion of Matthew, consequently, has Jesus himself direct the readers of the Gospel back to the past—back to his earthly ministry, to those five groupings of Jesus' sayings found in this Gospel. The teachings of Jesus to be observed by later generations of disciples are these:

On the Higher Righteousness (chaps. 5–7).

On Discipleship (chap. 10)

On the Secrets of the Kingdom (chap. 13)

On the Church (chap. 18)

On the End of the Age (chaps. 24–25).

The words by the risen Jesus at the end of the Gospel make it quite clear that Father, Son, and Holy Spirit are for all the nations of the earth (28:19). But the evangelist makes it equally clear throughout the Gospel that Jesus the Teaching Christ fulfills the promises made by God to Israel. A variety of themes in the Gospel supports the claim that Matthew represents the most Jewish of the Gospels or, at least, that Matthew is Jewish in distinctive ways.

Matthew begins with these words: "An account of the genealogy of Jesus the Messiah, the son of David, the son of Abraham" (1:1). Many within first-century Judaism expected God to raise up for the deliverance of Israel a king from the house of David. Jesus as son of David possessed the qualifications for messiahship. All Jews within first-century Judaism viewed Abraham as the founding father of Israel. Jesus as son of Abraham belonged to historic Israel. The genealogy that follows the opening words in Matthew serves a double purpose (1:2-17). On the one hand, the genealogy demonstrates that Jesus is indeed God's Messiah from the house of David. On the other hand, the genealogy summarizes the whole history of God's dealings with the chosen people Israel. Hence throughout Matthew, there appears the reminder that *Jesus is the Jewish Messiah descended from David.* The title "Son of David" appears as a designation for Jesus usually in passages peculiar to this Gospel (9:27; 12:23; 15:22; 20:30, 31; 21:9, 15; 22:42; also 1:20).

In Matthew, Jesus does more than fulfill the general Jewish hope for a messiah descended from David. Even *details in the life of Jesus take place in fulfillment of specific passages of Scripture:* virgin birth (1:23 = Isa. 7:14); birth in Bethlehem (2:6 = Mic. 5:2); flight to Egypt (2:15 = Hos. 11:1); massacre in Bethlehem (2:18 = Jer. 31:15); settlement in Nazareth (2:23 = ?); move to Capernaum (4:15-16 = Isa. 9:1-2); healing work (8:17 = Isa. 53:4); messianic secrecy (12:18-21 = Isa. 42:1-4); teaching in parables (13:35 = Ps. 78:2); entry into Jerusalem (21:5 = Zech. 9:9); betrayal and burial of Judas (27:9-10 = Zech. 11:12-13; also Jer. 18:1-3; 32:6-15). These quotations in Matthew are called fulfillment quotations because the evangelist usually introduces them with words such as: "This was to fulfill what had been spoken by the Lord through the prophet. . . ."

In Matthew, the message of Jesus is usually characterized by the phrase *kingdom of heaven.* This contrasts with the expression *kingdom of God* preferred in Mark and Luke (cf. Matt. 4:17 and Mark 1:15; Matt. 13 and Mark 4). Within first-century Judaism, the name of God was often avoided in speech out of respect. Some other name was often substituted for the name of God. The author of Matthew reflects this traditional Jewish respect for the divine name ("God") by using a substitute ("heaven").

In Matthew, the expression *the law and the prophets* sometimes appears (5:17; 7:12; 22:40). The "law," or Torah, and the "prophets" represent two of the three main divisions of Jewish Scripture. The law includes the five books of Moses that are known in our Bible by the names Genesis, Exodus, Leviticus, Numbers, and Deuteronomy. The prophets include eight books: the four former prophetic books of Joshua, Judges, Samuel, and Kings and the four latter prophetic books of Isaiah, Jeremiah, Ezekiel, and the Twelve.

In Matthew, and only in Matthew, are preserved *sayings of Jesus that reflect a very restricted understanding of his earthly ministry.* He orders his disciples: "Go nowhere among the Gentiles, and enter no town of the Samaritans, but go rather to the lost sheep of the house of Israel" (10:5-6; also 15:24). So in Matthew, Jesus focuses his earthly ministry on Israel. More specifically, he focuses his ministry on those within Israel whom he calls "the lost sheep"—the common folk. Matthew, therefore, understandably contains Jesus' most derogatory sayings against Israel's religious leaders. These sayings are introduced with a stereotyped expression characteristic of this Gospel: "Woe to you, scribes and Pharisees, hypocrites!" (23:1-36). Those responsible for shepherding the sheep of Israel have abdicated their responsibility (9:36). The traditional teachers within Israel stand condemned by Jesus the Teaching Messiah.

A Jewish-Christian Community in Dialogue with Judaism. Early

Christian writers attributed authorship of this Gospel to the disciple, or apostle, named Matthew. They also said that Matthew had written the Gospel in Hebrew.

The author of this Gospel has admittedly altered his Markan source so that the disciple Matthew achieves slightly more prominence (cf. Matt. 9:9 and Mark 2:13-14; Matt. 10:3 and Mark 3:18). But precisely this literary dependence of Matthew upon Mark renders impossible the ancient Christian tradition that Matthew was written in Hebrew by the disciple named Matthew. Like Mark, its main written source, Matthew was originally written in Greek. There is also little likelihood that a disciple of Jesus such as Matthew the tax collector would have relied upon a Gospel written by a nondisciple such as Mark. The author of the Gospel of Matthew is unknown.

Whoever the author, he displays literary skills characteristic of a Jewish-Christian scribe. He has brought together varied teachings of Jesus and organized them in his Gospel into five large discourses. Each discourse centers around a particular theme. Thus the writer of Matthew has formulated his Gospel as something of a church book—a manual intended for the guidance of his Jewish-Christian community in matters of belief and practice. Writings designed to serve as guides for living were not unknown within Judaism in the ancient world.

During the lifetime of Jesus himself, a dedicated band of Jews lived a monastic-style existence in a settlement on the northwest shore of the Dead Sea. Those who lived here at the place called Qumran probably belonged to the Jewish sect known as the Essenes. These sectarians were dedicated to the observance of the law of Moses. The scrolls discovered in caves in this vicinity in the 1940s, the so-called Dead Sea Scrolls, belonged to their library. The scroll named the Manual of Discipline contains rules and regulations that governed their common life. Their library was hidden in the caves during the Jewish revolt against Rome. Their settlement suffered destruction at the hands of the advancing Romans around the year 68 C.E.

After the fall of Jerusalem to the Romans in the year 70, rabbis belonging to the sect of the Pharisees relocated themselves in the small town of Jamnia. They began the reorganization of Judaism. Involved in the reorganizing process was collecting traditional interpretations of the law of Moses that had circulated among the rabbis. A century or so later these interpretations found written expression in that legal code known as the Mishnah.

The Jewish community of Qumran, therefore, had its Manual of Discipline. Rabbinic Judaism developed the Mishnah. The Jewish-Christian community of Matthew received its Gospel. British scholar W. D. Davies even suggested that the author of Matthew wrote his Gospel with one eye on the events transpiring at Jamnia.[6] Similarly, Anthony J. Saldarini has argued that this Gospel grew out of the life of a Christian-Jewish group whose author was seeking to legitimate his own form of Judaism by delegitimating the leaders of the wider Jewish community.[7]

But whatever the exact relationship of the Gospel writer to Judaism, the narrator tells the Jesus story from the perspective of a Jewish-Christian, or Christian-Jewish, scribe. This anonymous scribe reports a Jesus saying that represents a perfect self-description: "Therefore every scribe who has been trained for the kingdom of heaven is like the master of a household who brings out of his treasure what is new and what is old" (13:52).

The writings of Ignatius, Bishop of Antioch (died ca. 110 C.E.), offer some guidance regarding the place and the date of the origin of the Gospel of Matthew. Since Ignatius seems familiar with the Gospel, Syria is usually considered the place of origin—but not necessarily Antioch. The Palestinian seaport of Caesarea and the Egyptian city of Alexandria have also been mentioned as possible sites. The use of the gospel by Ignatius and its literary dependence upon Mark point to a date sometime between the years 110 and 70 C.E. The usual dating of the Gospel in the 80s fits well into this chronological frame.

The Gospel of Luke

The author of Luke adopts the Gospel of Mark as a principal written source. But the Gospel of Luke, unlike Matthew, cannot be called a revised edition of Mark. The omissions and additions are too numerous. Only around 50 percent of Mark appears in Luke. The author of Luke has prefaced the Markan material with infancy stories about both John the Baptist and Jesus his successor. Throughout the Gospel are interspersed various other traditions. Appended to the Markan material are significant stories related to the resurrection. Then, in a dramatic departure from Mark, the Lukan writer has supplemented the Gospel with the book of Acts to form a two-volume work.

The author of this ambitious writing project has certainly taken geography into consideration in organizing this retelling of the Jesus story. The author has retained the general geographical scheme found in Mark. But whereas Mark only briefly reported Jesus' journey from Galilee to Jerusalem, Luke has greatly expanded the travel section. In fact, the travel section dominates the middle portion of the Gospel (9:51–19:27). The author also follows a geographical outline in the book of Acts as he traces the growth of the church from Jerusalem to Rome (cf. Acts 1:8). The Gospel of Luke represents a journey inward toward Jerusalem. A journey outward from Jerusalem appears in the book of Acts.

Several features of Luke-Acts, however, serve notice that the author writes not only with a geographical but also a *historical* scheme in mind. We have already reviewed the proposal of Hans Conzelmann in our discussion of redaction criticism. According to him, the author of Luke-Acts understands God's dealings with the world in terms of three distinct periods: (1) period of Israel; (2) period of Jesus' ministry; and (3) period of the church. Conzelmann's interpretation of the theology of Luke has not gone unchallenged. There is difficulty, for example, in identifying in Luke-Acts the exact points at which transition occurs from one period of history to the next. But the suggestion of American scholar Raymond E. Brown has merit.[8] To him the infancy narratives that open the Gospel signal the transition from the period of Israel to the period of Jesus' ministry (Luke 1–2). The narratives that open the book of Acts signal the transition from the period of Jesus' ministry to the period of the Church (Acts 1–2).

The author of Luke-Acts has also woven into the continuous fabric of the work the *theological* theme of the Holy Spirit. During the transition from the period of Israel to the period of Jesus' ministry (Luke 1–2), Jesus' conception by the Holy Spirit (1:35) is accompanied by a general outburst of the Spirit among a few pious Israelites (1:15, 41, 67; 2:25-27). During the period of his ministry, Jesus appears as the bearer of the Spirit. He receives the Spirit at his baptism (3:22) and is guided by the Spirit through his testing in the wilderness (4:1, 14). Then in the synagogue at Nazareth he claims that his endowment by the Spirit fulfills Scripture (4:18-19 = Isa. 61:1-2). Later Jesus dies having returned his spirit (Spirit?) to his Father (23:46). During the period of transition from the period of Jesus' ministry to the period of the church (Acts 1–2), Jesus ascends into heaven and then at Pentecost the church receives the gift of the Spirit from on high (2:1-4).[9]

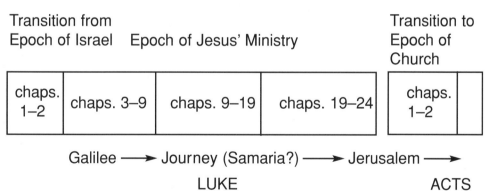

Jesus the Universal Christ. Both the Gospel of Luke and the book of Acts express their author's appreciation of the Jewish roots of Christianity. This appreciation is quite noticeable in the frequent focus on Jerusalem—the geographical and spiritual center of Judaism. Complementary to this particularistic recognition of the Jewish roots of Christianity, however, appears a sweeping universalism that presents Christianity as the faith intended by God not only for Jew but also for Gentile. The book of Acts, of course, unfolds in stages the Spirit-directed mission to the Gentiles. But the Gospel itself prepares for the extension of Christianity to the Gentiles. The narrator portrays Jesus pre-eminently as the Universal Christ. Along the way, Jesus relates to diverse sorts of people—outsiders, outcasts, and insiders. He dies on behalf of them all, in spite of his innocence before the law. If Matthew has been called the most Jewish of the Gospels, Luke in many ways represents the most Gentile.

In Luke, *Jesus is the Christ of outsiders*, the Gentiles. As in the other Gospels, Jesus' actual contact with Gentiles remains limited (cf. 7:1-10). But the author anticipates that period after Jesus' ministry when the church would carry salvation to the Gentiles. The genealogy in Luke traces Jesus' lineage back to Adam, the first human (3:23-38; cf. Matt. 1:1-17). Perhaps the boldest example of Luke's editorial work in the Gospel is the use of the story of Jesus' rejection at Nazareth as the introduction to the public ministry (4:16-30; cf. Mark 6:1-6). The worshipers in the synagogue become angry with Jesus only after he compares his ministry with the ministries of the prophets Elijah and Elisha. It so happens, as Jesus points out, that these two prophets went to the aid of Gentiles even though Israelites were equally in need. Also in Luke, Jesus sends forth for preaching and healing not only his twelve disciples but seventy (-two?) others as well (10:1-20). Twelve represents the number of the tribes of Israel. Seventy is a traditional number for all the nations of the earth.

In Luke, *Jesus is also the Christ of outcasts*, those marginals of first-century Palestinian society. The narrator makes this emphasis primarily by reporting stories and sayings peculiar to this Gospel. Among those with whom Jesus associates and whom he defends are the Samaritans, tax collectors, the poor, and women.

The Samaritans were the inhabitants of the territory of Samaria, which lay between Galilee in the north and Judea in the south. They understood themselves to be worshipers of the God of Israel and observers of the law of Moses. But as early as the fourth century B.C.E., they had separated themselves from worship at the Jerusalem Temple and had adopted Mt. Gerizim in Samaria as the appropriate place for sacrifice to God. Jews (a name derived from *Judea*) looked upon them with disdain. The author of Luke may have viewed Jesus' prolonged journey to Jerusalem as having been through Samaria (9:51–19:27). The trip begins with an unsuccessful attempt to secure lodging in a Samaritan village (9:51-56). Within this travel section, the narrator also reports the parable of the good Samaritan and the story of the Samaritan leper who thanked Jesus for healing him (10:29-37; 17:11-19; cf. Matt. 10:5-6).

Tax collectors, as clients of the Romans who occupied Palestine, evoked considerable hostility among the more zealous Jews. The payment of taxes to Rome was considered by some to be a compromise of their obligations to God. The narrator repeats the account of Jesus' debate concerning the payment of taxes to Caesar (20:20-26; cf. Mark 12:13-17) and the account of Jesus' dealings with such tax collectors as Levi (5:27-32; cf. Mark 2:13-17). But the writer amplifies this interest in taxes and tax collectors. Only Luke contains the parable of the Pharisee and the tax collector and the story about Zacchaeus, the tax collector at Jericho (18:9-14; 19:1-10).

The expression *the poor* had become a designation for those simple Jewish folk who looked to God as their protector and provider (cf. Matt 5:3). But in Luke there appears a sustained stress on the rewards of economic poverty and the dangers of economic prosperity: "Blessed are you who are poor.... But woe to you who are rich" (6:20-23, 24-26). Only Luke reports the parables of the rich farmer and the rich man and Lazarus (12:16-20; 16:19-31).

Women within Palestinian society, as in other ancient societies, had little if any public status. The author of Luke reports contacts between Jesus and women that are both shocking and touching. Only this Gospel notes how women of wealth subsidized his ministry (8:1-3). Only this Gospel reports the significant episode when Jesus praises Mary for learning at his feet instead of commending Martha for her work in the kitchen (10:38-42). The compassion of Jesus shines through his actions in the stories of the widow of Nain and the sinful woman (7:11-17; 7:36-50).

In Luke, however, *Jesus the Christ of outsiders and outcasts is also the Christ of insiders,* such as the Pharisees. Like Matthew, Luke contains very harsh words by Jesus about the Pharisees. In fact, the writer even condemns them as "lovers of money" (16:14). Nevertheless, this Gospel depicts the Pharisees in a more favorable light than does the Gospel of Matthew. Jesus dines with Pharisees (7:36; 14:1). Also, certain Pharisees warn Jesus that Herod Antipas, ruler of Galilee, seeks to kill him (13:31). Perhaps we should not be surprised that the great missionary to the Gentiles in the book of Acts is a Pharisee named Saul, or Paul.

Toward the conclusion of Acts, the narrator emphasizes the political innocence of Paul. Herod Agrippa declares to the Roman Governor Festus that Paul has done nothing deserving death or imprisonment (Acts 26:30-32). The narrator also stresses *the political innocence of Jesus* toward the conclusion of the Gospel. Only this Gospel reports that the Jewish religious authorities indict Jesus before Pontius Pilate on political charges (23:2). Only this Gospel has Jesus' innocence defended and declared by four different persons. Appropriately, these persons come from among outsiders, outcasts, and insiders: outsiders represented by Pontius Pilate (23:4, 14, 22) and the unnamed centurion (23:47; cf. Mark 15:39); outcasts represented by the thief on the adjacent cross (23:39-43); and insiders represented by Herod Antipas (23:6-16). In spite of his declared innocence, Jesus the Universal Christ died.

Theophilus and the Mission to the Gentiles. Early Christian authors attribute authorship of this Gospel, and its sequel, to Luke, the Gentile physician and companion of Paul. The letters of Paul do make reference to such a person (Col. 4:14; Philem. 24; 2 Tim. 4:11).

There can be considerable probability that the author of Luke-Acts was a Gentile Christian, although some have claimed him to be a Hellenistic Jewish Christian. Philip Francis Esler has consciously complemented the redaction critical approach of Hans Conzelmann with insights from the social sciences. He identified the setting of Luke-Acts as a mixed Christian community of Jews and Gentiles, with both segments having been associated with synagogues.[10] However, Luke and Acts are written in idiomatic Greek. Both reflect characteristics of Hellenistic history writing, including a formal preface (Luke 1:1-4; Acts 1:1-2). They connect the Jesus story to world history and the reigns of Roman emperors (Luke 1:5; 2:1; 3:1). The recipient of the two volumes has a Greek name: Theophilus (literally, "friend of God"). Various conjectures have been made about the identity of this Theophilus. Some have suggested that he was a person of high status because he is addressed as "most excellent" *(kratiste)*. This address was appropriate for a member of the Roman ruling class or the imperial household. Others have suggested that the name Theophilus was not a personal name but a general designation for any Gentile interested in the emerging Christian movement as a "friend of God."

Other aspects of Luke-Acts have been cited to support authorship not by any Gentile but by the Gentile named Luke, who was the physician-companion of Paul. The book of Acts contains what are popularly known as the "we" passages (Acts 16:10-17; 20:5-15; 21:1-18; 27:1–28:16). The narrator of Paul's missionary journeys in these passages changes from the third person "they" and "he" to the first person "we." This gives the impression to the reader that the writer was accompanying Paul at these points—that the writer was a traveling companion of Paul, a companion such as Luke. However, the "we" passages are not conclusive. If Luke were the person implied by the "we," it may simply indicate that the author of Luke-Acts was incorporating Luke's travel diary into the narrative. The actual author could be someone else. Furthermore, the name of Luke appears nowhere in Luke-Acts. Lukan authorship, therefore, remains remotely possible but by no means certain.

The author of Luke-Acts obviously wrote somewhat self-consciously as a historian. The two volumes constitute a history of Christian beginnings. The history moves the reader from Jesus' birth and ministry in Palestine along the path of the church's spread along the northeast perimeter of Mediterranean world as far as Rome. As a Gentile writing to a Gentile, this ancient Christian historian portrays Jesus as the Universal Christ. The narrator tells this story so that Theophilus "may know the truth" (Luke 1:4). This truth includes the recognition that Christianity is not a dangerous political movement. Both the Gospel and Acts present multiple witnesses who declare Jesus and Paul to be innocent of all political charges. This kind of political apologetic on behalf of Christianity would have been important among Gentiles, especially Romans. Both Jesus and Paul had been executed by the Roman state. The Jews, the people of Jesus and Paul, had recently been engaged in open rebellion against Rome (in the years 66–70 C.E.).

Those scholars who accept Luke as the author of the Gospel sometimes accept Rome as the place of writing. The final "we" passage takes Paul from Caesarea to Rome (Acts 27:1–28:16). In Rome, Paul does refer to Luke as one who is with him—if the so-called prison letters were written by Paul from Rome (Col. 4:14; Philem. 24). But Greece and Antioch in Syria have also been proposed as places of origin, and a date of origin in the 80s appears likely. Both the Gospel writer's use of Mark as a written source and a lack of knowledge of Matthew suggest a date that would correspond roughly with the date of Matthew.

The Gospel of Luke, therefore, joins the Gospels of Mark and Matthew as expressions of what we have called the Synoptic portrayal of Jesus. We turn now to consider the distinctive portrayal of Jesus presented by the Gospel of John.

The Johannine Portrayal

Whether literarily independent of the synoptic Gospels or not, the Gospel of John offers a dramatically different portrayal of Jesus. This portrayal can be sketched as follows.

John presents a different *outline of Jesus' ministry* and many *peculiar stories*. In the Synoptics, Jesus begins his public ministry only after the imprisonment of John the Baptist. But in John, Jesus inaugurates his public ministry before the arrest and imprisonment of John the Baptist. Jesus even gains a disciple or two from among the latter's followers (1:19-51). The ministries of Jesus and John parallel each other for a while (3:22-24). In the Synoptics, Jesus makes only one visit to Jerusalem—at Passover season. But in John, Jesus through-out his ministry moves back and forth between Galilee and Jerusalem (2:13; 5:1; 7:10; 12:12). His ministry embraces at least three Passover seasons (2:13; 6:4; 12:1; also 5:1[?]). Jesus' ministry, therefore, could have lasted three years. Since Jesus cleanses the Temple in Jerusalem on his first visit, another event leads to the final conspiracy against him—the raising of Lazarus from the dead (11:1-53). In the Synoptics, the Last Supper occurs on Passover evening and Jesus dies on Passover day. But in John, the Last Supper takes place on the evening before Passover evening. At this meal Jesus washes his disciples' feet and engages them in extended dialogue (13:1–17:26). The crucifixion falls on the day of preparation for Passover (19:14).

John also presents a different *characterization of Jesus* and his *message.* In the Synoptics, Jesus generally tries to keep his messiahship a secret. But in John, Jesus' activity is characterized by "messianic openness." To friend and foe, in Galilee and Jerusalem, he identifies himself as the "Son" of the "Father" through a series of sayings that begin with the words "I am":

"I am the bread of life" (6:35, 48)
"I am the light of the world" (8:12; 9:5)
"I am the gate for the sheep" (10:7)
"I am the good shepherd" (10:11, 14)
"I am the resurrection and the life" (11:25)
"I am the way, and the truth, and the life" (14:6)
"I am the true vine" (15:1).

In the Synoptics, Jesus teaches in parables. But in John, his brief "I am" sayings are part and parcel of longer discourses. There are no parables. In the Synoptics, the central theme of Jesus' message is that of the "kingdom of God." But in John, the central theme is that of "life," or "eternal life" (20:30-31). In the Synoptics, Jesus talks about the future apocalyptic hope. But in John, he emphasizes the possibility for renewed life in the present (especially 11:17-27). Jesus also promises his followers that after his death the Holy Spirit, or the "Advocate," will come (14:16, 26; 15:26; 16:7). The discourses in which Jesus talks about himself have close connections with specific acts of Jesus. These acts, or "signs" as they are called, include nature miracles, physical healings, and even dead raisings. But there are no exorcisms.

To appreciate the distinctiveness of John more fully, we will explore the Gospel in terms of its literary structure, its portrayal of Jesus, and the possible circumstances related to its origin.

The Gospel of John

Mark begins his narration of the Jesus story with the ministry of John the Baptist and the baptism of Jesus by John. Both Matthew and Luke begin their accounts with events related to the birth and infancy of Jesus. But John begins where the entire Bible begins: "In the beginning . . . " (1:1; cf. Gen. 1:1).

The portion of John with which we are most familiar is probably the prologue (1:1-18). The prologue exalts the preexistent Word and announces that the Word has become flesh. Some scholars claim that an early Christian hymn underlies this prologue. Some English translations of the Bible, such as the New American Bible (1970; revised NT, 1986), even indicate the verses adapted from this hymn by printing them in poetic form (vss. 1-5, 10-11, 14). But whatever its literary derivation, the prologue supports John's presentation of Jesus as the one who has come into the world. The prologue also introduces themes prominent later in the Gospel—such as light and life.

John, the distinctive Gospel, has a distinctive beginning. Outside the prologue, the author has also organized his material in a pattern peculiar to him. The first half of the Gospel proper contains an account of Jesus' work in the world at large (1:19–12:50). The literary pattern, as is widely recognized, consists of placing stories and discourses side by side. After Jesus performs some deed, he then interprets the deeper meaning of that deed through a lengthy discourse. The second half of the Gospel contains an account of Jesus' work on behalf of his own followers (13:1–20:29). Now, however, the literary pattern is reversed. The so-called farewell discourses (13:1–17:26) precede the passion and resurrection stories (18:1–20:29). Having come from the Father into the world, Jesus the Son on the eve of his death prepares his disciples for his departure out of this world.

The statement of purpose probably represents an earlier ending of the Gospel (20:30-31). The chapter with which the Gospel presently ends is generally considered to be a later addition (21:1-25).

The author of John obviously includes a *geographical* dimension to his work since he tells the story of Jesus as a sequence of events. Jesus makes several trips from Galilee to Jerusalem. As indicated above, the author also arranges his material about Jesus in a literary pattern. Stories and discourses alternate with one another. But in organizing his material, the author seems to be guided by the theological idea of Jesus as the One who has come into and departed out of the world. For us to recognize this, however, is already to touch on the dominant theological emphasis in the Fourth Gospel.

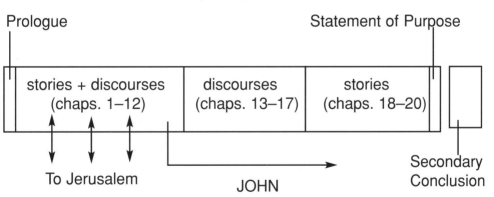

Jesus the Eternal Christ. Mark portrays Jesus preeminently as the Crucified Christ. Matthew portrays Jesus as the Teaching Christ. Luke portrays Jesus as the Universal Christ. In John, however, what really matters is neither Jesus' passion nor his words nor his deeds. The central concern of this Gospel writer is Jesus' origin and, hence, his identity. Who is Jesus? That is the question. As announced in the prologue, Jesus is the preexistent Word become flesh (1:1, 14), the only Son of the Father (1:14; also v. 18). He is the Eternal Christ. Virtually all dimensions of the Jesus story in John revolve around the question of identity.

The question of Jesus' identity underlies both his actions and his speeches. His actions are referred to as "signs"—acts that reveal his identity as the One sent by God. His speeches, or discourses, interpret the meaning of his actions as signs. Sometimes in the discourses, Jesus interprets his actions by the famous "I am" sayings. Jesus feeds the five thousand, for example, with five barley loaves and two fish. Later he explains: "I am the bread of life" (6:25, 48). Jesus gives sight to the man blind from birth. Before and after encountering the man, he declares: "I am the light of the world" (8:12; 9:5). Jesus raises Lazarus from the dead. Just prior to this happening, he says: "I am the resurrection and the life" (11:25). There are also in the discourses daring comments by Jesus about his intimate relationship to God (5:19-29; 8:58; 10:30; 14:9).

The question of Jesus' identity also underlies the controversy that swirls around him. In John, the expression *the Jews* often serves as a general name for Jesus' opponents, as though neither Jesus nor his disciples were Jews, although we know they were. The Jews ask both John the Baptist and Jesus, "Who are you?" (1:19; 8:25). Repeatedly the Jews respond to Jesus' plain talk about himself with confused questioning and the accusation of blasphemy (5:18; 6:41, 52; 10:33, 36). They are often joined in their questioning by the crowds (7:40-44; 12:34). Thus it comes as no surprise when the Jews accuse Jesus of blasphemy at his trial before Pontius Pilate: "We have a law, and according to that law he ought to die because he has claimed to be the Son of God" (19:7).

Against the backdrop of the hymnic prologue, therefore, the author of John portrays Jesus as the Eternal Christ. Jesus the Son has come into the world from God the Father and departed out of the world to God the Father. While he was in the world, Jesus performed God's work and made God known. More specifically, he brought life and he revealed love. Persons in the world become the recipients of this work and this understanding by believing in Jesus as the Christ, the Son of God. These brief comments about life, love, and believing point to three further aspects of the Johannine portrayal worthy of consideration.

In John, there is a dualistic view of reality, and *life*, or *eternal life*, is a present possibility. The Synoptics assume a view of reality more traditionally apocalyptic in nature. History is divided into two ages. There is a present age dominated by evil and a future age when God will triumph. Each of the synoptic Gospels reports apocalyptic teaching by Jesus (Mark 13 par.). Only at the end of this present age would the "kingdom of God" fully come. Only then would Jesus return as the exalted "Son of Man." But the Gospel of John narrates the Jesus story within a conceptual framework distinguished not by two ages but by two realms. There is, as we have observed, the realm above and the realm below (cf. 8:23). Jesus repeatedly talks about his coming and his going, his descending and his ascending. There is no return of Jesus at the end of history. In his farewell speeches, he talks instead about the coming of the Holy Spirit, or Advocate (14:16, 26; 15:26; 16:7). Also, Jesus seldom mentions by name the kingdom of God. He seldom mentions a general resurrection of the dead. Jesus prefers instead to talk about *life,* or its synonym *eternal life.* This life is eternal, extending beyond biological death. But this life is also a present possibility. For *life,* in John, designates the quality of existence available here and now through Jesus Christ. This is the main point of the Lazarus episode that appears midway through the Gospel (11:1-53). Martha expresses the traditional apocalyptic belief that Lazarus, her dead brother, would be resurrected at the last day. But Jesus, by raising Lazarus from the dead, demonstrates that eternal life begins in the present through him. The future is now.

In John, there is an emphasis on predestination and *love* is restricted to friends.

First John 4:16 reads: "God is love." These words represent an accurate commentary on the Gospel. The theme of God's love runs through the Gospel and finds its culmination in the farewell discourses (13:1–17:26). God's love, in that best known of all Gospel verses, is said to be a universal love for the whole world (3:16). But Jesus' love is directed specifically toward his own followers (13:1). And the "new commandment" that Jesus gives to his followers commands them to love one another — not neighbors, and certainly not enemies (13:34-35; 15:12-13). There is no love of enemies in John. God's love becomes effective in the world only among those who follow his Son. Those who follow the Son are those given to him by the Father. There is, therefore, a strong predestinarian emphasis in the Gospel (especially 17:1-26; also 6:44, 65; 10:29).

In John, there is also an ongoing preoccupation with the theme of *believing,* or *not believing,* in Jesus. Persons in the world attain eternal life and express love as the result of believing in Jesus as the Christ, the Son of God.

There are different levels, or kinds, of belief. There is a belief based on actually seeing Jesus and the works, or signs, he performed (2:11; 4:48, 53; 7:31; 10:38; 11:45). But the Gospel writer calls his readers to a belief which does not depend upon tangible, external evidence. This is apparent by the manner in which he concludes the Gospel — with the resurrection appearance of Jesus to Thomas. The words addressed to Thomas are obviously addressed not only to Thomas but to later generations: "Have you believed because you have seen me? Blessed are those who have not seen and yet have come to believe" (20:29). The statement of purpose that follows these words repeats the theme of belief and leads us to a consideration of the possible circumstances which led to the writing of this Gospel (20:30-31).

The Belief of a Christian Community. Early church tradition, although not unanimous, attributed the writing of this Gospel to John, son of Zebedee. John was identified as the "beloved disciple" mentioned in the Gospel.

Admittedly, the beloved disciple is often associated with Simon Peter in the Fourth Gospel as John is linked with Peter in the Synoptics. But there are problems in identifying John as this disciple and in attributing authorship of the Gospel to him. One problem relates to the absence in John of many stories reported in the Synoptics in which John plays an important role. The stories "missing" in the Fourth Gospel include the call of John and James his brother by Jesus beside the Sea of Galilee (Mark 1:16-20 par.). In fact, the Gospel of John makes no reference whatsoever to either John or James by name. Another problem relates to the emphasis in the Gospel of John on Jesus' activity in Judea and Jerusalem, although John himself was a Galilean, a northerner. In fact, the Gospel of John makes no explicit reference to the beloved disciple until the final visit of Jesus to Jerusalem, until the Last Supper (13:23). Understandably, therefore, some scholars have identified the beloved disciple as a non-Galilean, a southerner. One suggestion has been that this enigmatic figure was none other than Lazarus. He was a resident of Bethany near Jerusalem; and he was said to have been loved by Jesus (11:3, 5, 36). But perhaps the greatest problem in ascribing authorship of the Gospel of John to John, son of Zebedee, is simply the distinctive portrayal of Jesus in this Gospel. Consequently, the overwhelming majority of scholars deny that the Gospel of John in its present form could have been written by John the fisherman from Galilee.

The attempt to establish the exact historical origin of the Gospel of John has, throughout most of the modern era of Gospel criticism, involved the study of its possible intellectual background. Scholars have tried to discover the ancient cultural setting of the dualistic worldview in the Gospel. They have sought the source for such contrasting themes as light and darkness, life and death, truth and falsehood. Other scholars in more recent years have concentrated their labors on the possible documentary sources and oral traditions behind the Gospel. Taking into account these varied investigations, we can make a few observations about the probable historical origin of the Gospel of John.

First, the thought world of the Gospel of John is not necessarily Greek but more probably Jewish. The often rigid distinction between Greek and Jewish thought, once common, has been recognized as invalid. Early in the twentieth century, the Gospel was viewed as a thoroughly Hellenistic writing. But today the Gospel is known to have intellectual kinship with such Jewish writings as the Dead Sea Scrolls. The Gospel and the Scrolls share broad themes. They even share specific expressions, such as "Spirit of truth" and "sons of light."

Second, the Gospel of John was probably written not as a missionary tract to convert unbelievers but as a confessional document for Christian believers. The older view of the Gospel as a Hellenistic writing often involved the idea that it had been written to recommend Christian belief to sophisticated Gentile intellectuals. The more recent understanding of the Gospel as conceptually Jewish has sometimes included the idea that it originated as a document intended for nonbelieving Jews. But there are clear indications in the Gospel, especially the farewell discourses (chaps. 13–17), that the Gospel as we know it was written for Christian believers. The statement of purpose can be translated so that it suggests a strengthening of belief. The New English Bible (1970), for example, reads: "Those here written have been recorded in order that *you may hold the faith* that Jesus is the Christ, the Son of God" (20:31, italics added).

Third, the Gospel of John was probably not the product of just one person but in some sense grew out of the corporate life of an ongoing Christian community. In Johannine scholarship today, reference is often made to a "Johannine circle," a "Johannine School," or a "Johannine community." Evidence for the communal origins of the Gospel is of two kinds. On the one hand, there is evidence external to the Gospel itself. Five writings within the New Testament bear the name of John. These are the Gospel of John, the three Letters of John, and the Revelation (or Apocalypse) of John. Opinion varies about the precise relationship among these writings. But they may have originated out of a group of churches bound together by geography and by leadership. The Letters give clear indication that they were written at a time when believers had encountered the problem of "docetism" (from Greek, *dokein*, "to seem, appear"). Docetism is the claim that Jesus only "seemed" to be human and the denial that he was truly human (cf. 1 John 4:2; 2 John 7). This became a common viewpoint among second-century "Gnostic" Christians. Some scholars, among them Rudolf Bultmann,[11] have detected Gnostic themes within the Gospel itself. The dualistic worldview in the Gospel, for example, does have some similarity with the Gnostic distinction between the realm of spirit and the realm of matter. But the Gospel writer may be using Gnostic categories to combat Gnosticism. Although the author portrays Jesus as one coming into the world from above and taking leave of the world to return above, this writer also underscores the humanness of Jesus in the world (1:14; 6:52-58; 19:34). On the other hand, there is evidence internal to the Gospel which also suggests that it grew out of the corporate life of an ongoing Christian community. Several scholars claim to have found evidence within the Gospel that its traditions were developed out of the life of a Jewish-Christian community. A crucial moment in that community's experience allegedly occurred when its members as Christian Jews were expelled from the synagogue by their unbelieving kinsmen (cf. 9:22; 12:42; 16:2). American scholars J. Louis Martyn[12] and Raymond E. Brown[13] have even attempted to reconstruct in some detail the history of the Johannine community over the last half of the first century. Urban C. von Wahlde also views the Gospel as having passed through three versions, each of which corresponds to a period in the community's life.[14] Advocates of the Signs Gospel, said to underlie the Gospel of John, consider this writing to represent an earlier stage in the history of the Johannine community.

Fourth, the differences between the Gospel of John and the Synoptics in their portrayals of Jesus probably result from the creativity of the author and community of John. John may contain certain information about Jesus just as historically accurate as the information about Jesus in the Synoptics if John does, as many think, preserve traditions independent of those in the Synoptics. A few scholars, however, also defend the discourses of Jesus as representative of the way he actually talked during his lifetime. It has been claimed, for example, that the discourses by Jesus in John originated as his more informal conversations and debates, while the words of Jesus in the Synoptics began as his formal teachings which he required his disciples to memorize.[15] But this claim is not convincing, for Jesus in the Gospel of John talks more like the author of 1 John than he does Jesus in the Synoptics. In their present form, therefore, the discourses of Jesus in John must be attributed to the creativity of the Gospel writer and his community. The Gospel writer himself, however, appears to justify this creative activity in a couple of ways. He frankly admits that a full understanding of Jesus' ministry came to his followers only after the resurrection (2:22; 12:16). He also includes passages about the Holy Spirit, or "Advocate," that declare the Holy Spirit will guide later generations to a grasp of the full truth about Jesus (14:15-17, 26; 15:26-27; 16:4-15). Thus the Gospel of John itself implies that the evangelist within his community was not content simply to remember and to repeat words spoken by the early Jesus. Instead, he meditated and reflected on the deeper meaning of that ministry. Or, in accordance with his own understanding, he was inspired by the Spirit so that the exalted Jesus spoke through him. There appears to have been real profundity in Clement of Alexandria's description of the Fourth Gospel centuries ago when he called it the "spiritual Gospel." John to a greater extent than the other Gospels probably contains words spoken not by Jesus during his earthly ministry but "heavenly sayings" spoken by the exalted Jesus through the Gospel writer and his community (cf. book of Revelation).

In conclusion, the Gospel of John, as we know it, grows out of the experiences of the writer and that writer's community. There had been conflicts with unbelieving Jews in the past. There would be conflicts with "Gnostic" Christianity in the future. The Gospel itself preserves and proclaims belief in Jesus as the Christ, the Son of God. The traditional place of origin for the Gospel was Ephesus in Asia Minor. Some scholars still accept Ephesus as a likely site. Others speak in more general terms, such as simply Asia Minor or

Syria. Even Palestine itself and Alexandria in Egypt have been proposed as possibilities. A date for the writing of the Gospel near the end of the first century, before 100 C.E., continues to be the most widely held view.

Other Gospel Portrayals

As we have indicated, ancient writings other than the four canonical Gospels were sometimes designated Gospels and referred to as Gospels by early Christian writers.[16] Gospel literature has also come to include documents about Jesus discovered in more recent times. Even more broadly defined, gospel literature now includes documentary sources said to underlie the four canonical Gospels. We have mentioned how some scholars have identified a foundational document underlying the Gospel of John and called it the Signs Gospel. Others now refer to Q not simply as the Q document but as Sayings Gospel Q. One way to categorize this diverse body of noncanonical Gospel literature is to divide these Gospels into two basic categories: narrative Gospels and sayings Gospels.

Among the narrative Gospels are two noncanonical writings that reflected and shaped the imagination of the early church: the *Infancy Gospel of Thomas* and the *Protevangelium (Infancy Gospel) of James*. The former contains fantastic miracle tales about the childhood of Jesus, including how he cursed to death a playmate. The latter relates wondrous stories about the birth of Mary the mother of Jesus, her own dedication to God and upbringing in the Temple, and her marriage at age twelve to Joseph, an aged widower with children by his prior marriage.

Also among the narrative Gospels are three Jewish-Christian Gospels, so called because of their association with early Jewish Christianity: the *Gospel of the Ebionites*, the *Gospel of the Hebrews*, and the *Gospel of the Nazoreans*. These gospels are known only through references and citations in the writings of early church leaders such as Clement of Alexandria, Origen, Eusebius, Jerome, and Epiphanius, who lived and wrote at different times during the second to the fifth centuries.

Another narrative Gospel known through a letter of Clement of Alexandria (died ca. 215) and now designated the *Secret Gospel of Mark* apparently represents a version of Mark that circulated in Alexandria during the second century. This previously unknown letter by Clement was discovered by American scholar Morton Smith in 1958 in the Mar Saba monastery near Jerusalem.[17] The copy of the letter, written on the back page and inside back cover of a seventeenth-century book, contained two brief passages about Jesus not found in canonical Mark: the one a dead raising story, the other a brief notation, both involving a young man (presumably the same young man mentioned in canonical Mark, 14:51-52). There has been considerable discussion about the actual existence of such a Gospel and its relationship to canonical Mark. Based on a careful linguistic study, Smith himself concluded that either *Secret Mark* and canonical Mark were based on common tradition or that *Secret Mark* was an imitation of canonical Mark.

The *Egerton Gospel* represents the remains of still another Gospel; first published in 1935, it bears the name of the person who purchased the papyrus fragments on which it is preserved. These rudimentary remains of a Gospel include a story in which Jesus heals a leper and a story in which Jesus is asked about paying taxes to rulers.

Besides narrative Gospels, there are also sayings Gospels. They consist of dialogues between Jesus and his followers or discourses by Jesus, but few or no stories about him—certainly not about his passion. This kind of gospel was apparently quite popular among those Christians responsible for the collection of ancient Gnostic writings, commonly known as the Nag Hammadi library, discovered in Egypt in 1945.[18] These thirteen codices—or books—written in Coptic and containing some fifty tractates, were buried in the Egyptian countryside in the fourth century, probably by Christians seeking to hide them from church authorities. The *Apocryphon (Secret Book) of James* consists of private teaching imparted by Jesus to James and Peter 550 days after his resurrection and just before his ascension. The *Dialogue of the Savior* contains conversations among Jesus and his disciples, including Mary, presumably Mary Magdalene. The participation of Mary in these conversations gives evidence of the prominence of women within Gnostic Christianity. Mary even has her own gospel, although it is not one of the Nag Hammadi documents and is preserved only in fragmentary manuscripts. The *Gospel of Mary* presents Mary and Levi as the bearers of the true apostolic tradition in contrast to Andrew and Peter.

These narrative and sayings Gospels are important for understanding the diversity of belief in the early church. But most scholars dismiss these writings as having little, if any, contribution to make toward an understanding of the life of Jesus. However, three Gospels—not yet discussed—have been variously used in recent years by scholars at the center of the debate about the historical Jesus. One is a narrative Gospel, the other two sayings Gospels.

Gospel of Peter

This work has been known since the discovery of a significant portion of it by French archaeologists at Akhmim, Egypt, in 1886. The incomplete manuscript itself, in Greek, dates from the eighth or ninth century. Since then two smaller fragments have been found at Oxyrhynchus, Egypt, dating from the third or second centuries. These remains of a longer work contain an account of the passion and resurrection of Jesus.

Jesus the Crucified Lord. This Gospel bears the name of Peter because he is identified in the narrative itself as the storyteller (7:2; 14:3). The story takes up with Jesus before Herod and Pilate, continues through the crucifixion of Jesus, and breaks off with the discovery of the empty tomb by Mary and other women. The characters and many of the details in the story correspond to characters and details in the four canonical Gospels. With its focus on the crucifixion, this Gospel, as did Mark, portrays Jesus as the Crucified Lord. Characters in the story refer to Jesus, usually ironically, as "Son of God" (3:1, 4; 11:3-4) and "King of Israel" (3:2; 4:2).The narrator repeatedly identifies Jesus as "Lord" in the telling of the story. The title "Messiah," or "Christ," does not appear.

Relation to the Four Gospels. Since its discovery, scholars have debated the relationship between the traditions in the *Gospel of Peter* and traditions in the four canonical Gospels. For most of the twentieth century, scholars considered the *Gospel of Peter* to date from the second century and to be literarily dependent on the four canonical Gospels. In recent years, some have argued both for an earlier dating and reversed the assessment about its literary dependency. John Dominic Crossan has argued that behind the current *Gospel of Peter* lies an earlier version of the passion that he calls the Cross Gospel. The Cross Gospel, accordingly, served as the source for the passion accounts in all four canonical Gospels.[19] The importance of such a claim for Jesus research is that only one written source underlies all passion accounts.

Gospel of Thomas

The *Gospel of Thomas*—a sayings Gospel—was one of the documents in the Nag Hammadi library discovered in Egypt in 1945 and among the first to receive widespread scholarly attention. Although only preserved in its entirety in Coptic, this Gospel was probably first written in Greek. Three fragments in Greek of a then unknown collection of Jesus' sayings, dating from the second century, had been found at Oxyrhynchus decades earlier and were only later identified as remnants of this Gospel.

Jesus the Gnostic Wisdom Teacher. A prologue and an inscription at the end of the book associate its writing with Thomas, presumably one of the twelve: "These are the secret sayings that the living Jesus spoke and Didymos Judas Thomas recorded" and "The Gospel According to Thomas." The Gospel itself consists of a series of 114 sayings of Jesus, often linked by catchwords and customarily introduced with a straightforward, "Jesus said..." Thus Jesus speaks without being identified by any title of honor, such as "Christ." Both the prologue and the very first word spoken by Jesus suggest that the Gospel portrays Jesus as a Gnostic Wisdom Teacher whose words communicate eternal life: "Whoever discovers the interpretation of these sayings will not taste death" (GThom. 1).[20] Jesus later says: "Whoever drinks from my mouth will become like me; I myself shall become that person, and the hidden things will be revealed to that one" (GThom. 108).

Approximately half of the sayings in this Gospel are not attested in the four canonical Gospels. However, some have parallels with the Gospel of John. An even larger number represent versions of Synoptic parables and other sayings, some of which seemingly have more primitive forms than their Synoptic counterparts. For example, the parable of the mustard seed states what the kingdom is like:

It is like a mustard seed, which, when sown upon the ground, is the smallest of all the seeds on earth; yet when it is sown it grows up and becomes the greatest of all shrubs, and puts forth large branches, so that the birds of the air can make nests in its shade. (Mark 4:31-32 par.)	It is like a mustard seed. <It> is the tiniest of all seeds, but when it falls on prepared soil, it produces a large plant and becomes a shelter for birds of heaven. (GThom. 20:2-4)

Another familiar saying of Jesus in *Thomas* with a Synoptic counterpart that seems not more primitive but more developed is Jesus' saying about paying taxes to the emperor: "Give Caesar the things that are Caesar's, give God the things that are God's, and give me what is mine" (GThom. 100:2-4; cf. Mark 12:17 par.).

Relation to the Synoptic Gospels. Because of the physical evidence of the Greek fragments, the Gospel itself can be dated no later than the end of the second century. Many scholars date the Gospel earlier in the century with Syria as its place of origin because of its association with Thomas, remembered in the church as the apostle to Syria and India. The question of dating is closely related to the issue of its relationship to the four Gospels, especially to the Synoptics. Many scholars view *Thomas* as literarily dependent on the Synoptics for its Synoptic-like material. But others, such as Stephen J. Patterson, have dated Thomas toward the end of the first century and discovered in the gospel an independent tradition of Jesus' sayings that may go back to midcentury, even to the Jerusalem church.[21] The Gospel does mention James the Just, the brother of Jesus who was a leader in the Jerusalem church (GThom. 12). The importance of this claim for Jesus research is that *Thomas* possibly provides scholars with an independent and early source for evaluating the historical probability of Jesus' words alongside those other Synoptic sources: Mark, Q, M, and L.

Sayings Gospel Q

Earlier in our discussion of the canonical Gospels, we spoke of Q in three ways: as a written source for sayings of Jesus found in Matthew and Luke, as a cycle of oral tradition common to Matthew and Luke, and as a symbol for material found in Matthew and Luke but not Mark. In recent years, there has been renewed emphasis upon Q not only as a written source but as a Gospel with its own integrity—Sayings Gospel Q. Much labor has been expended both in meticulous literary reconstruction of the Greek text of this Gospel and in an imaginative reconstruction of the social history of the people, or community, responsible for writing and living it.[22]

Jesus the Apocalyptic Wisdom Preacher. Various proposals have been made about the content of Sayings Gospel Q. Instead of identifying—as we have done—Q material by citing chapters and verses from both Matthew and Luke (e.g. Matt. 3:7-10 = Luke 3:7-9), Q scholars have adopted the convention of identifying Q passages by citing chapters and verses from Luke, since Luke seems to preserve the original order of the sayings from the missing document (e.g. Q 3:7-9). The following outline for the content of Sayings Gospel Q comes from John Kloppenborg:[23]

(1) John's preaching of the Coming One	Q 3:7-9, 16-17
(2) The temptation of Jesus	Q 4:1-13
(3) Jesus' inaugural sermon	Q 6:20*b*-49
(4) John, Jesus, and "this generation"	Q 7:1-10, 18-28; (16:16); 7:31-35
(5) Discipleship and mission	Q 9:57-62; 10:2-24
(6) On prayer	Q 11:2-4, 9-13
(7) Controversies with Israel	Q 11:14-52
(8) On fearless preaching	Q 12:2-12
(9) On anxiety over material needs	Q 12:(13-14, 16-21), 22-31, 33-34
(10) Preparedness for the end	Q 12:39-59
(11) Two parables of growth	Q 13:18-19, 20-21
(12) The two ways	Q 13:24-30, 34-35; 14:16-24; 26-27; 17:33; 14:33-34
(13) Various parables and sayings	Q 15:3-7, 16:13, 17-18; 17:1-6
(14) Eschatological Discourse	Q 17:23-37; 19:12-27; 22:28-30

In Sayings Gospel Q, the focus is upon Jesus' words. The sayings themselves seem to be of two kinds: wisdom sayings, including parables, that provide directives for how to conduct one's life; and eschatological sayings, including future Son of Man sayings, that constitute warnings about the coming judgment. As in Thomas, so here in Sayings Gospel Q: Jesus is not identified by the title "Christ." But whereas in *Thomas* Jesus appears as a Gnostic Wisdom Teacher, he appears as an Apocalyptic Wisdom Preacher in Sayings Gospel Q.

Relation to the Synoptic Gospels. John Kloppenborg has not only reconstructed the text of Sayings Gospel Q but also claimed that the two main kinds of material therein—wisdom sayings and eschatological sayings—give evidence for at least a two-stage development of the document and the life of the community. At the earliest stage, the Q people viewed Jesus primarily as a teacher of wisdom, a sage. At a later stage the community came to view Jesus also as a prophet, an apocalyptic preacher. A final stage involved the addition of such narratives as the threefold temptations of Jesus in the wilderness.

Many scholars have questioned this kind of layering of the Jesus material in Q and the attendant social reconstruction of a Q community. But the importance of this claim for Jesus research has been that Sayings Gospel Q—along with the *Gospel of Thomas*—provides some scholars with evidence for reconstructing the life of Jesus along lines quite different from what we see in the four canonical Gospels. These four gospels are narrative Gospels, with passion-resurrection accounts, and they date from the last third of the first century. By contrast, Sayings Gospel Q and the *Gospel of Thomas* as sayings Gospels independently locate the authority of Jesus preeminently in his words, since neither has a passion-resurrection account. Sayings Gospel Q with certainty and possibly the core sayings in the *Gospel of Thomas* date from the middle third of the first century, 50 C.E. or earlier.

We have completed the first stage of our quest for Jesus and already anticipated the second. We have examined the literary sources on which our understandings of Jesus are ultimately based. Now we turn our attention from the Gospels to the historical level of his life.

PART TWO

Historical Reconstruction of the Life and Ministry of Jesus

4

Historical Problem

The Gospels of Matthew, Mark, Luke, and John are confessions of faith in Jesus as the resurrected, living Christ of God. Today as of old the four invite us as readers to participate in their confession of faith. These Gospels, unlike the other New Testament writings, make their confession by narrating the story of Jesus. Each Gospel thereby directs our attention back to Jesus' earthly life, to his words, his deeds, and his passion.

With their backward glance, however, the four Gospels present us not only with the challenge of faith in Jesus but with a problem about Jesus. This problem is historical in nature, and is commonly referred to as the *problem of the historical Jesus*.

Our survey of the four Gospels has already suggested that Jesus poses a peculiar historical problem for later generations who may want to know more about his life. As faith documents, they were not written as the jottings of disinterested reporters. Among these four are two distinctly different portrayals of Jesus, the one in the Synoptics and the other in John. And even the Synoptics, in the midst of their similarities, offer diversity of detail. Also, Mark, the earliest of them, was written forty years after the life of Jesus. During this period, the stories and sayings of Jesus were passed down by word of mouth and were translated into Greek out of the Aramaic language. Furthermore, there are other Gospels beyond the four in the New Testament, including the *Gospel of Peter*, the *Gospel of Thomas*, and—as some would contend—Sayings Gospel Q.

We can state the problem of the historical Jesus as a question: What is the relationship between Jesus as portrayed in the Gospels and Jesus as he actually lived and died? Or, to use terminology common in New Testament scholarship: What is the relationship between the *Christ of faith* and the *Jesus of history?*

The phrase *Christ of faith* refers to Jesus as proclaimed by, and within, the church. All the New Testament writings with their varied talk about Jesus, including the Gospels themselves, present Jesus as the Christ of faith. And the traditional creeds, of course, describe Jesus as the Christ of faith in such language as "the Son . . . of one substance with the Father" or "very God and very Man." The phrase *Jesus of history,* by contrast, refers to Jesus as he walked and talked in first-century Palestine. Or, more precisely, the phrase refers to what can be established about Jesus using available literary evidence and principles of historical evaluation and judgment.

In recent biblical scholarship, there has been considerable discussion about the adequacy of the phrases *Christ of faith* and *Jesus of history.* Marcus J. Borg has introduced another bipolar distinction that provides helpful commentary on these traditional phrases as we have defined them above. Borg makes a distinction between the *post-Easter Jesus* and the *pre-Easter Jesus.*[1] John P. Meier has introduced another distinction. He differentiates between the *historical Jesus* and the *real Jesus* as a way of acknowledging that there is more to Jesus than can be known through historical research.[2] At least one interpreter has challenged or even denied the validity of any such distinction by reversing the phrases: *the historical Christ* and *the Jesus of faith.*[3]

However, we shall continue to use the phrases the *Christ of faith* and the *Jesus of history,* while recognizing the limitations of the contrasting phrases. What then is the relationship between the Christ of faith and the Jesus of history? When we hurl this central question against the Gospels, it shatters into hundreds of specific historical questions about Jesus:

EXISTENCE

Was there, in fact, a historical person named Jesus from Nazareth? If so, did he really do and say what the Gospels claim he did and said? If not, what was he like? What evidence supports this alternative understanding of Jesus?

ORIGIN, WORDS, DEEDS, DESTINY

What was Jesus' origin? Was he a Jew? What kind of Jew? What about his family? Was Mary his mother a virgin at the time of her conception? Was Joseph his father descended from King David? Did he have brothers and sisters?

What did Jesus say? Did he proclaim the "kingdom of God" using parables? Or did he offer himself and "eternal life" through lengthy "I am" discourses? Both? How did he understand the "kingdom of God"?

Politically? Apocalyptically? Eschatologically, but not apocalyptically? Spiritually? As a place? An activity? An experience? Wholly future? Wholly present? Both future and present? Atemporally? Did he accept the authority of the Torah, the law? How? What was the relationship between his kingdom preaching and his Torah teaching? Between eschatology and ethics?

What did Jesus do? Did he submit to the water baptism of John the Baptist? Why? Did he call disciples? Were there actually twelve of them? What about the women with whom he associated? Did he perform miracles? What is a miracle? Did he speak of miracles as "mighty works" or as "signs"? What kind of miracles did he perform? How were the miracles related to his preaching and his teaching? Did he associate with social outcasts? Which groups? Samaritans? Harlots? Tax collectors? Did he debate with the religious authorities? Which groups? Pharisees? Sadducees? Essenes?

What about Jesus' destiny? His crucifixion and resurrection? How did this Galilean end up on a Roman cross outside Jerusalem? What were the roles of Caiaphas the high priest and Pontius Pilate the Roman governor? Of Judas? Did Jesus really die on the cross? Who was the man Joseph of Arimathea? What convinced Jesus' disciples that he had been resurrected from the dead? An empty tomb? Appearances? Something else? Was Jesus actually resurrected from the dead? Brought back to life?

CHRONOLOGIZING AND PSYCHOLOGIZING

When did Jesus' life begin and end? How long did his ministry last? Three years? One year? Some other length of time? Did his ministry fall into distinct periods? What was the sequence of events? The geographical movement? How many times did he visit Jerusalem during his ministry? Several times? Once? Was the Last Supper a Passover meal? Did he die on Passover day?

What did Jesus think about himself? Did he believe himself to be a messiah? What kind? A prophet? What kind? A rabbi? What kind? Did his understanding of himself and his mission develop over the course of his life and ministry? How? Did he refer to himself by any names of honor? "Messiah"? "Son of God"? "Son of Man"? What was his motive for specific events? Why did he go to Jerusalem on the occasion of his death? To preach? To die? Did he enter the city on an ass and undertake some disruptive act in the Temple? How did he view these acts? Did he really think that his death was a sacrifice on behalf of the sins of the whole world? Did he believe that he would be resurrected from the dead and return in glory on the clouds of heaven?

SOCIAL WORLD AND HISTORICAL CONTEXT

What was the Mediterranean world like in Jesus' day? What values and social processes governed this world?

What about the history of the Mediterranean world, the Roman Empire, ancient Israel, and postexilic Judaism? What was Palestine like in Jesus' day? Religiously? Politically? Economically? Socially? Geographically? Were there significant differences between Jewish life and practice in Galilee, on the one hand, and in Judea and Jerusalem, on the other? How did these various social and historical factors influence Jesus?

Some persons may consider a rigorous historical questioning of the Gospels about Jesus as irrelevant or even blasphemous. Some of the possible historical answers to the preceding historical questions could have profound implications for faith in Jesus as the Christ. But the questions asked in this chapter have been asked repeatedly throughout the extensive search for the historical Jesus conducted over the past two hundred years.

The next chapter surveys the different turns and twists involved in this search. We will discover that particular methods have been developed which, according to their advocates, will enable us to give relatively certain answers to many historical questions about Jesus. A subsequent chapter, chapter 6, briefly reviews a variety of historical portrayals of Jesus. We will see that historians have often reached different conclusions about what Jesus was really like.

5

Historical Search

History as an academic discipline concerns itself with what people have done in the past, as most schoolchildren can tell us. Since the historian does not have a time machine, he or she gains access to past human actions primarily through the use of written documents. These documents may be as varied as love letters and government records, eyewitness reports and bills of sale. But the authority for evaluating what these sources say belongs neither to the sources themselves nor to whoever wrote them. The authority belongs to the historian, the interpreter. The historian pieces together a coherent account of what happened in the past based on a detective-like questioning of the literary witnesses. The historian may also consider the reasons for and motivations behind what happened.

The ability to reconstruct a detailed history, of course, depends upon the available evidence. If historians have little information and that information seems very unreliable, then this increases the possibility that they will use their imaginations in uncontrolled ways. They may become more like novelists than historians. Their writing may be more fiction than fact.

As biographers, historians reconstruct the lives of particular persons. They consider the overall sequence of events in the lives of their subjects. They also consider the innermost thoughts of their subjects. In other words, the biographer both chronologizes and psychologizes the subject studied.

The ongoing effort to use the four Gospels and other available evidence to reconstruct in some detail the life and ministry of Jesus has become known as the *quest of the historical Jesus*. This chapter focuses on this historical search for

Jesus. Each of the five periods in this quest corresponds roughly to one of the five periods in the development of Gospel criticism. We will see that the inter-relationship between Gospel criticism and the historical search for Jesus is not a coincidence. The methodological approaches to the Gospel texts delineated in chapter 2 were developed in the interest of, or had implications for, the quest of the historical Jesus: source criticism, form criticism, redaction criticism, narrative criticism, and social-scientific criticism.

Period 1: Pre-Quest (Before 1778)

Once the four Gospels were established as Scripture within the early church, they were interpreted to support faith and doctrine. No distinction was made between the Christ of faith and the Jesus of history. Strictly speaking, there was *no problem* and *no quest* of the historical Jesus.

The church's leaders as well as Christianity's opponents, however, were well aware of the obvious differences among the four Gospels. Over the centuries, any number of attempts were made to harmonize and to defend the apparent discrepancies in the Gospel accounts. We have already mentioned Augustine's study of the four Gospels and his attempt to explain their differences. But per-haps the most important harmony of the four Gospels in the early church was the *Diatessaron* (paraphrased, "Four-In-One") by a man named Tatian.

A native of Mesopotamia, Tatian had studied in Rome in the middle of the second century. He actually took the four Gospels and skillfully wove them together into a continuous narrative of the Jesus story. Modern scholars have debated both Tatian's motive for writing and the original language of his writ-ing. But whatever his intention and whether he wrote initially in Greek or Syriac, it was the Syriac version that gained considerable popularity. Some scholars have even claimed that the *Diatessaron* was introduced into the Tigris-Euphrates region before the four individual Gospels. All agree that this har-mony was widely used within the Syriac-speaking church until the fourth and fifth centuries. But more than this, the work of Tatian exerted an influence well beyond its original time and place through its translation and adaptation into such languages as Armenian, Arabic, and Latin.

The Protestant Reformation witnessed the formulation and circulation of many new harmonies. The renewed emphasis upon Scripture and the new availability of printing made this both desirable and feasible. Sometimes the Gospels were woven together into a continuous account of the Jesus story. At other times the Gospels were printed separately but in parallel columns. John Calvin, the great reformer of Geneva, followed something of the latter approach in his biblical commentary called *A Harmony of the Gospels of Matthew, Mark, and Luke* (1555).[1] He placed similar passages from these Gospels next to one another and followed them with verse by verse comment.

Those who developed Gospel harmonies did not always agree with one another in their treatments of the four Gospels and the Jesus story. Some interpreters favored joining together similar stories found in different Gospels with the belief that Jesus performed that particular activity only once. Tatian, for example, apparently reported the cleansing of the Temple only once although the incident appears in all four Gospels. But others often repeated similar stories found in different Gospels with the belief that Jesus must have performed the activity on more than one occasion. Thus they may report the cleansing of the Temple at least twice since John records the incident near the beginning and the Synoptics at the end of Jesus' ministry. In spite of varying approaches to the four Gospels and the Jesus story, however, the general assumption throughout the pre-quest period was one of *correspondence between the Christ of faith and the Jesus of history*. The Christ of faith was, quite simply, identical with the Jesus of history.

The Enlightenment, not the Reformation, provided the intellectual setting for a rigorous historical search in, through, and behind the four Gospels for Jesus. The emergence of the quest of the historical Jesus occurred virtually simultaneously with renewed interest in the literary relationship among the four Gospels. Now both the Gospels and Jesus were often considered without regard for the traditional ways they had been viewed within the church.

Period 2: Old Quest (1778–1906)

The name and date most often associated with the beginning of the historical quest are Hermann Samuel Reimarus and 1778. Reimarus was a respected professor of Oriental languages in the German city of Hamburg, where he was born and where he died. He maintained public silence throughout his life about his negative views of Christianity. There were limits to free speech even in a so-called enlightened age. A transgression of those limits could lead to loss of employment, social ostracism, and even arrest, so that the negative views of Reimarus became known only after his death. Between 1774 and 1778, several fragments of a sizable manuscript by him were published. The year 1778 saw the publication of the seventh fragment, entitled "On the Intention of Jesus and His Disciples."[2] The importance of this document for the quest lies in its sharp delineation between the Christ of faith and the Jesus of history.

According to Reimarus, Jesus, during his lifetime, shared with his disciples the intention of establishing in the immediate future an earthly kingdom with himself as the kingly messiah. Reimarus found support for this interpretation in the Gospels themselves: Jesus summarized his message with the phrase "kingdom of heaven" (or "kingdom of God"). When Jesus entered Jerusalem riding on an ass in fulfillment of the royal passage in Zechariah 9:9, the crowds acclaimed him as king. The sign over the cross publicized the charge on which he was executed, "King of the Jews." The words of Jesus on the cross in Matthew 27:46 (also Mark 15:34) expressed his attitude toward his death, "My God, my God, why have you forsaken me?" Reimarus accepted these words as historical and concluded, "It was clearly then not the intention or the object of Jesus to suffer or to die, but to build up a worldly kingdom, and to deliver the Israelites from bondage. It was in this that God had forsaken him, it was in this that his hopes had been frustrated."[3]

During his earthly ministry, therefore, Jesus believed that God had designated him to become a kingly, or political, messiah. He died disappointed that he had not achieved his goal of establishing a worldly kingdom.

By contrast, according to Reimarus, the Gospels generally portray Jesus as a spiritual messiah who died for the sins of humankind, who was resurrected from the dead, and who will return in glory. This view of Jesus as a spiritual messiah was intentionally fabricated by his disciples after his unexpected death. Reimarus said, "The new system of a suffering spiritual savior, which no one had ever known or thought before, was invented only because the first hopes had failed."[4]

The disciples of Jesus, according to Reimarus, had stolen his body from the tomb so that no one could dispute their claims of his atoning death, his bodily resurrection, and his second coming. Reimarus thereby perceived a certain historical truth underlying the stolen body story in Matthew 28:11-15. The reason the disciples undertook their deception and fabrication was their desire to avoid returning to their more mundane ways of making a living in Galilee.

The historical reconstruction of Reimarus is objectionable in retrospect, not only on theological but also on literary and historical grounds. But he had made the crucial distinction. Jesus the spiritual messiah of church teaching and the Gospels was quite clearly *not* identical with the historical, political messiah behind the Gospels. The Christ of faith was *not* the Jesus of history. Reimarus' specific understanding of the historical Jesus did not prevail. But his recognition of *discontinuity between the Christ of faith and the Jesus of history* became a prominent assumption in the nineteenth century. This fundamental assumption of discontinuity also involved related assumptions, or corollaries. It was widely held that it was *methodologically possible* and *theologically necessary* to seek and to recover the shape and substance of Jesus' historical ministry.

Those persons engaged in the quest of Jesus assumed that it was possible to recover what he was like as a historical figure. If they rightly used the Gospels, they believed, then they could reconstruct his life and ministry. Individual interpreters, of course, often defined what was a right use of the Gospels as historical sources. Sometimes they seemed to pick and choose arbitrarily those details in the Gospel accounts that supported what they claimed to be establishing historically. At other times they allowed a rigid understanding of natural law to lead them to approach the miracle stories in the Gospels with great skepticism. They explained away the miracles as natural occurrences, dismissed them as products of primitive superstition, or just ignored them. Reimarus himself often appeared arbitrary in his use of the Gospel accounts and approached the miracle stories with skepticism.

The debate over the literary relationship among the four Gospels, however, was perceived to have important consequences for the quest to rediscover what Jesus was like. John, as the last of the four to be written, was increasingly regarded as irrelevant to the search for the historical Jesus. Mark, the earliest, was often viewed as presenting a very trustworthy account of Jesus' earthly ministry. As an early collection of Jesus' teachings, Q was also regarded highly as a source for what Jesus had taught during his ministry.

Furthermore, there emerged the indisputable recognition that the historian should understand Jesus against the background of his own distinctive environment—first-century Palestinian Judaism. Reimarus had already shown considerable historical sensitivity at many points. For him, Jesus was a Jew whose cultural and religious "home" was not the Christian church but Palestinian Judaism. He examined Gospel passages about Jesus in relation to Jewish thought and custom as he knew them. Consequently, he understood Jesus' kingdom message and ministry as reflections of the traditional Jewish hope for a worldly deliverer.

Methodologically, therefore, it was considered possible to reconstruct the life and ministry of Jesus. What Jesus was really like *could* be known. But furthermore, what Jesus was really like *ought* to be known. Theologically, it was assumed to be necessary to reconstruct the life and ministry of Jesus.

Reimarus had sought the historical Jesus in order to discredit traditional Christianity. But many after him sought Jesus in order to support Christian belief. The nineteenth century saw the rise of that theological movement known as Protestant "liberalism," a term not to be understood negatively as it sometimes is in our day. Liberal theologians desired a firm foundation for Christian belief and practice. They sought that foundation neither in the traditional creeds nor in the New Testament generally nor in the Gospels particularly, but rather in the personality and religion of Jesus himself. Liberal theology emphasized Jesus not so much as savior but as teacher and example. It stressed not so much faith *in* Jesus but the faith *of* Jesus as he taught the Fatherhood of God and the brotherhood of man (to use nineteenth-century phrasing). Liberal theology also understood the kingdom of God as that realm to be realized on earth as Jesus' followers, ancient and modern, obeyed his command to love God and neighbor.

This kind of theology may be most familiar to us through such American hymns as Washington Gladden's "O Master, Let Me Walk with Thee" and S. Ralph Harlow's "O Young and Fearless Prophet." But German scholar H. J. Holtzmann serves as an appropriate symbol for the relationship in the nineteenth century among liberal theology, the quest of the historical Jesus, and Gospel criticism. We have already mentioned Holtzmann as the popularizer of the "two-document hypothesis," which claimed Mark was the first Gospel written. He concluded his 1863 study of the synoptic Gospels with a short description of the life of Jesus, following the basic outline of Mark's Gospel. He arranged Jesus' ministry into specific stages of activity and suggested how Jesus' awareness of his messiahship developed over the course of his ministry. Holtzmann's source analysis of the Gospels and his presentation of the historical Jesus became quite influential in liberal theological circles. Theologically, therefore, many assumed that it was necessary to search for the historical Jesus.

The nineteenth-century quest—or the "old quest," as it has come to be called—was characterized by great variety. There was variety of motive and variety of result. There was variety of philosophical and theological perspective. Hundreds of biographies, or "lives," of Jesus were written. Both professional historians and amateurs retold the story of Jesus by arranging his life into distinct periods and by probing his understanding of himself. Like most biographies, therefore, these biographies of Jesus displayed extensive chronologizing and intensive psychologizing. Among the most famous, or infamous, writings from this era were the *Life of Jesus Critically Examined* by David Friedrich Strauss (1835–1836; English trans., 1846)[5] and the *Life of Jesus* by Ernest Renan (1863).[6] In upbringing and family background, Strauss was a German Protestant and Renan a French Catholic. But both suffered for their writings about Jesus. The former forfeited his hopes for an academic career. The latter lost his academic position. The biography of Jesus was principally the literary expression of the "old quest," but any book that presents itself as a "life" of Jesus with detailed chronologizing and psychologizing, whatever its date, represents in some sense a throwback to the "old quest."

For a comprehensive accounting of the nineteenth-century quest as pursued in continental Europe, one should consult the remarkable survey written in 1906 by Albert Schweitzer, translated from German into English with the title *The Quest of the Historical Jesus* (English trans., 1910).[7] Schweitzer's reflections as a commentator and a contributor established him as a transitional figure in the history of Jesus research. The date of his publication serves as a convenient date for marking the shift from the "old quest" period to the period of "no quest."

Period 3: No Quest (1906–1953)

Albert Schweitzer was known to the world as the humanitarian missionary doctor of West Africa. He spent the last fifty years of his life battling tropical diseases, continuing his work until his death in 1965. But before he studied medicine he had already distinguished himself as a biblical scholar at the

University of Strasbourg. His writings about Jesus in many respects both ended the "old quest" period and anticipated the period of "no quest."

Schweitzer, on the one hand, ended the "old quest" period by demonstrating how his nineteenth-century predecessors, such as H. J. Holtzmann, had failed to recover Jesus as he really was during his historical ministry. Schweitzer claimed that they had modernized Jesus and made him over in the likeness of their own philosophical and theological ideas. He concluded his exhaustive review with these words rejecting the nineteenth-century liberal understanding of Jesus:

> The Jesus of Nazareth who came forward publicly as the Messiah, who preached the ethic of the Kingdom of God, who founded the Kingdom of Heaven upon earth, and died to give His work its final consecration, never had any existence. He is a figure designed by rationalism, endowed with life by liberalism, and clothed by modern theology in an historical garb.[8]

Schweitzer, on the other hand, anticipated the "no quest" period by saying that the historical Jesus he had discovered was for the most part insignificant for twentieth-century faith and practice. He said:

> The truth is, it is not Jesus as historically known, but Jesus as spiritually risen within men, who is significant for our time and can help it. Not the historical Jesus, but the spirit which goes forth from Him and in the spirits of men strives for new influence and rule, is that which overcomes the world.[9]

The historical Jesus whom Schweitzer discovered, therefore, both differed from the figure of his predecessors and rendered Jesus as a historical figure insignificant for later generations. Jesus during his lifetime, according to Schweitzer, had proclaimed that God in the near future would establish his supernatural kingdom through the supernatural messiah known as the "Son of Man" (cf. Dan. 7:13). Jesus believed that God had designated him to be revealed at the kingdom's arrival as that supernatural messiah; and he acted to hasten that climactic moment. Schweitzer described his viewpoint as one of thoroughgoing or consistent eschatology. Jesus both proclaimed and acted out his apocalyptic beliefs.

Albert Schweitzer found support for his interpretation in the Gospels themselves. For him Matthew 10:23 was a crucial text. Here Jesus, before sending out his disciples two by two, said to them: "When they persecute you in one town, flee to the next; for truly I tell you, you will not have gone through all the towns of Israel before the Son of Man comes." Until this point in his ministry, Jesus had thought that the persecution of his disciples would constitute those sufferings before the end which were expected within traditional Jewish apocalyptic speculation. He had thought that he, therefore, would be revealed as the "Son of Man" before they completed their rounds. Schweitzer explained the meaning of Jesus' words in Matthew 10:23 accordingly:

> He does not expect to see them back in the present age. The Parousia of the Son of Man, which is logically and temporally identical with the dawn of the Kingdom, will take place before they shall have completed a hasty journey through the cities of Israel to announce it.[10]

But the disciples returned to Jesus. They had not suffered. The kingdom of God had not arrived. He had not been glorified as the Son of Man. So Jesus had to rethink the course of his ministry. He subsequently decided that he had to take on himself the sufferings before the end. He shared this decision with his disciples near Caesarea Philippi. Schweitzer explained:

> In the secret of His passion which Jesus reveals to the disciples at Caesarea Philippi the pre-Messianic tribulation is for others set aside, abolished, concentrated upon Himself alone, and that in the form that they are fulfilled in His own passion and death at Jerusalem.[11]

But Jesus' own death still did not usher in God's supernatural kingdom and his glorification as the "Son of Man." The historical, apocalyptic Jesus had miscalculated—not once, but twice.

Hermann Samuel Reimarus had initiated the nineteenth-century quest by considering Jesus against the background of Jewish expectation for a political messiah and an earthly kingdom. Albert Schweitzer surveyed that quest by considering Jesus against the background of Jewish expectation for a supernatural messiah and a supernatural kingdom. Both Reimarus and Schweitzer agreed that Jesus during his ministry had failed to achieve his intended goal. They also agreed that there was a difference between the Gospel portrayals of Jesus and Jesus the historical figure.

This assumption about *discontinuity between the Christ of faith and the Jesus of history* was carried forward from the "old quest" period into the period of "no quest." Some scholars early in the twentieth century called for the suspension of efforts to seek the Jesus of history. This "no quest" attitude stemmed from a growing realization that it may be *methodologically impossible* to write a life of Jesus and *theologically unnecessary* to base Christian faith on the results of historical research. These scholars and theologians began to emphasize the importance of the Christ of faith.

The seekers after the historical Jesus in the nineteenth century had proceeded with the methodological confidence that they could use the Gospels to rediscover what Jesus had been like, but gradually this confidence was eroded. Historical skepticism asserted itself.[12] There were even those who denied that a historical figure named Jesus from Nazareth ever lived. Others did not deny the existence of Jesus but did say that it was impossible to write a detailed biography about him. A number of developments led to these expressions of historical skepticism. Certainly the development of form criticism brought this skepticism to full flower. Some form critics, as we have seen, called into question the historical reliability of the outline of Jesus' ministry in Mark. Others emphasized how the early church may have created many of the stories and sayings of Jesus now preserved in the Gospels. Therefore the nature of the Gospels themselves made a quest of the historical Jesus difficult, if not impossible.

Those seekers after the historical Jesus in the nineteenth century who had Christian commitment generally proceeded with the theological conviction that it was necessary to rediscover what Jesus had been like. But this conviction about the importance of the historical Jesus for Christian faith was increasingly challenged and even rejected. It was pointed out that the church and individual believers over the centuries had had their faith sustained by preaching and liturgy, by the creeds and the biblical writings. It was said that Christian faith was not—and had never been—grounded in the shifting sands of historical investigation about the life of Jesus. In other words, the claim was now made that the decisive basis for Christian faith was not the Jesus of history but the Christ of faith. The nature of faith, therefore, made a quest of the historical Jesus unnecessary and perhaps illegitimate.

A principal representative of the "no quest" attitude toward the historical Jesus was Rudolf Bultmann, a longtime member of the faculty at the University of Marburg. Throughout his lengthy career as biblical scholar, theologian, and preacher, he clung steadfastly to the view that the quest of the historical Jesus was methodologically impossible and theologically unnecessary. His historical skepticism, of course, was related to his pioneering work in form criticism. Bultmann could make positive comments about Jesus the historical figure and published a small book on Jesus' teaching called *Jesus and the Word* (1926; English trans., 1934).[13] But he denied that any interpreter could write a biography of Jesus. Bultmann's theological reluctance to undertake biographical writing about Jesus, even if possible, was related to his existentialist theology. The term *existentialism* generally refers to a theology or philosophy that emphasizes the human individual as a decision-making agent. Bultmann himself emphasized that Christian faith was the individual's affirmative answer to the church's *kerygma* (literally, "proclamation") of Jesus as the Christ. Faith, for Bultmann, was a personal response to the Christ of faith. He even said that faith which needed the external props of historical research into the life of Jesus was simply not faith. To Bultmann, therefore, both the nature of the Gospels and the nature of faith made the writing of a life of Jesus impossible and illegitimate.

Rudolf Bultmann was probably the outstanding biblical scholar of his century in terms of technical scholarship and theological reflection. Ironically, one of his contributions was a renewal of interest in the Jesus of history. His own students came to recognize certain weaknesses in their teacher's position, methodologically and theologically. Consequently, at mid-century the period of "no quest" was superseded by a "new quest" of the historical Jesus.

Period 4: New Quest (1953–1985)

Not all scholars had suspended the historical search for Jesus. However, even in circles characterized by historical skepticism, the search was begun anew as the result of a lecture by Ernst Käsemann in 1953. The occasion for the lecture was a reunion of Rudolf Bultmann's former students, many of whom had assumed important teaching positions in European universities. The lecture was published and translated with the title "The Problem of the Historical Jesus."[14] In his concluding remarks, Käsemann distinguished between his interest in the Jesus of history and the attitudes of earlier representatives of the "old quest" and the "no quest."

Käsemann firmly rejected the possibility of writing a biography of Jesus in the manner of the "old quest." The Gospels, he said, do not allow for the extensive chronologizing and the intensive psychologizing of the Jesus story:

> Have not some central points emerged, around which we might, if with the utmost caution and reserve, reconstruct something like a life of Jesus? I should reject such a view as being a misunderstanding. In writing a life of Jesus, we could not dispense with some account of his exterior and interior development. But we know nothing at all about the latter and next to nothing about the former, save only the way which led from Galilee to Jerusalem, from the preaching of the God who is near to us to the hatred of official Judaism and execution by the Romans. Only an uncontrolled imagination could have the self-confidence to weave out of these pitiful threads the fabric of a history in which cause and effect could be determined in detail.[15]

Käsemann also rejected the kind of historical skepticism that was partly responsible for the "no quest" disinterest in the earthly career of Jesus. The Gospels, he said, may not allow for a full biographical treatment of the Jesus story, but they do refer to a real person of flesh and blood:

> But conversely, neither am I prepared to concede that, in the face of these facts, defeatism and scepticism must have the last word and lead us on to a complete disengagement of interest from the earthly Jesus. If this were to happen, we should either be failing to grasp the nature of the primitive Christian concern with the identity between the exalted and the humiliated Lord; or else we should be emptying that concern of any real content, as did the docetists. We should also be overlooking the fact that there are still pieces of the Synoptic tradition which the historian has to acknowledge as authentic if he wishes to remain an historian at all. My own concern is to show that, out of the obscurity of the life story of Jesus,

certain characteristic traits in his preaching stand out in relatively sharp relief, and that primitive Christianity united its own message with these.[16]

Käsemann summarized his view of the issue in these terms: "The question of the historical Jesus is, in its legitimate form, the question of the continuity of the Gospel within the discontinuity of the times and within the variation of the kerygma."[17]

The scholarly movement initiated by Ernst Käsemann became known as the "new quest" of the historical Jesus. He and his successors maintained the distinction between the Christ of faith—the kerygmatic Christ—and the Jesus of history. But they neither sought the Jesus of history at the expense of the Christ of faith nor elevated the Christ of faith to the exclusion of the Jesus of history. Instead, they desired to establish *continuity between the Christ of faith and the Jesus of history.* They believed that within limits it was *methodologically possible* to reach relatively certain historical conclusions about Jesus, especially about his message. They also believed that it was *theologically necessary* to seek these historical conclusions as a reminder to Christian faith that Jesus the Christ was indeed a human being.

Within four years of Käsemann's challenge there appeared a full-scale treatment of Jesus from among those who had studied with Rudolf Bultmann. The author was Günther Bornkamm; the book, *Jesus of Nazareth* (1956; English trans., 1960).[18] The work of Bornkamm stayed within the guidelines set forth by Käsemann. The very title of the book had significance in this regard. The book was not called a "life," a biography, of Jesus. There is throughout the volume only the slightest interest in the sequence of events in the ministry of Jesus and virtually no interest in the self-understanding of Jesus. The message of Jesus constitutes the major focus of the book. Bornkamm wrote this volume for a general audience as well as scholars, and it became one of the most widely read historical treatments of Jesus over the quarter-century after its initial publication. The international reputation of Bornkamm as an authority on Jesus was indicated by his being asked to contribute the article "Jesus Christ" for the *Encyclopaedia Britannica* (15th ed., 1974).

This renewed interest in Jesus, initiated by Käsemann and popularized by Bornkamm in the 1950s and 1960s, attracted followers throughout the scholarly world. The very name given to this approach to the Jesus problem was bestowed by American scholar James M. Robinson in his sympathetic review of its beginnings, *A New Quest of the Historical Jesus* (1959).[19] Because of its origin and development within Bultmannian scholarly and theological circles, the "new quest" approach to Jesus possessed a kind of homogeneity lacking in that diverse movement known as the "old quest." Three unifying characteristics should be briefly mentioned.

First, "new quest" scholars recognized the faith, or kerygmatic, nature of the Gospels. The Gospels are not modern biographies but faith documents with every story and saying reflective of that faith. Simultaneous with the renewed interest in the historical Jesus was the development of redaction criticism. We have noted in our examination of this method how Günther Bornkamm was a pioneer in the study of the theology of Matthew. Thus he was well aware of the possible distance between the Christ of faith and the Jesus of history when he affirmed the possibility and necessity of bridging that distance by historical investigation into the earthly career of Jesus.

Second, "new quest" scholars understood the academic discipline of history and history writing more in terms of "event" than "sequence of facts." The Gospels do not allow interpreters to write a modern biography, a "life," about Jesus. But the Gospels do allow them to write about the life of Jesus. Every story and every saying as an interpreted event may have originated with Jesus in his earthly ministry.

Third, "new quest" scholars accepted the view that the burden of proof rested upon those who claimed that material in the Gospels was "authentic"—that is, originated with Jesus in his earthly ministry. These scholars, therefore, inherited and further developed certain principles or criteria that would enable them to establish the authenticity of the Gospel material; and they passed on these criteria to the next generation of Jesus scholars. Later in this chapter we will list and discuss several criteria that continue to be used, in various ways, to establish the historical probability of Jesus' words and deeds.

Period 5: Third Quest / Renewed Quest / Post-Quest (Since 1985)

During the 1960s and 1970s, interest in the historical Jesus began to extend well beyond "new quest" scholars and their sympathizers. That Jesus research has entered another stage, or period, in recent decades has received general recognition among scholars working in the field. To distinguish this preoccupation with the historical Jesus from the nineteenth-century "old" or "first quest" and the mid-twentieth-century "new" or "second quest," scholars have variously used the phrases "third quest" and "renewed quest" to describe the widespread interest in the historical Jesus that erupted both in scholarly and popular circles toward the end of the twentieth century.[20]

However, we propose the phrase "post-quest" to identify the most recent period of the quest. This phrase points to something distinctive about what has happened in our time. We have also used the year 1985 as a convenient date to mark the transition from the "new quest" period to the "post-quest" period. In that year two events occurred that signaled a transition in the history of Jesus research, each of which gives meaning to the phrase *post-quest*.

In 1985, there appeared E. P. Sanders' volume *Jesus and Judaism*. Sanders' academic career had carried him from McMaster University in Canada to Oxford University in England and, eventually, back to Duke University in America. Having published significant volumes on Paul's relation to Judaism, Sanders turned his attention to Jesus. In the introduction to this Jesus book, Sanders lists a number of works on the historical Jesus that had appeared in the years immediately prior to his own. Sanders suggests that these scholarly works shared a feature with his own presentation:

> In these and other works it is assumed or argued (usually assumed) that it is worthwhile to know and to state clearly whatever can be known about Jesus, and great effort is expended in establishing what can be known. The present work is written in the latter vein. To speak personally for a moment, I am interested in the debate about the significance of the historical Jesus for theology in the way that one is interested in something that he once found fascinating. The present work is written without that question in mind, however, and those who wish an essay on that topic may put this book down and proceed farther along the shelf.[21]

Here Sanders recognizes that the renewed interest in the historical Jesus, unlike the "old quest," the "no quest," and the "new quest," was neither driven nor dominated by the traditional question of the relationship between the Christ of faith and the Jesus of history. Just as philosophy had earlier declared its independence from theology as a result of the Enlightenment, so Sanders suggests that historical inquiry into the life of Jesus is now being pursued independent of christology. The question of the historical Jesus is interesting in itself without any necessary linkage to the church's traditional confession of Jesus as the Christ. *The focus now rests on Jesus as a historical figure.*

In March of 1985, the same year that Sanders published his Jesus book, there convened in Berkeley, California, the first meeting of the Jesus Seminar—initially a group of thirty or so scholars who had gathered at the invitation of Robert W. Funk. After many years as a scholar and teacher at such institutions as Vanderbilt University and the University of Montana, Funk had begun to think that it was time for him to set forth his own historical reconstruction of the ministry of Jesus. In order to facilitate his task, he had sought two scholarly aids. He tried to locate a "raw list" of all the sayings by, and stories about, Jesus as reported in ancient literature—within and without the New Testament. He also looked for a "critical list" of words and deeds generally considered by scholars, after two hundred years of critical sifting, to have been actually said and done by Jesus. He failed to find an exhaustive list of either kind.

Therefore Funk invited a group of scholarly colleagues to participate in an ongoing Seminar that eventually met twice annually in four day sessions. He later described their common purpose in these words:

> The aims of the Seminar were two: (1) We were to compile a raw list of all the words attributed to Jesus in the first three centuries (down to 300 C.E.). These sayings and parables were to be arranged as parallels, so that all versions of the same item would appear side by side on the page for close comparison and study. We decided to defer listing the deeds of Jesus until a second phase of the Seminar. (2) We were then to sort through this list and determine, on the basis of scholarly consensus, which items probably echoed or mirrored the voice of Jesus, and which items belong to subsequent stages of the Jesus tradition.[22]

John Dominic Crossan, who served as cochair of the Jesus Seminar, designed and edited the raw list of Jesus' words: *Sayings Parallels: A Workbook for the Jesus Tradition* (1986).[23] Funk himself edited those subsequent volumes that represented the critical lists of Jesus' words and deeds respectively: *The Five Gospels* (1993) and *The Acts of Jesus* (1997).[24] The Jesus Seminar became known in academic and popular circles for such procedures as face-to-face discussion of position papers, voting by dropping colored beads in a box on the authenticity of individual sayings and specific deeds, and color-coding the voting results, with only around 20 percent of Jesus' reported words and deeds being judged historically probable (red/highly probable; pink/probable; gray/possible, or black/improbable).

Sharp differences have distinguished the work of E. P. Sanders from that of the Jesus Seminar. Nonetheless, in 1985, both Sanders and the Jesus Seminar, without conscious reference to each other, seemingly agreed that their interest in Jesus was historical, not theological.

Other biblical scholars, along the way, have also noticed how the current phase of Jesus research exhibits a general disinterest in theological matters. Walter P. Weaver, for example, observed: "What seems characteristic of this new movement is a lack of interest in the theological significance of its subject."[25] M. Eugene Boring has also observed that this phase of Jesus scholarship "proclaims its separation from the theological enterprise—although it does this in strikingly different ways."[26] Dennis C. Duling describes this period of Jesus research as "theologically neutral."[27]

Thus an assumption for this phase of the quest for the historical Jesus can be described in terms of *methodological possibility* but *theological neutrality*. Since the historical quest for Jesus has traditionally been driven by theological concerns, the current period of Jesus research can appropriately, but somewhat ironically, be called "post-quest." The phrase *post-quest*, however, is intended to identify a distinctive dimension of what has been going on in recent Jesus studies and not to suggest that all involved are uninterested in what has traditionally been described as the relationship between the Christ of faith and the Jesus of history.

John P. Meier provides further confirmation of the concern by contemporary Jesus scholars to bracket out their own faith commitments as they pursue their work as historians. On the opening pages of what have become more than a thousand pages of his own judicious rethinking of the historical Jesus, Meier—a Catholic priest who teaches at Catholic University in Washington, D.C.—confesses that he writes out of "a Catholic context." However, as a way of not allowing his Christian commitments to get in the way of his historical investigations, he imagines what he calls an "unpapal enclave." He says:

> Suppose that a Catholic, a Protestant, a Jew, and an agnostic—all honest historians cognizant of 1st-century religious movements—were locked up in the bowels of the Harvard Divinity School library, put on a spartan diet, and not allowed to emerge until they had hammered out a consensus document on who Jesus of Nazareth was and what he intended in his own time and place. An essential requirement of this document would be that it be based on purely historical sources and arguments.[28]

Perhaps this bracketing of interest in the theological implications of Jesus research relates to another distinctive dimension of recent Jesus scholarship—a strong emphasis upon Jesus as a Jew who was continuous with the Judaism of his own time, however that continuity might be understood. Meier's own multivolume work on the historical Jesus carries the title *A Marginal Jew* (2 vols., 1991, 1994). The titles of other major works also testify to Jesus' Jewishness: E. P. Sanders's *Jesus and Judaism* (1985); James H. Charlesworth's *Jesus Within Judaism* (1988); John Dominic Crossan's *The Historical Jesus: The Life of a Mediterranean Jewish Peasant* (1991). These writings were anticipated by the pioneering work of Geza Vermes that over a twenty-year period has become, as projected, a trilogy: *Jesus the Jew* (1973); *Jesus and the World of Judaism* (1983); and *The Religion of Jesus the Jew* (1993).[29]

These volumes also contain among themselves three of the principal historical models that have emerged in recent years for understanding Jesus the first-century Jew. Sanders portrays Jesus as the eschatological prophet who announces the restoration of Israel. Crossan portrays Jesus as a Galilean peasant sage whose unconventional teaching and itinerant behavior resembles that of Cynic philosophers. Vermes portrays Jesus as a *Hasid*, or holy man, a rabbi in the charismatic tradition of Galilee, who teaches the law and heals the sick. By contrast, the marginal Jew emerging from the pages of Meier's work does not easily fit into one category. Furthermore, to varying degrees, these volumes also use the insights of such social sciences as cultural anthropology and archaeology. The differences among these and the many other historical portrayals of Jesus, past and present, are based on a variety of factors.

One factor involves the literature the historian admits as evidence and how the interrelationship of this literature is understood. All four canonical Gospels? Only the synoptic Gospels? Or, also—and even primarily—traditions represented by Q and the *Gospel of Thomas*? What about the *Gospel of Peter*? Certainly a reassessment of Gospel literature has been a major factor in the renewed interest in the historical Jesus.

Another factor involves the kind of Judaism—the specific Jewish context—within which to place Jesus. Do the eschatological traditions expressed by ancient Israel's prophets and their successors provide the context within which to understand Jesus? Whereas apocalyptic has been understood by some to be a kind of eschatology that projected a coming *end* of the world, other scholars view apocalyptic to be a dramatic way of talking about the end of the present evil age and the inauguration of a new age *within* history when God would somehow intervene and restore Israel.

Or do wisdom traditions compiled by Israel's sages in such books as Proverbs, with their focus on how to live now, provide the context within which to understand Jesus? In recent years, some scholars have rediscovered Jesus' parables and aphorisms as expressions of wisdom that do not reinforce but challenge traditional ways of viewing God and the world. Without denying Jesus' Jewishness, but observing how Galilee generally represented a much Hellenized territory, others have established similarities between Jesus' teaching and the countercultural wisdom of those wandering philosophers known as Cynics.

Or do the legal traditions grounded in the five books of Moses and later codified by the rabbis in the Mishnah provide the context within which to understand Jesus? Scholars generally have come to view Jesus' antagonism toward the Pharisees, as displayed in the Gospels, to be more of a reflection of conflict between the post-Jesus church and the synagogue than a recollection of conflict between Jesus and his Pharisaic contemporaries.

Still another factor that determines a historical reconstruction of Jesus' career involves the way the interpreter uses specific principles, or criteria, for determining whether or not Jesus spoke this word or performed that act. Here are *five* criteria of the many that have been developed and invoked during the long search for the historical Jesus.[30]

First, the *criterion of dissimilarity* states that sayings or emphases of Jesus in the Gospels may be considered authentic if they are dissimilar from sayings or emphases of the early church, on the one hand, and of ancient Judaism, on the other. This criterion assumes knowledge of both the early church and ancient Judaism with which comparison is made. Its limitation is that it confirms only those aspects of Jesus' teaching that are peculiar to him and excludes those aspects that he may have shared with the early church or Judaism. Because this criterion tends to separate Jesus from Judaism, it no longer has the prominence it did among "new quest" scholars. Among the sayings and emphases often said to have been authenticated by this criterion are: Jesus' proclamation of the "kingdom of God" as not only future but also present; Jesus' interpretation of the Torah without appeal to precedent; Jesus' address of God by the intimate name *Abba* ("Father"); and, generally, Jesus' parables.

Second, the *criterion of multiple attestation* states that sayings, themes, or kinds of behavior by Jesus may be considered authentic if they are attested in multiple Gospel sources—traditionally Mark, Q, M, L, and John. Most, if not all, of these sources depict Jesus as one who preached in parables, associated with social outcasts, debated with religious authorities, and performed healings and exorcisms. This principle obviously grew out of the source analysis of the Gospels so characteristic of the "old quest" period. But, as we have seen, the *Gospel of Thomas* and the *Gospel of Peter* have come to be viewed by some scholars in recent years as sources independent of the Synoptics and John. The Q document itself has been elevated by some to the status of Sayings Gospel Q, which antedates the canonical narrative Gospels.

Third, the *criterion of embarrassment* states that information about Jesus that would have been viewed by the early church as an embarrassment may be considered authentic since it is unlikely that the church would have made up such activities or sayings. Among details said to meet this criterion are: Jesus' baptism by John, since it was a baptism of repentance for the forgiveness of sins; Jesus' conflict with his immediate family, since his mother Mary and his brother James later become prominent in the church; and Jesus' denial by Peter and his betrayal by Judas, since they were among his chosen disciples.

Fourth, the *criterion of language and environment,* more negative than positive, states that material about Jesus in the Gospels may not be considered authentic unless it is compatible with the language and culture of Palestine and Palestinian Judaism. This principle also emerged out of the "old quest." Participants in the nineteenth-century search took seriously the study of Jesus within the first-century setting in which he lived and died. No scholar in this century used this criterion with any more rigor than Joachim Jeremias. Although a German contemporary of Rudolf Bultmann, he never accepted the "no quest" outlook and continued to work his way back through the Gospel tradition to the historical Jesus. He even tried his hand at translating from Greek back into the Aramaic such portions of the Gospel tradition as Jesus' parables, the Lord's Prayer, and the words over the bread and wine at the Last Supper.[31]

Five, the *criterion of coherence* states that sayings or emphases of Jesus in the Gospels may be considered authentic if they cohere, or agree, with material established as authentic by other criteria. This criterion allows for the enlargement of the amount of authentic material. There is considerable debate about the different kinds of "Son of Man" sayings preserved in the Gospels. But the apocalyptic "Son of Man" sayings could be accepted as authentic insofar as they cohere with the futuristic dimension of Jesus' kingdom proclamation.

Retrospective: A Continuing Quest

Retrospectively, the quest can be viewed from two vantage points. First, the quest can be viewed as a succession of historical periods in the ongoing history of Jesus research. We have identified Albert Schweitzer's survey of the nineteenth-century quest, published in 1906, as marking the transition from the "old quest" period to the period of "no quest." We should reemphasize, however, that not all scholars suspended the effort to rediscover the Jesus of history.

An interest in Jesus as a historical figure continued without interruption, especially within British and American scholarship. An important difference between the scholars who continued the quest and those representatives of the "new quest" lay in their fundamental attitude about the historical value of the four Gospels. Many British and American scholars rejected in principle the possibility of writing a biography about Jesus. But they tended to accept the material in the four Gospels as authentic unless there were reasons for denying authenticity. But "new quest" scholars, to the contrary, questioned the authenticity of the material unless they could establish it as authentic. These differences about burden of proof among scholars of varying backgrounds have continued into what we have called the "post-quest" period.

Second, the quest can be viewed as providing representative assumptions and attitudes about Jesus as a historical figure. The assumptions and attitudes dominant in each period of the quest also continue as options in our day among professional scholars and nonprofessional scholars, among clergy and laity. The attitudes and assumptions, as well as the critical viewpoints, dominant in one period may also be present in another.

There are those, primarily in the nonacademic sector, who are simply unaware of the problem of the historical Jesus—although the attention paid to Jesus in the popular media in recent years must surely have raised public awareness. There are even biblical scholars aware of the problem of the historical Jesus who find various ways to deny it by ingeniously defending the basic historicity of the four Gospels. They rail against much that goes on in the historical search for Jesus. Such persons live with a "pre-quest" mentality.

Then there are those with the perspective of the "old quest." They approach Jesus and his story with a strong biographical interest and, if Christian, view him as the basis of faith. They may, in some sense, follow and not worship him.

There are others with the orientation of the "no quest" who stress Christ as proclaimed through preaching and liturgy, through creed and Scripture. They may consider historical scholarship to be irrelevant to their own lives of faith.

Still others have the outlook of the "new quest." They believe it important, in spite of the historical difficulties, to establish some kind of continuity between the Christ of faith and the Jesus of history in order to undergird their faith.

If a distinguishing characteristic of what we call the "post-quest" is an interest in the historical Jesus without a stated theological agenda, this may—in part—explain the commercial media and publishing success of Jesus over the last decade. Disillusioned with overly simplistic answers, or no answers, from the church to their most basic questions about life, many have turned to the varied world of Jesus scholarship to see what all the fuss is about.

QUEST OF THE HISTORICAL JESUS

Period 1: Pre-Quest (before 1778)	Period 2: Old Quest (1778–1906)	Period 3: No Quest (1906–1953)	Period 4: New Quest (1953–1985)	Period 5: Post-Quest (since 1985)
Period of Pre-Criticism	Period of Source Criticism	Period of Form Criticism	Period of Redaction and Narrative Criticisms	Period of Social-Scientific Criticism
Correspondence between Jesus of History = Christ of Faith	Discontinuity between *Jesus of History* // Christ of Faith	Discontinuity between Jesus of History // *Christ of Faith*	Continuity between *Jesus of History* < *Christ of Faith*	Focus on *Jesus of History* [Christ of Faith]
No Problem and No Quest	Methodologically Possible and Theologically Necessary	Methodologically Impossible and Theologically Unnecessary	Methodologically Possible and Theologically Necessary	Methodologically Possible and Theologically Neutral

6

Historical Portrayals

The search for the historical Jesus has resulted in many different portrayals of his life and ministry, as we have already seen. A historical portrayal can be described as a *telling of the Jesus story based on the evaluation of available sources following certain principles of historical interpretation.* The historical portrayal of Jesus, therefore, is an expression of *reason,* historical reason. Some writers about Jesus are professional historians. Other writers are amateurs. Some write to serve and to nurture Christian faith, while others write to challenge and to undermine Christian faith. But all authors of historical portrayals claim to be telling the Jesus story, or a portion thereof, "as it really happened."

Even the historian, of course, tends to make Jesus over in his or her own image. This was Albert Schweitzer's main criticism of many writers on the subject in the nineteenth century. He claimed that they had depicted Jesus as a teacher congenial to the modern era instead of an ancient apocalyptist. Certainly the historian brings to the task assumptions and commitments which influence what is said and how it is said. Nonetheless, historical inquiry persistently pursued does establish a kind of distance between the interpreter and the subject matter. Historical portrayals *should* be "objective" by reflecting an objective quality in contrast to Gospel portrayals, on the one hand, and admittedly fictitious portrayals, on the other. Gospel portrayals and fictitious portrayals are primarily expressions of Christian faith and the literary imagination respectively. Historical portrayals are products of historical reason.[1]

A number of narratives about Jesus by nonacademics have achieved considerable popularity over the course of this century. These include, to mention

110

only two, *The Greatest Story Ever Told*, 1949, by Fulton Oursler[2] and *Jesus the Evidence*, 1984, by Ian Wilson.[3] Oursler was an author, journalist, and play-wright. His Jesus book provided at least the title for George Stevens' 1965 Jesus film epic of the same name. Wilson has written on other religious sub-jects, including a widely read book on the Shroud of Turin. Works such as these may be considered historical portrayals to the extent that they claim to portray Jesus "as he really was" or to report "what really happened."

Various schemes have been adopted for classifying those writings that line the path taken by seekers after Jesus. We classify historical portrayals according to three types: the biographical portrayal characteristic of the "old quest"; a con-sciously nonbiographical—or even antibiographical—portrayal taken by the "new quest"; and the neobiographical portrayal that marks the latest phase of the Jesus quest. We include in our survey only portrayals of Jesus written by professional historians with expertise in literary analysis and historical reconstruction.

The Biographical Portrayal

We used the expression "old quest" in the preceding chapter to designate a particular period in the history of Jesus research. That period was bracketed by the dates 1778 and 1906, associated with publications by Hermann Samuel Reimarus and Albert Schweitzer. We described the basic approach to the Jesus story during this period as biographical. Jesus and his story were chronologized and psychologized. His ministry was arranged into distinct periods. His mind was probed for his self-understanding and his intentions. The biographical approach, however, was by no means confined to the nine-teenth century. It persists to the present day. The following writings represent the biographical approach to the Jesus story. To appreciate the distinctiveness of each, we will briefly consider the critical principles followed by its author and the resulting historical portrayal of Jesus.

DAVID SMITH, *The Days of His Flesh: The Earthly Life of Our Lord and Savior Jesus Christ* (1905).[4]

David Smith served as a minister in Scotland and later as a professor of the-ology in Londonderry, Northern Ireland. He writes with a twofold purpose: "to vindicate the historicity of the evangelic records" and "to justify the church's faith in Him as the Lord from Heaven."[5] We have included his sizable work on Jesus in our survey for reasons related to his own statement of pur-pose. He harmonizes all four Gospels and seldom, if ever, omits a story or say-ing about Jesus contained therein. He also portrays Jesus as the incarnation of God, as indicated by the title itself.

The Four Gospels Harmonized. Smith introduces his work with a detailed defense of the essential reliability of the four Gospels. He writes before the development of form criticism but acknowledges the role of oral transmission of Gospel tradition. Moreover, he allows for what he calls "sundry mishaps" in that process. These include slips of memory, the alteration of objectionable details, and slight changes in stories to make them conform more closely with the Old Testament passages they are said to fulfill. But the Gospels contain the "True Deposit," since the Gospel tradition originated with the apostles in a Jewish environment accustomed to a careful preservation of oral teaching.

Smith writes at the time of a growing acceptance of the "two-document hypothesis" regarding the literary relationship among Matthew, Mark, and Luke. But he views the synoptic Gospels as independent deposits of Gospel tradition. The Gospel of Matthew was derived from the disciple Matthew but not actually written by him. The Gospels of Mark and Luke were written by their namesakes. Smith views the work of the evangelists as that of editors. He does, however, acknowledge a certain editorial freedom on their parts. They even quoted Jesus' words out of their original historical setting and cited incidents out of their original chronological order. To Smith, the Fourth Gospel was written by John the "beloved disciple." John wrote with the intention of correcting and supplementing the other Gospel accounts that he had before him. This is apparent, for example, in what Smith considers to be John's correct placement of the Temple cleansing at the outset of Jesus' public ministry.

Jesus as the Incarnation of God. Smith reports the earthly life of Jesus in chronological order. He shuttles back and forth, weaving the four Gospels into a single tapestry with his own comments binding the threads together. He begins his narration with the affirmation of Jesus' preexistence (John), his birth and infancy (Matthew and Luke), and his journey to Jerusalem with his parents at age twelve (Luke). Smith continues with a recounting of Jesus' public ministry (all four Gospels). That ministry spanned a three-year period and included several trips from Galilee to Jerusalem (John). The confession of Peter at Caesarea Philippi occurred prior to the final trip to Jerusalem (Mark par.). The Last Supper was a Passover meal, and the crucifixion was on Passover day (Mark par.; but John agrees, according to Smith's interpretation). Smith concludes his narration with the resurrection appearances (all four Gospels) and the ascension (Luke). Along the way, Smith assigns absolute dates to the main events: birth, 5 B.C.E.; baptism, 26 C.E.; and, by implication, crucifixion, 29 C.E.

Within this chronological framework, Smith makes rather sweeping statements about the nature and constancy of Jesus' understanding of himself and his mission. He says that at age twelve Jesus discovered who he was and why he had come into the world. Jesus knew that as God's Son, Israel's Messiah, and Savior of the world, he had come to die as a sacrifice for the sins of all humankind. This messianic consciousness was simply confirmed for Jesus at his baptism and fulfilled by his crucifixion.

Smith reports, of course, both Jesus' talk about himself through the "I am" sayings (John) and his preaching about the "kingdom of God" through parables (Mark par.). But Smith de-emphasizes the apocalyptic aspect of Jesus' kingdom proclamation. He declares that Jesus anticipated a period of some length between his resurrection and his second coming. He also denies that Jesus derived his favorite self-designation as the "Son of Man" from apocalyptic texts such as Daniel 7:13. Rather, it originated as a nickname of derision that Jesus appropriated for his own use in the hope that humanity would be led to see the true meaning of messiahship.

Smith accepts the historicity of the miracles but with certain interesting qualifications. He suggests that Jesus himself did not believe in demons. Jesus in his exorcisms accommodated himself to the beliefs of his ancient day in order to heal the persons who did believe in the reality of demons. Smith also interprets the nature miracles as having what he calls "prophetic" significance. The miracle of the fish and the loaves anticipated the Last Supper. The miracle of the walking on the water foreshadowed the resurrection appearances.

For David Smith, the discontinuity between the Christ of faith and the Jesus of history is minimal. The four Gospels testify to Jesus as he was—the incarnation of God.

HUGH J. SCHONFIELD, *The Passover Plot* (1966).[6]

For over forty years, since his days as a student at the University of Glasgow, Hugh J. Schonfield sought to discover what the God-man of Christianity was really like. His interpretation of the life and death of Jesus represents the result of that prolonged personal and scholarly quest. We consider it as an interesting biographical portrayal of Jesus.

Four Gospels and Ancient Scrolls. Schonfield devotes the latter half of his work to an elaboration of a number of literary and historical issues integrally related to his presentation of Jesus' ministry in the first half.

He accepts Mark as the first of the four Gospels to be written. His view of the origin of John, however, has considerable importance for his historical conclusions. According to Schonfield, John was written in Ephesus early in the second century by a Greek elder named John. This explains the Hellenistic portrayal of Jesus in the Gospel as the incarnation of God. John, however, does contain important information transmitted to the Greek elder by the "beloved disciple." But Schonfield identifies the beloved disciple not as John the son of Zebedee but as a Jewish priest in whose home the Last Supper was held. John, therefore, may not be historically reliable in its characterization of Jesus as the incarnation of God, but it does have indispensable historical details about his ministry from an eyewitness. Although Schonfield appears conversant with the generally accepted conclusions of source criticism, he does not avail himself of the insights of form and redaction criticism. Consequently his use of the four

Gospels in support of his own understanding of the historical Jesus often appears arbitrary.

In addition to the four Gospels, the Dead Sea Scrolls are important for Schonfield. The Scrolls and the Essene spirituality therein had their influence on Jesus. One such influence was the "oracular" use of Jewish Scripture, the Old Testament. That is, Scripture was viewed as prophecies to be fulfilled. Just as the early church after Jesus used the Old Testament to demonstrate that he had fulfilled prophecies, so the Essenes before Jesus used Scripture to show how they were fulfilling the prophecies. Jesus adopted his "oracular" method from the Essenes, or "Saints," according to Schonfield. Thus the plot was born!

Jesus as the Plotting Messiah. Central to Schonfield's portrayal of Jesus is the conviction that Jesus was "the man who believed he was Messiah."[7] Jesus came to this awareness even as he was growing up. His achievement during this formative period was of two kinds. First, he brought together various aspects of the Essene messianic hope into one coherent self-concept: the Messiah whose name was "Son of Man," whose character was that of the "Suffering Just One" and the "glorious king," and whose transition from suffering to glory would be through death and resurrection. Second, Jesus searched Scripture and pieced together a messianic "plan," "program," or "blueprint" that he as Messiah in obedience to God would act to fulfill. Jesus implemented that plan, according to Schonfield, in two phases.

The appearance of John the Baptist signaled for Jesus the time to initiate the implementation of "the first phase" of his messianic scheme. Jesus' baptism by John, probably early in 35 C.E., became the moment when God indicated approval of him as his messianic Son. Thereafter, Jesus chose twelve disciples and undertook with them a public ministry of preaching and healing centered primarily in Galilee. Jesus experienced a certain popularity because of his healing. But the general response was what he had expected—apathy and rejection!

The reported execution of John the Baptist signaled for Jesus the time to begin "the second phase" of his messianic plan. The turning point occurred near Caesarea Philippi. After the confession of Peter, Jesus began to teach his disciples that he must suffer, die, and be resurrected. But now the plan required a "plot." For Jesus believed that the plan called not for actual death and real resurrection but for a faked death and a staged resurrection. Accordingly, Jesus went with his disciples to Jerusalem for the Feast of Tabernacles in October and remained through the Feast of Rededication in January. During this period, Jesus, unknown to the twelve, began to lay plans for what would become the "Passover plot" three months later. As that plot unfolded, it had several dimensions. Judas would be induced to betray his master. Lazarus would make arrangements for the colt to be used for the triumphal entry into Jerusalem. John, a priest of Jerusalem, would open his home for the Passover meal—the Last Supper. Another, now anonymous, conspirator would offer a drugged drink to Jesus in response to the words, "I thirst." Joseph of Arimathea would provide a tomb for the removal of the drugged and unconscious form of Jesus for burial. Later recovered, Jesus would present himself as one resurrected from the dead. The "Passover plot" unfolded as planned by Jesus with only one unexpected turn of events. That turn, however, proved to be fatal: a Roman soldier thrust a spear into Jesus' side. Jesus' body, now mortally wounded, was taken from the cross and buried as planned. Jesus even recovered for a moment in the tomb and gave a message to a bystander to be delivered to his disciples in Galilee. Then he died. His body was buried again in a different tomb. The first tomb to which he was taken was subsequently discovered empty. The person who tried to communicate his farewell message to his disciples was mistakenly identified as the resurrected Jesus. This person may have been the same man who drugged Jesus at the cross. These events transpired at Passover, 36 C.E.

Schonfield, as is evident, chronologizes the Jesus story on several levels. The ministry lasts but a year and falls into two phases with Caesarea Philippi as the watershed (Mark par.). But there is an earlier visit to Jerusalem at the time of the Feast of Tabernacles and prior to the final visit to Jerusalem at Passover time (John). To the ministry of Jesus are affixed the beginning and concluding dates of 35 and 36 C.E.

To Schonfield, Jesus died as a messiah whose plot had failed. But through the unanticipated birth of the church and Christianity, Jesus succeeded in a manner beyond his wildest dreams. There is obviously, however, sharp discontinuity between the Christ of faith and the Jesus of history as the latter is portrayed by Hugh J. Schonfield.

ARCHIBALD M. HUNTER, *The Work and Words of Jesus* (1950).[8]
T. W. MANSON, *The Servant Messiah: A Study of the Public Ministry of Jesus* (1953).[9]
VINCENT TAYLOR, *The Life and Ministry of Jesus* (1955).[10]
C. H. DODD, *The Founder of Christianity* (1970).[11]

The study by Archibald M. Hunter represents the earliest of the four to be written. In the preface of his book, Hunter mentions by name three other New Testament scholars whose writings have placed him in their debt: T. W. Manson, Vincent Taylor, and C. H. Dodd. Dodd also served as the director and vice-chairman of the committee that oversaw the translation and publication of The New English Bible (1970)—a joint venture undertaken not only by the Church of England and the Church of Scotland but also by the Methodist, Baptist, and Congregational Churches.

These four British scholars certainly differ regarding specific points of interpretation relative to what Jesus was like historically. But their reconstructions are important because they represent, in their commonality, the view dominant in British scholarship at midcentury. This commonality includes both their use of the four Gospels and their characterization of Jesus as the suffering servant messiah. This understanding of the historical Jesus also has its advocates among American and continental scholars.

The Synoptics Plus John. All four scholars accept and defend the "two-source" solution to the synoptic problem. Mark was the earliest Gospel to be written. Matthew and Luke contain sayings similar enough to establish the existence of Q—whether a document or a well-defined body of oral tradition. Both Hunter and Taylor express appreciation for B. H. Streeter's expansion of the "two-source" hypothesis into a "four-source" theory. Hunter in a helpful appendix even provides the text of those Gospel passages that can be designated respectively as Q, M, and L.

The significance of source analysis for these British scholars is the conclusion that Mark and Q constitute two relatively ancient sources that report the ministry and message of Jesus. They view the early church as a preserver rather than a creator of the Jesus tradition. It will be remembered from our survey of the development of form criticism that C. H. Dodd and Vincent Taylor were critical of the claims made by German critics that the church created the outline of Jesus' ministry in Mark and many of his words and deeds. For all four of these British scholars, the Gospel of Mark does reflect a broadly reliable outline of Jesus' ministry—at least for the ministry centered in Galilee. All four believe that Mark and the other Synoptics preserve a coherent and generally accurate accounting of Jesus' teachings and activities.

These scholars also consider the Gospel of John to be more of a theological document than the Synoptics, but they are willing to use John as a source for the historical Jesus. This historical use of John expresses itself primarily in relation to certain details of Jesus' ministry. These details include such matters as the length of Jesus' ministry, his activity in Judea, his visits to Jerusalem, and the dating of the Last Supper. Among the four interpreters, C. H. Dodd is the one most willing to use even the discourse material in John to explore Jesus' intention and teaching.

Jesus as the Suffering Servant Messiah. Hunter, Manson, Taylor, and Dodd deny that a full biography about Jesus can be written, but each proceeds with confidence in his own ability to psychologize Jesus and to chronologize his ministry.

There is no doubt in their minds that Jesus in his mind knew himself to be the Messiah. Jesus did not, however, use the title "Messiah" for himself; and he accepted the title from others only with hesitation. The reason for this reticence and reluctance was the association of the title "Messiah" with the nationalistic hope within Israel for a Davidic royal messiah. By sharp contrast,

Jesus viewed his messiahship in terms of servanthood and suffering. Jesus found scriptural basis for this creative redefinition of messiahship in the "Servant of the LORD" passages in Isaiah—especially in Isaiah 53, the dramatic depiction of the servant's vicarious suffering. Although A. M. Hunter argues that Jesus was aware of the suffering dimension of his servanthood even at his baptism, Vincent Taylor suggests that Jesus came to this awareness only in the course of his ministry. But all four scholars portray the historical Jesus as the suffering servant messiah. The basic conflict in Jesus' ministry, therefore, was a conflict derived from the clash between his understanding of his messianic vocation and the messianic expectation of others, including his own disciples. Jesus offered servanthood, not dominion; sacrifice, not conquest. Furthermore, all four scholars claim that Jesus selected as his own special designation the expression "Son of Man." The expression had varied connotations but was free of obvious political overtones. Jesus went to Jerusalem knowing that humiliation but also vindication awaited him.

This interpretation of Jesus' messianic consciousness rests upon the acceptance by these scholars of the historicity of the verbal exchange between Jesus and his disciples near Caesarea Philippi. This interpretation also depends upon the authenticity of the subsequent "passion predictions" when Jesus says that the "Son of Man" must suffer, die, and be raised on the third day. Moreover, this interpretation indicates the confidence these scholars have in reconstructing the overall shape of Jesus' ministry.

All four scholars agree that Jesus' ministry lasted from eighteen months to three years. A. M. Hunter, as the most precise among them, views Jesus' public activity as embracing three Passover seasons—in the years 28, 29, and 30. The four of them also move Jesus from his baptism by John and his testing in the wilderness (Mark par.), through a brief period of activity in Judea (John) to the inauguration of his Galilean ministry of kingdom preaching and healing (Mark par.). Occasional visits southward to Jerusalem (John) cannot be ruled out, but Galilee remained the primary place of Jesus' ministry (Mark par.). Furthermore, all four scholars see three events marking the conclusion of the Galilean ministry and the shift of interest to Judea and Jerusalem—the feeding of the multitudes (Mark par. and John); a withdrawal into the region of Tyre (Mark par.); and the incident near Caesarea Philippi (Mark par.). C. H. Dodd places great emphasis on the feeding episode. To him this was the occasion of Jesus' final appeal to the Galileans. Their response was the unfortunate attempt to make him king (John 6:15). After the confession of Peter at Caesarea Philippi, according to their common interpretation, Jesus began to teach his disciples the nature of his messiahship and moved southward with them toward Jerusalem (Mark par.). Jesus and his disciples initially visited Jerusalem for the Feast of Tabernacles in the fall (John). T. W. Manson even proposes that this visit was the occasion for the triumphal entry and the cleansing of the Temple (contrary to Mark par. and John). But in the spring Jesus returned to Jerusalem to fulfill his messianic destiny and was crucified (Mark par. and John). The crucifixion probably took place on the day of preparation of Passover (John), although this is subject to debate.

Within this psychologizing and chronologizing framework, these four British scholars interpret Jesus' message of the "kingdom of God" as the proclamation of a reality already present in and through Jesus' ministry with his twelve disciples. C. H. Dodd popularized the phrase "realized eschatology" to designate this emphasis upon the kingdom as present through Jesus' activity of preaching, healing, and dying. Dodd even translates Mark 1:15 as: "The time has come; the kingdom of God is upon you!" Dodd's scholarly kinsfolk have adopted the phrase "realized eschatology" with approval. Dodd himself does not exclude a future dimension to Jesus' message but clearly understands Jesus' intention to be nonapocalyptic. Dodd repeatedly says that the consummation of the present kingdom lies "beyond history." Of the four interpreters, Vincent Taylor is the one most willing to acknowledge that Jesus toward the end of his ministry increasingly conceived of himself as not only the suffering but also the exalted "Son of Man" who would come in glory at the end of history.

Although Hunter, Manson, Taylor, and Dodd recognize a certain discontinuity between the Christ of faith and the Jesus of history, the Synoptic portrayals of Jesus enable them to rediscover the Jesus of history. As a result, they have established continuity between the church's confession of Jesus as the Christ and his own self-understanding as the suffering servant messiah.

SHIRLEY JACKSON CASE, *Jesus: A New Biography* (1927)

For thirty years Shirley Jackson Case was a member of the faculty at the University of Chicago. His interest and expertise lay in the area of Christian origins. He intended in this biography "to depict Jesus as he actually appeared to the men of his own time in Palestine nineteen hundred years ago."[12] This volume is a testimony to the judicious use of historical reason as Case carefully leads the reader from the Gospels back to Jesus in his historical ministry. His portrayal of Jesus as a social prophet represents a common characterization of Jesus within American scholarship.[13]

The Four Gospels from a Social Point of View. Case describes the Gospels as "ancient biographies" but clearly recognizes their confessional character and the problem they pose for the modern biographer. The modern biographer, he says, must be able to distinguish in the Gospels between "unhistorical features" and "objective data" to recover the historical Jesus. Case then reviews, and finds wanting, several alleged avenues to the historical Jesus.

Neither the inclusion of the four Gospels in the New Testament nor their reputed apostolic authorship assures historical accuracy. Case himself acknowledges the probability of Markan authorship of Mark, questions the

Lukan authorship of Luke, and denies Matthean and Johannine authorships for Matthew and John.

Neither does source criticism nor form criticism enable the historian to establish the historicity of material in the Gospels. Case accepts the "two-source" solution to the synoptic problem; but he denies that Mark, the earliest Gospel, can simply be accepted as the most accurate. Case affirms the value of form criticism in distinguishing between later and earlier features in the Gospel tradition, especially between Hellenistic and Palestinian features. But for him there must be a further test to establish probable historicity.

The final test of historicity is what could be called the criterion of suitability: every statement in the Gospels is to be evaluated by the degree of its suitableness to the Palestinian Jewish environment of Jesus, on the one hand, and to the Christian theological interests of the shapers of the Gospel tradition, on the other. The Synoptics and John, for example, give different dates for the Last Supper and crucifixion. Case admits that both the Synoptic dating of Passover and the Johannine dating of the day before Passover can be explained as theologically motivated. But he finally decides on the probability of the correctness of the Johannine dating. He reasons that it would have been more suitable to first-century Jewish requirements and practice for crucifixion to have occurred before, not in violation of, the holy day of Passover. In his retelling of the Jesus story, therefore, Case brings to bear on the documentary evidence what he calls "the social point-of-view."

Jesus as a Social Prophet. To Case, Jesus was a Jewish prophet who had the prophetic awareness of God's immediate presence and the prophetic sense of responsibility for the well-being of others. He proclaimed the prophetic message of God's future kingdom, a kingdom that was near. Jesus the Jew, however, would have used the expression "kingdom of heaven" (as in Matthew, not Mark and Luke). Jesus undertook the prophetic task of preparing his hearers for God's coming kingdom by summoning them to repentance and righteousness. It was Jesus' exercise of his prophetic authority over against institutionalized authority that led to his death as a "potential insurrectionist." He thereby became a "martyred prophet."

Regarding Jesus' self-understanding, therefore, Case repeatedly denies that he possessed a messianic consciousness. If Jesus ever used the phrase "Son of Man," he used it either to designate humankind in general or to denote that apocalyptic figure who would appear on earth at the last judgment. It is highly unlikely, according to Case, that Jesus would have used the expression for himself. It would have been more suitable for his followers to use it of him after his death. Jesus would have been more comfortable with the designation "prophet," for which role his upbringing in his home at Nazareth would have prepared him. His baptism by John became his call to be a prophet. His crucifixion was his destiny as a prophet.

Regarding the outline of Jesus' ministry, Case is less certain of it than he is about Jesus' prophetic self-understanding. He does establish the year 29 C.E. as a possible date of death. But he cannot with any probability establish the date of Jesus' birth. He observes, however, that the longer ministry attested by John is more likely than the shorter ministry of one year implied by Mark. Taken together, the four Gospels suggest that Jesus carried on his ministry both in Galilee and in Judea.

Jesus' task as a prophet was essentially one of preaching. Case calls into question the historicity of the miracle tradition on the basis that the miracle stories were suitable, hence created, for missionary work among the Gentiles by the early church. He also calls into question the genealogical record of Jesus' Davidic descent and the claim of his birth in Bethlehem on the basis that they were personal items more suitable, hence created, for missionary work among the Jews by the early church. Moreover, he refers to the resurrection experiences of Peter and the others only in passing. He calls them "remarkable visions." These visions stand between Jesus the prophet and the Christian church, between the historical Jesus and the Christ of faith.

The Nonbiographical Portrayal

We used the phrase "new quest" in the preceding chapter to identify the period in the history of Jesus research initiated by the lecture of Ernst Käsemann in 1953. The phrase itself originated as a designation for a specific approach to the Jesus story.

The followers of Rudolf Bultmann who adopted this approach shared similar views on the nature of the Gospels, the character of history as an academic discipline, and stated criteria for establishing authentic Gospel material. What resulted was a presentation of Jesus that focused on his words and deeds, especially his words. Chronology and psychology were of little interest. In other words, the "new quest" approach was self-consciously antibiographical in response to the exaggerated claims of the "old quest" that Jesus' life could be arranged sequentially in great detail and his mind probed to great depth.

GÜNTHER BORNKAMM, *Jesus of Nazareth* (1956; English trans., 1960).

This treatment of Jesus by Günther Bornkamm remains the classic work from "new quest" historians. He recognizes the faith character of the Gospels. He understands history as "occurrence and event." Thus he states: "Our task, then, is to seek the history *in* the Kerygma of the Gospels, and in this history to seek the Kerygma."[14]

The Synoptic Gospels Critically Examined. Bornkamm rules out the Gospel of John as a source for his historical reconstruction. This Gospel is a theological work to an even greater degree than the Synoptics. The latter, therefore, constitute his principal sources.

Bornkamm presupposes throughout his presentation the different methodologies of Gospel criticism—source criticism, form criticism, and redaction criticism. But he relegates a discussion of them to an appendix. There he acknowledges his acceptance of the "two-source" theory of Synoptic relationships. He does not define the principles for distinguishing between authentic and inauthentic sayings of Jesus. Neither does he pass explicit judgment on every saying he cites. But he does use such principles throughout his study— most noticeably the criterion of dissimilarity. And in his introductory consideration of "faith and history," he even declares inauthentic sayings as significant for faith insofar as they represent the response of faith to the history of Jesus.

Jesus of Nazareth. Bornkamm begins his historical reflections with a presentation of what he considers to be "the rough outlines of Jesus' person and history"—the "indisputable facts," the "historically indisputable traits."[15] He views the infancy stories as too legendary to be useful as historical sources. But he accepts that Jesus was of Jewish origin from the Galilean town of Nazareth and that his mother and father were named Mary and Joseph. His father (and perhaps he) was a carpenter. The names of his brothers are known. Jesus' mother tongue was Aramaic, and he must have known Hebrew. Jesus was baptized by John. The exact meaning of the experience for Jesus, however, cannot be ascertained beneath the present accounts. The length of Jesus' ministry is also uncertain. But the "last decisive turning point" in that ministry was his decision to go to Jerusalem prior to the occasion of his crucifixion.[16] Jesus' most characteristic trait was his sovereign authority, an authority expressed in word and backed by deed.

The central thrust of Jesus' message and ministry, according to Bornkamm, was this: "to make the reality of God present." Bornkamm echoes Jesus' own words and develops in successive chapters the related themes of "the dawn of the kingdom of God" and "the will of God."[17]

To Bornkamm, Mark 1:14-15 and Matthew 4:17 substantially catch up the center of Jesus' message, namely, the nearness of the "kingdom of God." Jesus was unlike those prophets who proclaimed the coming kingdom in nationalistic, earthly terms. He anticipated the arrival of the kingdom more in apocalyptic, cosmic images. But Jesus was also unlike most apocalyptists, for he refrained from speculating on the signs and the time of that kingdom. For Bornkamm, the apocalyptic section in Mark 13 par. may contain actual words of Jesus. This section as it now appears, however, has been shaped within the early church, which was more apocalyptic than Jesus himself in terms of calculating the signs and the time of the end. Furthermore, Jesus announced that the kingdom, which has a future dimension, already dawns in the present through his own words and actions. This tension between the future and present is rejected in the beatitudes and in many of the parables of Jesus. Bornkamm discusses Jesus' custom of table fellowship with the lowly and the despised within the context of his discussion of the kingdom of God.

To Bornkamm, Jesus not only proclaimed the "kingdom of God" but also confronted his hearers in a radical way with the "will of God." Jesus entered into debate over points of Torah interpretation, like the scribes of his day. But unlike those scribes, Jesus interpreted the Torah with such freedom and authority that he seemed to call into question the very letter of the Torah, as in the matters of ritual uncleanness (Mark 7) and divorce (Mark 10). The Sermon on the Mount (Matt. 5–7), according to Bornkamm, was formulated in a Jewish-Christian community more committed to the letter of the Torah than Jesus himself. Even within the Sermon, however, are those contrasting statements that challenge the very letter of the Torah: "You have heard it said. . . . But I say unto you . . . " Jesus offered further evidence of his authority by not appealing to past scribal interpretations of these Torah texts before rendering his own judgment.

Bornkamm makes a passing reference to the miracles within the context of his discussion of the will of God. He declares that the miracle stories cannot be accepted at face value, especially the accounts of nature miracles, but he sees in these stories testimony to Jesus' undoubted power to effect exorcisms and healings.

Contrary to those scholars who view the notion of specifically *twelve* disciples as a creation of the early church, Bornkamm presents Jesus as having called twelve from among his larger following for special appointment. Jesus decided to go with them to Jerusalem. Interestingly, Bornkamm adopts in the broadest possible sense the Markan outline for Jesus' ministry. But he does not highlight Caesarea Philippi as the turning point in that ministry, as have many others. He also dismisses the subsequent "passion predictions" that the "Son of Man" must suffer as formulations of the church after the fact of the passion. Consequently, the "turning point" in Jesus' ministry was the decision to go to Jerusalem. The purpose of the visit was to proclaim the message of the kingdom, not to die.

For Bornkamm, the passion accounts are so overlaid with the faith perspective of the early church it is virtually impossible to recover Jesus' intentions behind such acts as the entry into Jerusalem and the cleansing of the Temple. But these two events—a "certainty"—led to his arrest by the Jewish authorities and eventual execution on a Roman cross. Again it is impossible to ascertain what Jesus thought about his death. But by the time of the Last Supper he was aware of its inevitability. As Mark 14:25 makes clear, Jesus celebrated the meal in the expectation of the coming kingdom and of his imminent separation from his disciples. To Bornkamm, it is unlikely that the meal was a Passover supper. He can only say that the meal was at Passover time and that Jesus was crucified before the beginning of the festival proper.

In conscious opposition to the psychologizing interest of the "old quest," Bornkamm defers any explicit consideration of what he calls "the messianic question" to a place near the end of his study. He also relegates to an appendix a brief survey of such honorific titles as "Messiah," "Son of God," and "Son of Man." Here Bornkamm denies that Jesus ever referred to himself by the name "Son of Man. " He considers as authentic only those "Son of Man" sayings in which Jesus seems to distinguish between the "Son of Man" and himself (as Mark 8:38). But to Bornkamm, as he stresses at the outset of his presentation, Jesus expressed through his words and deeds a sovereign authority—the authority of God. Jesus no doubt during his lifetime aroused among his hearers messianic expectation and questioning. But his historical ministry can best be described as "a movement of broken messianic hopes."[18] It was after the resurrection event that Jesus' followers—the church— bestowed on him various titles of respect in response to him and his message that the kingdom of God had dawned. Now was the hour of salvation!

For Bornkamm, therefore, the continuity between the Christ of faith and the Jesus of history lay not in Jesus' self-understanding as messiah but in his authoritative ministry of word and deed. A striking implication of Bornkamm's portrayal is Jesus' historical distinctiveness. He reflects in his style of ministry characteristics of various social roles in first-century Judaism. But Jesus differs from them all—apocalyptist, prophet, scribe, and even messiah. Thus Bornkamm presents him as Jesus of Nazareth.

The Neobiographical Portrayal

We have used the date 1985 to identify the transition from the "new quest" to the current phase of Jesus research that has variously been labeled "third quest," "renewed quest," and now "post-quest." In spite of the variety that marks Jesus research at the close of the twentieth century, most participants have learned much from their predecessors.

Scholarly "lives" of Jesus have once again appeared but, virtually without exception, they do not reflect the detailed chronologizing nor the presumptuous psychologizing of the nineteenth century. Moreover, scholars of various inclinations appeal to the criteria of authenticity that were honed by such representatives of the "new quest" as Günther Bornkamm. Furthermore, whether consciously or unconsciously, scholars have variously followed Bornkamm's precedent by beginning their lives of Jesus with brief sketches about what can be known about their subject with some certainty. However, scholars today are not writing over against the nineteenth-century-style biography of Jesus, as did Bornkamm. Furthermore, they tend to develop their historical portrayals out of a careful exegesis of the texts and defend their analyses as they reconstruct their lives of Jesus. The phrase *neobiographical portrayal* has been adopted as a broad category to embrace the varied historical portrayals that have appeared in recent years.

S. G. F. BRANDON, *Jesus and the Zealots: A Study of the Political Factor in Primitive Christianity* (1967).[19]

GEZA VERMES, *Jesus the Jew: A Historian's Reading of the Gospels* (1973).

MORTON SMITH, *Jesus the Magician* (1978).[20]

The works of these three scholars, in all their diversity, are harbingers of the "post-quest" period which would follow them. S. G. F. Brandon was at the time of writing a professor of comparative religion at the University of Manchester, Morton Smith a history professor at Columbia University, and Geza Vermes a lecturer in Jewish studies at Oxford University. It was Morton Smith who discovered the *Secret Gospel of Mark* at the Mar Saba monastery in 1958. Each of these historians pursues a different line of inquiry. Not one of the volumes constitutes a comprehensive, detailed reconstruction of Jesus' life or teaching. The work of Vermes, however, represents the first book of the trilogy that he completed during his long tenure as professor of Jewish studies at Oxford.

Mark and Parallel Sources. There is some similarity of approach to the Jesus story by these writers. All three examine the Gospels and Jesus in relation to special dimensions of first-century life and thought. Brandon explores the zealot movement that scholarship at the time believed was a well-defined movement of Jewish revolutionaries committed to opposing Roman rule with arms. Smith focuses on the way Jesus was portrayed by his opponents in the ancient world and on the ancient belief in magic. Vermes highlights the peculiar character of Judaism in Galilee, its charismatic quality. All three scholars also accept Mark as the first Gospel and use Mark in a pivotal way in their own historical reflections about Jesus. Each historical portrayal that results from their labors stands over against, to a greater or lesser degree, the other historical portrayals we have surveyed thus far.

Jesus—Zealot? Magician? Galilean Hasid (Holy Man)? These are the questions raised and to which answers are given by S. G. F. Brandon, Morton Smith, and Geza Vermes.

The point of departure for Brandon's study is the cross of Jesus and the "fact" for which it stands: Jesus was executed by the Romans as a political rebel. Was Jesus, therefore, a revolutionary, a zealot? Brandon concludes that Jesus was not a zealot. Rather Jesus proclaimed the apocalyptic message of the coming "kingdom of God" and called his fellow Jews to repentance in preparation for its arrival. The arrival of the kingdom would involve, of course, Israel's fulfillment of her destiny as God's people. According to Brandon two obstacles stood between Jesus and the accomplishment of his mission of preparation: the Jewish priestly hierarchy and the Roman occupational government. Jesus' direct challenge to these obstacles was made not against the Roman rulers but the Jewish authorities. That challenge expressed itself by his entry into the city of Jerusalem and his disruption of the Temple. The entry of Jesus may even have been "designed to demonstrate his Messianic role."[21] But whatever Jesus' intentions, the Jewish authorities saw in these bold acts a political threat. They took measures that led to Jesus' arrest, interrogation, and delivery to Pilate as a person guilty of subversion. As a consequence, Jesus died on the Roman cross as a political rebel. For Brandon, therefore, although Jesus was not a zealot, there were political dimensions to his ministry. The church, however, tried to cover up these political dimensions. The author of the Gospel of Mark was a chief culprit in this political cover-up. Mark, according to Brandon, was written in Rome in 71 C.E. in the aftermath of the Roman conquest of Jerusalem. In fact, Mark was written shortly after the booty from the fallen Temple was carried through the streets of Rome in the victory procession of Titus. The author of the Gospel found it necessary to defend the political innocence of Jesus Christ, the Son of God. In a redaction analysis of the Markan passion account, Brandon shows how the pre-Markan tradition was edited to shift the responsibility for the death of Jesus from Pilate to the Jewish authorities. The Markan portrayal of the apolitical Jesus was expanded in the Gospels of Matthew and Luke into what Brandon calls "the concept of the pacific Christ."[22]

Morton Smith begins his carefully documented study with the observation that two main views of Jesus prevailed in the ancient world. The church, as seen in the Gospels, confessed him to be "Jesus the Son of God." The church's opponents, whose writings were eventually suppressed by the church, dismissed him as "Jesus the magician." Smith sets for himself the task of seeking the "real Jesus" whose activity gave rise to both viewpoints. He seeks Jesus within what he considers to be the indisputable "historical framework" of Jesus' ministry. First, Jesus as a miracle worker attracted large crowds and aroused messianic speculation. Second, the Jewish authorities, bothered by the crowds and the messianic speculation, arrested Jesus and turned him over to Pilate for execution as a messianic pretender, "King of the Jews." Unlike Brandon, therefore, Smith focuses on Jesus' miracle-working activity as a central aspect of his life and death. Was Jesus, therefore, really a "magician" more in keeping with the way he was presented by the church's opponents than with the way he was characterized by the church itself? Smith concludes that Jesus did fit the category of "magician" more suitably than any other categories such as "apocalyptic seer," "prophet," "rabbi," or even "miracle worker." To support this claim, Smith undertakes a detailed examination of the Gospel of Mark. The author of Mark, like the church generally, suppressed the evidence of magical activity by Jesus. But indications of magical practices continue to shine through the text of Mark. There are, according to Smith, numerous verbal parallels between the material in Mark and material in ancient magical texts. But on a larger scale, the overall presentation of Jesus in Mark accords with the shape of a magician's career. Jesus receives the Spirit of God from on high and the Spirit drives him into the wilderness where he has "visionary" experiences. Subsequently, he pursued a wandering ministry characterized by exorcisms and healings (often by physical means such as touch and saliva). Jesus was accompanied by an inner circle of enchanted followers whom he taught secretly (probably certain magical rites). To Smith, Jesus was a magician to the very end. The Last Supper itself was evidently a magical rite involving the idea of union between Jesus and his followers. This rite was carried over into the church as the eucharist.

Geza Vermes opens the initial volume of his trilogy with an overview of the way Jesus is portrayed in the synoptic Gospels, especially Mark. The Synoptics characterize Jesus as a Galilean Jew who was "exorcist," "healer," and "teacher." According to Vermes, a true historical understanding of Jesus requires considering him within the context of first-century Palestine, particularly Galilee and, more specifically, Galilean Judaism. By contrast to the Judaism of the South, Judaism in Galilee was more charismatic with greater emphasis on miracle working. Representatives of this charismatic tradition were such *Hasidim* (Holy Men) as Honi the Circle-Drawer and Hanina ben Dosa. Was Jesus, whose own mission was to bring physical and spiritual healing, also a Galilean *Hasid* (Holy Man)? Vermes argues that he was indeed! Vermes notes half a dozen similarities between the ancient depictions of Hanina ben Dosa and Jesus. Both men were of intense devotion and prayer. Both possessed the power of healing and could heal from a distance. Both stood in opposition to demons and evil spirits. Both advocated detachment from worldly goods by precept and example. Both concentrated on moral issues with a corresponding lack of interest in ritualistic matters. Both aroused the distrust of the religious establishment. Like Hanina ben Dosa, therefore, Jesus was a Galilean *Hasid*. Vermes postpones to a later volume a detailed discussion of Jesus' teaching. But he does review how the traditional titles bestowed on Jesus by the church may have been used within Aramaic-speaking Galilean Judaism. Vermes believes that Jesus probably thought of himself as a prophet following in the miracle-working tradition of Elijah and Elisha. Thus Jesus would have preferred this name over all others. But Jesus could have spoken of himself as Son of God and been addressed as Lord since both names of respect were used within the charismatic tradition. Vermes thinks, however, that it is unlikely that Jesus thought of himself as messiah. Furthermore, Vermes denies that Jesus would have used the phrase *Son of Man* in those apocalyptic sayings reminiscent of Daniel 7:13. If Jesus used the expression *Son of Man*, he used it as a circumlocution, as another way of saying "I" when he was talking about himself and his earthly ministry.

Like S. G. F. Brandon, Geza Vermes takes seriously the Galilean setting of Jesus' life and ministry. Like Morton Smith, he focuses his attention on Jesus' activity as a miracle worker. But Vermes is not interested in pursuing the possible connections between Jesus and the zealots. Nor is he willing to describe Jesus as a magician. For Vermes, Jesus was one of a company of Galilean charismatics, or *Hasidim*. All three scholars agree, however, in their delineation of discontinuity between the Christ of faith and the Jesus of history. The scholarship of each continues to reverberate in the writings of those who have come after them.

E. P. SANDERS, *Jesus and Judaism* (1985)
————. *The Historical Figure of Jesus* (1993)[23]

We have already noted how the date of Sanders' 1985 volume on Jesus serves as a convenient chronological marker for the transition from the new quest to the post-quest period. His 1993 book represents an appeal to a broader audience attracted to what had become a public discussion over the historical Jesus.

"Facts," the Synoptic Gospels, and Jewish Restoration Eschatology. In conscious opposition to those who begin their historical reconstructions of Jesus' life and career based on Jesus' words, such as the parables, Sanders takes as his point of departure a list of "almost indisputable facts" about Jesus' career and an outline of his life about which there are "no substantial doubts."[24] This outline includes: Jesus' birth ca. 4 B.C.E.; his childhood and early adult years in the Galilean village of Nazareth; his baptism by John; his calling of disciples; his teaching in the villages and countryside of Galilee; his preaching of "the kingdom of God"; and his journey to Jerusalem ca. 30 C.E. During Jesus' visit to Jerusalem, he created a disturbance in the Temple area, shared a final meal with his disciples, was arrested and questioned by Jewish authorities, and was executed on the orders of Pontius Pilate, the Roman prefect.

This outline of events suggests that Sanders looks to the Synoptics as more historically reliable than John. Indeed, he concludes: "The synoptic gospels are to be preferred as our basic source of information about Jesus." However, it is the context—or contexts—within which Sanders places Jesus that provides the key to understanding "who he was and what he did."[25]

Jesus as Eschatological Prophet. Sanders first considers Jesus within the Jewish theological context in which the Gospels themselves place him: the history of salvation and the eschatological expectation that God would someday restore Israel. Sanders also considers Jesus within the context of Jesus' own career: between the time of his predecessor John, whose baptism he accepted, and the time of his successors, including Paul. In their own distinctive ways, both John and Paul proclaimed the eschatological message that the climax of history was at hand.

Therefore, Sanders carefully reviews the varied uses of the phrase *kingdom of God* and finally declares that "we can be quite confident that Jesus had an *eschatological* message." But Sanders denies that Jesus' eschatological message was apocalyptic in the sense of declaring a cataclysmic *end* of history. Instead, Jesus expected God's coming intervention to occur *within* history through "a divine, transforming miracle."[26]

That miracle would involve the inauguration of God's new age with the gathering of Israel's twelve tribes, the building of a new Temple by God, the establishing of peace and justice under God, and the turning of at least some Gentiles to worship Israel's God. Jesus' own calling of disciples and his symbolic use of the number twelve anticipated the restoration of Israel. And Jesus declared that his own disciples would judge the twelve tribes of Israel (Matt. 19:28 = Luke 22:28-30).

Sanders considers the miracles at length within their ancient setting. He acknowledges that Jesus performed healings and exorcisms, but concludes that such deeds did not demonstrate to the general populace that Jesus was "the end-time prophet," although Jesus himself evidently viewed them as "signs of the beginning of God's final victory over evil."[27]

Sanders also treats much of Jesus' teaching as a message given in anticipation of the coming kingdom. Jesus called for a "reversal of values" and a kind of "perfectionism"—expressed through parables and radical sayings, but based upon his understanding of God as loving and merciful.[28]

According to Sanders, Jesus himself gave expression to his view of God as loving and merciful in one rather remarkable way. The repeated accusation in the Synoptics that Jesus associates with "tax collectors and sinners" presupposes that Jesus actually consorted with truly wicked people, people living beyond the law in some blatant way. Furthermore, the general absence in Mark and Matthew of Jesus' use of the language of "repentance" suggests that Jesus was not a preacher of repentance. Therefore, Jesus simply told the wicked that God loved them and that God would receive them into the kingdom because of their acceptance of Jesus and his message.

Sanders says that Jesus would have thereby offended his fellow Jews by not enforcing the law's requirements for the repentant and by presenting himself as having the authority to say who would enter the kingdom. But elsewhere Sanders denies that Jesus taught his followers to violate Sabbath or dietary laws and claims that the conflict stories in Mark 2:1–3:6 reflect disputes in the later church.[29]

It is precisely Jesus' conviction that he had the authority to speak and act on God's behalf that discloses how he viewed his role in God's plan, not his use of any titles, although Sanders acknowledges that Jesus may have used the phrase "son of man." Thus Sanders claims that Jesus, in terms of first-century religious types, was "an eschatological prophet"; but Sanders prefers the term "viceroy" to describe how Jesus thought of himself.[30]

This Jesus and his followers went up to Jerusalem for Passover. There Jesus performed three symbolic acts anticipating God's eschatological restoration of Israel: entry on an ass, action in the Temple, and his final meal. The action in the Temple led Caiaphas to have him arrested and executed as a troublemaker. In response to Caiaphas' recommendation, Pilate ordered Jesus' crucifixion. The execution was carried out on Friday, Nisan 15, Passover day. Sanders puts forth a "guess" that the words of despair from Psalm 22:1 that appear on Jesus' lips in Mark 15:34 and Matthew 27:46 represent Jesus' own reminiscence of that Psalm.[31]

Sanders does not reflect on the theological implications of Jesus' having been wrong about his eschatological expectation that God was about to restore Israel. In an epilogue on the resurrection, however, he does accept as "a fact" that Jesus' followers and later Paul had resurrection experiences. He disclaims knowledge of the reality that prompted them.[32]

JOHN DOMINIC CROSSAN, *The Historical Jesus: The Life of a Mediterranean Jewish Peasant* (1991).

————. *Jesus: A Revolutionary Biography* (1994).[33]

No one has contributed more to a rethinking of the complete Gospel evidence available for reconstructing the career of Jesus than John Dominic Crossan. No one has approached that evidence with greater methodological rigor than he. Born and reared in Ireland, Crossan served for many years on the religious studies faculty at DePaul University in Chicago.

"Words" and a Threefold Methodology. Crossan prefaces his daunting 1991 volume with a list of a hundred or so of Jesus' sayings. These sayings, primarily parables and aphorisms drawn from Sayings Gospel Q and the *Gospel of Thomas*, represent "a reconstructed inventory"[34] of words that probably go back to the historical Jesus. As we will see, for Crossan these two documents—not the Gospel of Mark—preserve the earliest sources, and the criterion of multiple attestation constitutes the main principle for establishing which sayings represent the voice of Jesus.

Crossan's overall methodology for Jesus research involves what he calls "a triple triadic process."[35] The first triad involves his use of social *anthropology* (Mediterranean social world), Graeco-Roman *history* (events in that world), and the *literature* about Jesus (containing specific stories and sayings). The second triad focuses on the literature about Jesus by establishing a complete *inventory* of all major documents (non-canonical and canonical), the *stratification* of documents in their chronological sequence (30–60 C.E., 60–80 C.E., 80–120 C.E., 120–150 C.E.), and the *attestation* of independent sources within each of the 522 complexes of material in his inventory of Jesus tradition (single, double, or multiple attestation). The final triad involves the manipulation of the inventory already established in terms of the *sequence of strata*, the *hierarchy of attestation,* and—finally—the *bracketing of singularity* (exclusion of singly attested items).

For example, four independent sources claim that Jesus drew some correlation between the kingdom and children (Thomas, Mark, M, and John), with one of these sources considered by Crossan to date from the earliest stratum of tradition (Thomas).

Crossan quantifies this complex as 1 / 4, which means, first stratum / four independent sources. According to Crossan's calculus, the lower the number on the left, and the higher the number on the right, the greater the probability that Jesus said something like that. Crossan uses the complex of Jesus' sayings about children to support his historical conclusion that the kingdom announced by Jesus was a "kingdom of nobodies."[36]

Jesus as a Peasant Jewish Cynic. Crossan develops his characterization of Jesus along more traditional biographical lines in his 1994 book and toward its conclusion says: "The historical Jesus was a *peasant Jewish Cynic*" (his italics).[37] But in this volume too, Crossan is most reticent about detailed chronologizing or in-depth pyschologizing.

Like many other biblical scholars, Crossan understands the infancy narratives by Matthew and Luke to be compositions intended to demonstrate how the history of Israel, Israel's Scripture, and even particular Scriptural texts found their fulfillment in the coming of Jesus. But Jesus himself was *not* born of a virgin, *not* born of Davidic lineage, *not* born in Bethlehem. Instead, he was probably born in Nazareth, with parents named Mary and Joseph, when Herod was king, before 4 B.C.E. He died when Pontius Pilate was the Roman prefect, between 26 and 36 C.E.

Crossan carefully considers the implications of Jesus' coming of age when and where he did. In an agrarian society with a sharp division between the upper and the lower classes, the vast majority of the populace would have been peasants—most of whose crops went to support the upper classes. If Jesus were a carpenter, then this would identify him as a member of the even lower artisan class whose members—without land—lived on the margin between the peasants and the expendables. Jesus like most of his contemporaries would have been illiterate.

Within the broader framework of the Jewish homeland, there appeared an "apocalyptic prophet" named John. Crossan can speak about John's baptism of Jesus as "historically certain."[38] He is just as certain that Jesus later broke with John. Whereas John fasted, Jesus feasted. Whereas John had proclaimed a future apocalyptic kingdom, Jesus developed an understanding of the kingdom as a present one. Central to Crossan's reconstruction is the repeated affirmation that Jesus had both a "vision" and a "program."

Jesus' "vision" was that of a "radical egalitarianism" under God that expressed itself most dramatically in Jesus' practice of "open commensality." That is, Jesus would eat with anybody. His open table fellowship represented an inclusive community and contradicted the practices and values of a hierarchically ordered society. Thus Crossan can say: "For Jesus, the Kingdom of God is a community of radical or unbrokered equality in which individuals are in direct contact with one another and with God, unmediated by established brokers or fixed locations."[39]

Jesus' "program" involved a "radical itinerancy" as he and those empowered by him moved in "mission" from house to house. Crossan understands Jesus to be a healer and an exorcist, and he draws on medical and cross-cultural anthropology to understand the physical and social dynamics involved in such acts. Jesus' mission involved reciprocity: healing for food. Thus: "Here is the heart of the original Jesus movement, a shared egalitarianism of spiritual (healing) and material (eating) resources."[40]

It is in relation to Jesus' itinerancy that Crossan makes an intriguing suggestion. He claims that Jesus' family recognized his healing power and social importance, but wanted to benefit from it through his establishing Nazareth as a healing center. He refused and became estranged from them.

As others have done in recent scholarship, Crossan notes similarities in the attire and behavior between wandering Cynics and the Jesus missionaries. But he emphasizes a crucial difference. Whereas Cynics carried a staff and a knapsack to symbolize their self-sufficiency, the Jesus people were enjoined to carry neither staff nor knapsack. They were dependent on others as they moved about the rural countryside rebuilding peasant society from the ground up.

Crossan disclaims much reliable information about the end of Jesus' life other than "the fact of the crucifixion," which probably did occur at Passover time, possibly on the one occasion that Jesus and his fellow Galilean peasants went up to Jerusalem.[41] Jesus' followers would have known virtually nothing about the details related to his crucifixion, death, and burial. And the passion narratives represent compositions based not on memory but on Scripture. Based on multiple attestation, however, Crossan concludes that an action and a saying related to the Temple's destruction must go back to the historical Jesus and that such behavior resulted in his arrest.

After surveying the variety of resurrection texts, Crossan says: "Those who had originally experienced divine power through his vision and his example continued to do so after his death. In fact, even more so, because now this power was no longer confined by time or place."[42]

MARCUS J. BORG, *Jesus: A New Vision* (1987).[43]
————. *Meeting Jesus Again for the First Time* (1994).[44]

Marcus J. Borg has become a highly visible advocate of historical investigation into the life of Jesus. However, unlike some of his scholarly contemporaries, Borg repeatedly underscores the relevance of the historical Jesus for the contemporary life of faith and church. In 1996, at Oregon State University, he convened an interactive teleconference called "Jesus at 2000," which featured scholars of varying scholarly and religious viewpoints. Borg's volume teasingly entitled *Meeting Jesus Again for the First Time* represents a more autobiographical restatement of his earlier "vision" of what Jesus' historical ministry was all about.

"Two Images," the Synoptic Gospels, and Charismatic Jewish Tradition. In developing his own historical presentation, Borg moves beyond what he calls "the popular image of Jesus," on the one hand, and the "dominant scholarly image," on the other.[45] The former, based primarily on the Gospel of John, projects Jesus as a divine savior who has come into the world to die for the sins of humankind and to offer believers the possibility of eternal life. The latter, with an indebtedness to Albert Schweitzer, considers Jesus to have been an eschatological prophet who expected the end of the world in his own day.

Therefore, Borg rejects John and draws on the Synoptics for his delineation of what Jesus was like; and within the Synoptics, he considers as nonhistorical—or "inauthentic"—those eschatological sayings where Jesus seemingly says that the world will soon end. (Borg often uses the word "eschatological" to designate a viewpoint more often identified by the word "apocalyptic.")

Generally considered, the words and deeds of Jesus attested in the Synoptics make sense within the context of Jewish charismatic tradition. Like Moses, the later prophets, and such rabbis as Honi the Circle-Drawer and Hanina ben Dosa, Jesus lived a life open to the transcendent and became a mediator between the realm of the spirit and the world of culture.

Jesus as a Spirit-Filled Person. In his depiction of Jesus as a charismatic holy man, Borg acknowledges an indebtedness to Geza Vermes, who some years ago identified Jesus as such a figure. According to Borg, Jesus' first public appearance as an adult clearly places him in the stream of charismatic Judaism: Jesus' baptism by John. Borg speaks of the "historicity" of this event and considers Jesus' experience on this occasion to have been "a vision."[46]

However, Borg does not reduce Jesus to one social category but instead sees four dimensions reflected in his life and activity. Jesus was a miracle worker—a healer and exorcist. Jesus was a sage—using parables and proverbs to teach a subversive wisdom on such conventional topics as family, wealth, status, and religion. Jesus was also the founder of a movement centered in twelve followers—with their objective being the revitalization of Israel and their behavior serving to challenge the reigning "politics of holiness" with a "politics of compassion" as they dined with outcasts and associated with women.[47] And Jesus was a prophet—going to Jerusalem not to die but to call upon Israel to change in order to avert the social catastrophe that was surely coming.

Thus Jesus' ministry that began with baptism by John ends with crucifixion by the authorities in Jerusalem. Borg considers Jesus' entry into Jerusalem and his action in the Temple to be "prophetic acts" that sealed his doom; and Borg claims that "the most certain fact about the historical Jesus is his execution as a political rebel."[48] He also thinks that Jesus' execution involved collaboration between the Romans under Pilate and Jewish leaders associated with the high priest.

Having said that the length of Jesus' ministry cannot be known, but that it was "brief," Borg dates Jesus' death as having occurred "on a Friday in A.D. 30." Easter and resurrection involve Jesus' followers continuing "to experience him as a living reality, and *in a new way,* namely as having the qualities of God." Or, to state it differently, the historical Jesus became "an epiphany of God."[49]

One of the intriguing aspects of Borg's work is his reconstruction of Jesus' message and ministry without using the common Synoptic phrase *the kingdom of God.*[50] He avoids the phrase for two reasons. First, this expression has been interpreted in so many different ways. Second, its centrality for understanding what Jesus was like may have been overemphasized. Borg wants the phrase to be defined by the *gestalt* of Jesus as a Spirit-filled person, instead of the other way around. Borg also downplays the importance of traditional titles for understanding Jesus. The title that may have been appropriate during Jesus' lifetime, and possibly consistent with his self-understanding, was that of "son of God"—not in the unique sense as later defined by the church, but as an honored name for a holy person within charismatic Judaism.[51]

N. T. WRIGHT, *The New Testament and the People of God* (1992)[52]
──────. *Jesus and the Victory of God* (1996)[53]

N. T. Wright has emerged as the most visible and vigorous representative of British scholarship in the recent debate about the historical figure of Jesus. After teaching New Testament for twenty years at Cambridge University, McGill University, and Oxford University, Wright became—in 1994—the Dean of Lichfield Cathedral in his native England.

His substantial 1992 and 1996 volumes represent the first two volumes of a multivolume work on "Christian Origins and the Question of God." His first volume explores issues presupposed by the second: a theory of interpretation, an overview of first-century Judaism, and a study of the early church. The second volume focuses specifically on Jesus. Wright places himself in the eschatological interpretive tradition of Jesus research asserted by Albert Schweitzer and resumed by E. P. Sanders.

"Story," the Synoptics, Double Similarity and Double Dissimilarity. Wright takes the task of a "serious" historian to be the advancement of "serious historical hypotheses" about Jesus by constructing "large-scale narratives"—or stories—and examining the relevant data to see how they fit.[54] Wright bases his own story of Jesus primarily on the synoptic Gospels, which he claims provide reliable information. He turns to John only when considering Jesus' final visit to Jerusalem; and he dismisses any notion that the hypothetical Q document and the *Gospel of Thomas* represent an early form of Christianity.

Wright articulates what he calls the criterion of double similarity and double dissimilarity: "when something can be seen to be credible (though perhaps deeply subversive) within first-century Judaism, *and* credible as the implied starting point (though not the exact replica) of something in later Christianity, there is a strong possibility of our being in touch with the genuine history of Jesus." Wright invokes this criterion in support of the historical probability of particular acts and sayings of Jesus; for example, his practice of table fellowship and his biting anti-family statements.[55]

But more broadly, Wright uses this approach to support the historical plausibility of his overall story of Jesus when viewed in relation to Judaism, on the one hand, and the early church, on the other. By the conclusion of Wright's story, he has seemingly included everything from the Synoptics in it, although he ignores the infancy accounts in Matthew and Luke. And he has offered extended answers to the basic historical questions underlying his presentation: How does Jesus fit into Judaism? What were his aims? Why did he die?

Jesus as Eschatological Prophet/Messiah. What provides the framework for Wright's response to these three questions is what he calls "the story of Israel" or "the basic Jewish story."[56] This story—as expressed in the Scriptures and other literature—included the expectation of Israel's return from exile, YHWH's return to Zion, and the defeat of Israel's enemies.

Jesus fits into Judaism as "a prophet"—"a prophet bearing an urgent eschatological, and indeed apocalyptic, message for Israel." Wright makes it quite clear how he understands and uses "eschatology" and "apocalyptic." *Eschatology* refers to the climax of Israel's history involving events that would inaugurate a new phase *within* space-time history. *Apocalyptic* refers to end-of-the-world *talk* that speaks about eschatological events as though the space-time history itself were going to end.[57]

Wright supports the use of the prophet model for Jesus by briefly outlining the main dimensions of Jesus' career and by looking at Jesus in relation to popular movements of his day and to John the Baptist. Like John, Jesus seems to have combined the styles of "oracular" prophets and "leadership" prophets. But unlike John, Jesus is itinerant, gives more extensive teaching, and engages in healing. Thus Jesus the prophet is both similar and dissimilar to the Judaism of his day.

Jesus is a prophet, but more than a prophet. He is one through whom the "kingdom of God" is being inaugurated. His announcement of "the kingdom of God" evokes the story of Israel and her destiny; but he retells the story in unexpected ways and places himself at its center.

Wright examines in detail Jesus' teaching within the context of Jesus' own unfolding kingdom story.[58] Jesus' call to repentance (Mark 1:15 and Matt. 4:17) indicates what Israel must do to be restored. His corresponding call to faith entails believing that the God of Israel is indeed acting through him and reconstituting the new Israel around him. His forgiveness of sins becomes a way of talking about return from exile. Allegiance to Temple and Torah are being replaced by allegiance to Jesus.

Wright envisions Jesus' establishment of "cells of followers" in towns and villagers whose members were committed to living as "new covenant people," resulting in the formation of another sect alongside Essenes and Pharisees.[59] The sayings in the Sermon on the Mount (Matt. 5–7), including the Lord's Prayer, would have had their setting within cell gatherings; and these sayings represent a call for Israel to be Israel. Other followers, such as the twelve, would have been called to join Jesus in his itinerant kingdom activity.

Jesus' apocalyptic discourse (Mark 13 par.), which Wright reads as a conversation between Jesus and his disciples, becomes both a warning and prediction by Jesus. National disaster—the destruction of Jerusalem and the Temple—is imminent; but Jesus and his people will be vindicated. Wright understands the phrase "coming of the son of man" (from Dan. 7:13) to be Jesus' way of talking about the defeat of the enemies of the people of God and their own vindication. The discourse is not about the end of the world nor the second coming of Jesus. It is a declaration that the long-expected exile is over.[60]

According to Wright, it is Jesus' eschatological program that results in Jesus' conflict with the Pharisees. That program involves a reinterpretation of those traditional symbols of Jewish identity: Sabbath, food, nation, land, and Temple. Wright's examination of Jesus' teaching, including the parables, within the context of his own unfolding kingdom story not only demonstrates how Jesus the eschatological prophet relates to Judaism but also discloses an overriding aim: "to bring the story of Israel to its god-ordained climax, in and through his own work."[61]

So Jesus the prophet—the eschatological prophet—is also the Messiah. But, of course, just as Jesus revises Israel's story, so he redefines what messiahship means. As the Messiah, Jesus goes to Jerusalem to die. He sees his own journey as YHWH's return to Zion. In Jerusalem, his symbolic action in the Temple is an act of judgment against the traditional system by the one through whom YHWH will save Israel and the world. In Jerusalem, his symbolic action at the Passover meal with his followers is a declaration of how the true exodus would come about through him, how evil would be defeated, and how sins would be forgiven. In Jerusalem too, his cross becomes the means and the symbol of "the victory of God."[62] Jesus has taken the story of Israel upon himself!

In straightforward fashion, Wright declares that "Jesus was executed as a Rebel against Rome."[63] But he also explores more fully what might have

135

occurred at the "Jewish hearing(s)" by appealing not only to the scenes of Jesus before the high priest in Mark and Matthew but also to John 11 and 18, Deuteronomy 13, Daniel 7, and a reference to Jesus in the Talmud. Wright suggests that the Jewish authorities want not only to develop a case that would stick before Pilate but to find Jesus guilty of a crime under *Jewish* law in order to protect themselves from the general populace. They succeed; and Jesus, by his own words, convicts himself of being a false prophet and a blasphemer. In his brief conclusion, Wright affirms that both the success and the relevance of Jesus the eschatological prophet/Messiah depends on whether one accepts or rejects the claim of the early church that God raised him from the dead.[64]

ELISABETH SCHÜSSLER FIORENZA, *In Memory of Her: A Feminist Theological Reconstruction of Christian Origins* (1983).[65]
──────. *Jesus: Miriam's Child, Sophia's Prophet: Critical Issues in Feminist Christology* (1994).[66]

Elisabeth Schüssler Fiorenza, on the faculty at the University of Notre Dame before moving to the Harvard Divinity School, makes her contribution to the current debate over the historical Jesus out of her own commitment to a critical feminist theology of liberation. The response to her chapter on Jesus and the Jesus movement in her 1983 work prompted her to expand on those issues in her 1994 monograph. The latter volume contains her reflections on Jesus' crucifixion and resurrection.

Feminist Readings and a Feminist Model of Historical Reconstruction. Schüssler Fiorenza presupposes and variously uses the specialized methods and conclusions of Gospel criticism that have developed over the past century. But she applauds the more recent appropriation of social-scientific models to understand the social context of early Christian sources and traditions.[67] At the same time, however, a feminist reading of these texts recognizes their androcentric and patriarchal character. That is, they are written from a male point of view and reflect a hierarchically ordered social world dominated by males.

Schüssler Fiorenza also applauds the current phase of Jesus research, which she refers to as "the Newest Quest," because scholars now seek to understand Jesus within the social setting of first-century Judaism.[68] Correspondingly, she is critical of the preceding "New Quest" which, by its use of the criterion of dissimilarity, highlighted Jesus' difference from Judaism.

With appreciation for developments in Gospel criticism and Jesus research, Schüssler Fiorenza has defined her task and the task of other feminist scholars in these terms: "critical feminist scholarship must conceptualize early Christianity and early Judaism in such a way that it can make women and marginalized men visible as central agents who shaped Christian and Jewish beginnings."[69] In her earlier work, Schüssler Fiorenza was especially mindful of criticisms by Jewish feminists who saw Christian attempts to claim Jesus as a feminist over against patriarchal Jewish society as a way of reinforcing Christian anti-Judaic notions. Thus, in order to avoid playing Jesus over against patriarchal Judaism, Schüssler Fiorenza sought to discover for herself "the feminist impulse within Judaism."[70] She found evidence of that impulse in pre-70 C.E. Judaism, especially in the book of Judith. This book—from the first century B.C.E.—portrays its namesake as a strong, independent leader modeled on the figure of Moses and embodying Pharisaic piety.

Schüssler Fiorenza also delineated what she considered to be the "dominant ethos" of first-century Judaism and identified the central question asked by every Jew and answered, albeit differently, by every Jewish group. The ethos: Israel as "kingdom of priests and holy nation" (cf. Exod. 19:6). The question: "What must I do to enter the kingdom of heaven?" The Jesus movement originated as an extension of the impulse, or impulses, represented by the book of Judith.[71]

Jesus as Prophet and Child of Sophia. Schüssler Fiorenza is acutely conscious of the difficulty in moving from the earliest memories of the Jesus movement, preserved in such texts as Sayings Source Q and the Gospel of Mark, to the historical figure of Jesus. But she exhibits no hesitation in identifying the Jesus movement itself as "a renewal movement within Judaism" or as "a Jewish emancipatory movement of wo/men."[72] Or, to use the phrase that recurs in her writings, the Jesus movement involved a "discipleship of equals."

John the Baptist provides the foil for understanding what Jesus and his movement were all about.[73] John is a prophet who announces that God's judgment and wrath precede the coming *basileia* and the restitution of Israel. Jesus, however, emphasizes that in his ministry and movement God's *basileia* is already present. John's ascetic lifestyle is that of an apocalyptic preparing for the future. But Jesus' lifestyle is that of joyous celebration (Mark 2:18-20; Matt. 11:18-19 = 7:33-35). Both his table fellowship with sinners, tax collectors, and prostitutes and his casting out of demons give experiential confirmation of the *basileia's* presence. (Schüssler Fiorenza often leaves untranslated the Greek word *basileia*, which is feminine, but traditionally translated into English by the masculine "kingdom.")

Schüssler Fiorenza documents, in detail, women who figure prominently in the Jesus movement: Mary of Magdala (Luke 8:2); the woman with a flow of blood for twelve years (Mark 5:25-34 par.); the woman crippled for eighteen years (Luke 13:10-17). And then there is the woman who washed Jesus' feet (Luke 7:36-50 and John 12:1-8). According to Mark's Gospel she anointed Jesus' head, and this act, Jesus said, would be told wherever the good news is preached, "in memory of her" (Mark 14:3-9).

The praxis, or practice, of the Jesus movement was grounded in an understanding and experience of God as "all-inclusive love." The parables of Jesus give expression to the goodness and mercy of God, again and again. But for Schüssler Fiorenza there is much more to Jesus' understanding of God than this. She cites the very old Q saying in its Lukan wording: "sophia is justified [or vindicated] by all her children" (Luke 7:35). She concludes: "The earliest Jesus traditions perceive this God of gracious goodness in a woman's *Gestalt* as divine *Sophia* (wisdom)." This perception of God has its home in Israel's wisdom traditions, not in apocalyptic traditions, and also says something about Jesus himself. Schüssler Fiorenza continues: "The earliest Christian theology is sophialogy. It was possible to understand Jesus' ministry and death in terms of God-Sophia, because Jesus probably understood himself as the prophet and child of Sophia."[74]

Schüssler Fiorenza's claims about God as Sophia and Jesus as messenger of Sophia lead to many interesting readings of familiar texts. Jesus says: "And call no one your father on earth, for you have one Father—the one in heaven" (Matt. 23:9). She understands this saying to be a repudiation of all earthly fathers, and thereby a rejection of patriarchal authority, in the name of the "Father" God and in the interest of the discipleship of equals. Now, God as "Father" no longer legitimates a domination system. God can be addressed as "Father" in the Lord's Prayer (Matt. 6:9-13 = Luke 11:2-4) because the masculine "Father" no longer functions contrary to the discipleship of equals but supports the discipleship of equals. That discipleship itself constitutes a new family based on equality and not natural family bonds (Mark 10:29-30 par.).

Schüssler Fiorenza disclaims knowledge of how Jesus understood his death; but his execution as "King of the Jews" became the originating event for how his death was understood by his followers.[75] Based not on the Gospels but on traditions preserved in Paul's letters, she surveys several early Christian interpretations of that death and identifies as the earliest interpretation a confession such as "God raised Jesus from the dead" (cf. 1 Cor. 6:14; Rom. 8:11; et al.). Resurrection faith, therefore, has its fundamental basis in the Jewish belief that God vindicates the righteous who die as martyrs. Whereas Paul excludes women from the list of those to whom Jesus appeared after the resurrection, a list intended to legitimate male authority (1 Cor. 15:3-8), the Gospels associate women—particularly Mary of Magdala—with the discovery of the empty tomb and the message that Jesus the Living One will be encountered in Galilee (Mark 16:1-8 par.).[76] Schüssler Fiorenza concludes: "A critical feminist discourse of liberation that positions itself within the space of the empty tomb is able to insist that G*d and the Resurrected One can be found only among the Living Ones."[77]

We have completed the initial two stages of our quest for Jesus. We have examined the literary sources both canonical and extracanonical. We have reviewed several historical reconstructions of the life of Jesus in its first-century Palestinian setting. Now we move to the third stage and consider continuing issues in the study of his life. Much of our study thus far can be diagrammed as follows.

GOSPELS, GOSPEL CRITICISM, AND THE HISTORICAL JESUS

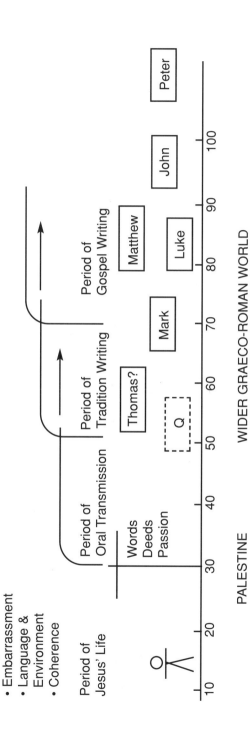

Focus of Historical Quest	Focus of Form Criticism	Focus of Source Criticism	Focus of Redaction Criticism and Narrative Criticism

< Social-Scientific Criticism >

Criteria of
• Dissimilarity
• Multiple Attestation
• Embarrassment
• Language &
  Environment
• Coherence

Period of
Jesus' Life

Period of
Oral Transmission

Words
Deeds
Passion

Period of
Tradition Writing

Thomas?

Q

Period of
Gospel Writing

Matthew

Mark

Luke

John

Peter

10   20   30   40   50   60   70   80   90   100

PALESTINE   WIDER GRAECO-ROMAN WORLD

PART THREE

Continuing Issues in the Life
and Ministry of Jesus

7

Resurrection and Virgin Birth

As attested on tombstones, human life is customarily reckoned as extending from birth to death. The life of Jesus is no exception. The familiar Apostles' Creed encloses the life of Jesus within these brackets: "...born of the Virgin Mary, suffered under Pontius Pilate, was crucified, dead, and buried." Possibly formulated in some form as early as the second century in opposition to those who denied the full humanity of Jesus, this creed affirms that Jesus—like every person—entered life from the womb and departed through a tomb. His mother Mary and his judge Pontius Pilate are remembered as the ones responsible for these crucial moments of passage.

The Apostles' Creed, however, also underscores certain differences that set the birth and death of Jesus apart from other births and deaths. Accordingly, Jesus had a unique prehistory and an unusual posthistory: "...conceived by the Holy Spirit...the third day he rose from the dead." The differences surrounding the origin and destiny of Jesus, of course, are similarly underscored in the New Testament. The infancy narratives bear witness to Jesus' conception within his virgin mother by the power of God. The resurrection narratives bear witness to his resurrection from the dead by the power of God.

The resurrection from the dead and the virginal conception are not in the strictest sense happenings in the life of Jesus. But his resurrection and his conception are reported in the traditions by which the Gospel writers, viewed collectively, have enclosed their narration of his life. A quest for Jesus, therefore, cannot ignore these traditions and the happenings to which they testify. We will consider the resurrection traditions first because belief in the resurrection of Jesus was of greater importance for the early church than belief in his virginal conception.

The Resurrection

The conviction that God had resurrected Jesus from the dead was of overriding significance for the establishment and proclamation of the early church. Without resurrection belief, the church probably would not have emerged following the apparent tragedy of the crucifixion. Virtually every page of the New Testament is permeated with resurrection belief. Five of the New Testament writings narrate, or enumerate, the events related to the resurrection of Jesus.

Literary Evidence

The four canonical Gospels constitute the best known literary evidence for the events surrounding the resurrection of Jesus. These narratives, however, are not the earliest written resurrection accounts. This honor belongs to the letter of Paul known as 1 Corinthians.[1]

The Gospel of Mark (chap. 16) represents the earliest Gospel witness to the resurrection. The original author probably, as we have stated, concluded his story with the account of how three women discovered the empty tomb. The author of the Gospel of Matthew (chap. 28) grafted his resurrection material onto the Markan trunk. He reworked the empty tomb story and added three scenes: an appearance of the risen Jesus to the women near the tomb; the bribing of the Roman soldiers by the chief priests; and an appearance of Jesus to the eleven disciples on a mountain in Galilee. The author of the Gospel of Luke (chap. 24) and the book of Acts (chap. 1) also grafted his resurrection material onto the Markan trunk. He also reworked the empty tomb story and made significant additions: the lengthy narrative of the appearance of Jesus to the two disciples near Emmaus; an appearance of Jesus to the eleven and others in Jerusalem; and the ascension of Jesus near Bethany. Both the author of Matthew and the author of Luke-Acts, therefore, have added resurrection appearance stories to their Markan source. The resurrection materials reported in Matthew and Luke-Acts, however, differ to such a degree that it is evident that the writers are drawing on special traditions, to be designated M and L respectively, not on Q.

The Gospel of John (chaps. 20 and 21) represents the latest of the Gospel witnesses to the resurrection. The peculiarity of the resurrection material in John offers further confirmation that its author was probably literarily independent of the Synoptics. The story of the empty tomb highlights the roles of Mary Magdalene, Simon Peter, and the beloved disciple. Subsequent scenes (in chap. 20) include: an appearance of Jesus to Mary Magdalene in the garden; another appearance that same evening in Jerusalem to the disciples minus Thomas; and an appearance eight days later also in Jerusalem to the disciples including Thomas. A final appearance, no doubt a secondary addition (chap. 21), occurs beside the sea in Galilee to seven disciples including Simon Peter and the beloved disciple.

But before the four Gospels, there was 1 Corinthians (chap. 15). Paul wrote this letter from Ephesus in the mid-50s to deal with a variety of issues within the Corinthian congregation. Some of the Corinthians evidently claim that "there is no resurrection of the dead" (vs. 12). The exact basis for this denial is not clear, but the general response of Paul is obvious. He argues: Christ has been resurrected from the dead; therefore, there will be a resurrection of all believers; and believers will be resurrected in a spiritual instead of a physical body. Paul recalls the gospel he had initially preached to the Corinthians in order to establish the reality of the resurrection of Jesus Christ:

> For I handed on to you as of first importance what I in turn had received: that [*hoti*] Christ died for our sins in accordance with the scriptures, and that [*hoti*] he was buried, and that [*hoti*] he was raised on the third day in accordance with the scriptures, and that [*hoti*] he appeared to Cephas, then to the twelve. Then he appeared to more than five hundred brothers and sisters at one time, most of whom are still alive, though some have died. Then he appeared to James, then to all the apostles. Last of all, as to one untimely born, he appeared also to me. For I am the least of the apostles, unfit to be called an apostle, because I persecuted the church of God. (vss. 3-9)

The importance of this Pauline passage stems not simply from its status as the earliest written account of the resurrection events. There are several other reasons. First, the core of Paul's account possibly consists of an early creed that Paul inherited from those who were believers before him. The precise scope and origin of this creed has been much discussed by scholars. But the creed inherited by Paul may have included the four phrases introduced by "that" (*hoti*) and concluded with the appearances to Cephas (the Aramaic form of Peter) and the twelve. Some scholars think that this creed originated within the Aramaic-speaking church, although it could have been passed on to Paul already translated into Greek. This creed, therefore, may have been formulated as early as the 30s. Paul could have received it as a result of his association with any number of Christian communities in the 30s and 40s: Damascus, Jerusalem, or Antioch. Second, Paul himself had ample opportunity to confer with persons who had experienced an appearance of the resurrected Jesus. In his letter to the Galatians, Paul reports a consultation he had in Jerusalem with Cephas, on which occasion he also saw James the brother of Jesus (Gal. 1:18-24). Both Cephas and James are included in Paul's list of witnesses to the resurrected Jesus (1 Cor. 15:5, 7). Furthermore, Paul observes that most of the five hundred to whom Jesus appeared at one time are still alive and could be contacted by any interested party (1 Cor. 15:6). Third, Paul understands his own conversion or call to have been a resurrection appearance of the same order as the appearances to Cephas, the twelve, and the others (note the repetitious "appeared." 1 Cor. 15:5, 6, 7, 8). If we deny apostolic authorship to the Gospels of Matthew and John, then Paul's account in 1 Corinthians represents the only account actually written by a person who claims to have experienced an appearance of the resurrected Jesus.

Literary Traditions

The literary witnesses to the resurrection considered above consist of two basic kinds of tradition or types of stories: *empty tomb stories* and *appearance stories*.

First Corinthians contains only a list of appearances. The oldest text of Mark contains only an empty tomb story. Matthew, Luke, and John incorporate both empty tomb and appearance stories into their narratives.

A notable feature of these New Testament witnesses is the absence of another kind of tradition: an *exit story*, an account that reports Jesus' leaving the tomb. All four Gospels jump in their narratives from an account of the burial of Jesus in the tomb to an account of the discovery of the tomb empty of his body.

Jesus has already been resurrected! The stone must be rolled away not to let Jesus out but to let the women into the tomb. Later visual art, such as Piero della Francesca's *Resurrection*, with its portrayal of Jesus with one leg in and one leg out of the sepulcher and a banner of victory in his hand, finds no support in the New Testament resurrection accounts. The exit tradition, however, does find literary expression in the *Gospel of Peter* about which we spoke earlier:

> Now in the night in which the Lord's day dawned, when the soldiers, two by two in every watch, were keeping guard, there rang out a loud voice in heaven, and they saw the heavens opened and two men come down from there in a great brightness and draw nigh to the sepulchre. That stone which had been laid against the entrance to the sepulchre started of itself to roll and gave way to the side, and the sepulchre was opened, and both the young men entered in. When now those soldiers saw this, they awakened the centurion and the elders—for they also were there to assist at the watch. And whilst they were relating what they had seen, they saw again three men come out from the sepulchre, and two of them sustain-

ing the other, and a cross following them, and the heads of the two reaching to heaven, but that of him who was led of them by the hand overpassing the heavens. And they heard a voice out of the heavens crying, "Thou hast preached to them that sleep," and from the cross there was heard the answer, "Yea." Those men therefore took counsel with one another to go and report this to Pilate. (9:35–11:43)[2]

The empty tomb and appearance stories that constitute the New Testament resurrection narratives are also to be distinguished from *miracle stories* that report the resuscitation of a dead person. The Old Testament reports incidents where such prophetic figures as Elijah and Elisha restore the dead to life (1 Kings 17:17-24; 2 Kings 4:18-37). The New Testament also reports occasions when Jesus (Mark 5:21-43 par.; Luke 7:11-17; John 11:1-44) and even Paul (Acts 20:7-12) restore life to the dead. But resurrection stories are different. In the miracle stories, the dead are granted life through the mediation of a human agent or miracle worker. But in the resurrection accounts, Jesus is granted life directly by God. In the miracle stories, the act whereby new life is granted—a prayer, a touch, a word of command—stands at the center. But in resurrection accounts, the act whereby new life is granted is presupposed; and the evidences of this, such as the empty tomb and the appearing of Jesus, are emphasized. In the miracle stories, the act whereby new life is granted is often public. But in the resurrection accounts that act is unseen and already accomplished when the appearances occur. In the miracle stories, the dead are given new life only to face death again in the future. But in the resurrection accounts, Jesus is carried beyond death. All these differences, of course, are derived from the differences in the events to which miracle stories and resurrection stories point. The resurrection of Jesus represents the eschatological event expected in certain circles of Judaism to take place not within but at the end of history (cf. Matt. 27:52-53).

Understandably, therefore, the New Testament resurrection narratives contain motifs which underscore *the form of the resurrected Jesus as being bodily, but not that of a resuscitated corpse.*

By beginning their resurrection accounts with empty tomb stories, all four Gospels affirm that Jesus' resurrection from the dead was a bodily resurrection. His spirit or soul did not simply leave his body. Within certain Hellenistic circles there was a jingle: *sōma sēma,* "the body is a tomb"—a tomb for the soul. But in the Gospel resurrection narratives, and in the Pauline account, the tomb is not the body of Jesus but rather that into which his body is placed upon death.

The appearance traditions in the Gospels also emphasize the bodily nature of the resurrected Jesus. Those to whom Jesus appears recognize him (Matt. 28:9, 17; Luke 24:31, 37; John 20:16, 20, 28; 21:12). He invites touch (John 20:27) and is touched (Matt. 28:9). He dines with them (Luke 24:30; John

147

21:13) and actually eats a piece of fish (Luke 24:43). But the appearance traditions in the Gospels also stress the nonphysical nature of the resurrected Jesus. Those to whom Jesus appears do not immediately recognize him (Matt. 28:17; Luke 24:16; John 20:14; 21:4) or imagine that they have seen a spirit (Luke 24:37). He forbids touch (John 20:17). He suddenly appears and disappears, even behind closed doors (Luke 24:31; John 20:19, 26). It is striking how the Gospel writers, particularly Luke and John, have placed these seemingly contradictory motifs side by side in their resurrection accounts.

The Pauline account of the resurrection is based on a creed and reported in a letter. That account, therefore, is not a dramatic narration of Jesus' appearances like the Gospel accounts. Simply put: "He appeared." But Paul does discuss his understanding of the nature of the resurrection body for believers at the end of history: "So it is with the resurrection of the dead. . . . It is sown a physical body *(sōma psuchikon)*, it is raised a spiritual body *(sōma pneumatikon)*" (1 Cor. 15:42, 44). Perhaps Paul would have also understood the form of the resurrected Jesus as that of a "spiritual body" since he does see an analogy between the resurrection of believers and the resurrection of Jesus. The expression "spiritual body" also seems to correspond with the intentions of the Gospel writers in their more pictorial presentations of the resurrected Jesus. The form of the resurrected Jesus for them was bodily, but not that of a resuscitated corpse.

Thus far we have noted how the literary evidence for the resurrection, within and without the New Testament, consists of three kinds of tradition: an appearance tradition, an empty tomb tradition, and even an exit tradition. But there also seems to be another kind of resurrection tradition in the New Testament, thought by many scholars to be the earliest of all. Scattered throughout Paul's letters are brief confessional statements about the resurrection. For example: " . . . whom [God] raised from the dead — Jesus" and "Jesus died and rose again" (1 Thess. 1:10; 4:14). These brief confessional statements, unlike the early creed in 1 Corinthians 15, do not even mention appearances. Some scholars, therefore, have argued that the earliest confession by Jesus' followers that God had resurrected him from the dead was based not on his appearances but on the Jewish belief that God would vindicate righteous martyrs. Accordingly, this confession could have been made even on the day of crucifixion itself.[3] We have seen how Elisabeth Schüssler Fiorenza also understands resurrection belief to be grounded in the Jewish traditions of the vindication of the righteous. She acknowledges the difficulty in establishing historically whether the empty tomb tradition, associated with the women, or the appearance tradition, associated with the men, is primary. But in her feminist reading, she emphasizes the role of the women in the transmission of the passion and resurrection traditions.[4]

Historical Reflections

Since we have reviewed the literary evidence and varying traditions of the resurrection, we are now in a position to consider certain historical and theological questions. What events immediately followed Jesus' crucifixion and entombment? How can the disciples' belief that God had resurrected Jesus from the dead be explained? Was Jesus actually resurrected from the dead by God?[5]

A few scholars still attempt to harmonize the varied Gospel and Pauline resurrection accounts into a coherent, internally consistent story of what happened during those days immediately following the crucifixion and resurrection. But most scholars recognize the difficulty, if not impossibility, of such a bold undertaking. One of the greatest difficulties is the scheme of salvation history presented in Luke-Acts. Jesus is said to have been resurrected on the first day of the week (Luke 24:7). On the same day the empty tomb is visited by a group of women (Luke 24:1-10, 22-23) and by some male disciples (Luke 24:24). Also on the same day Jesus appears to two disciples on the road to Emmaus (Luke 24:13-35), to Simon Peter (Luke 24:34), and to others including the eleven (Luke 24:36-49). The Gospel suggests that the ascension of Jesus into heaven occurred on that initial day (Luke 24:50-53). But the book of Acts, alone among the New Testament writings, refers to a forty day period of appearances that ended with the ascension (Acts 1:1-11). Ten days later, on the Day of Pentecost, the Holy Spirit descends on the gathered followers of Jesus (Acts 2:1-42).

All these happenings in Luke-Acts take place in Jerusalem or the immediate vicinity. Moreover, the resurrected Jesus within the Lukan account expressly commands his followers to remain in Jerusalem and not to depart until they receive the gift of the Holy Spirit (Luke 24:49; Acts 1:4-5). The Lukan account, therefore, rules out those appearances by Jesus in Galilee which are implied in Mark, emphasized in Matthew, and reported in the secondary ending of John. Luke must rework his Markan source in order to prepare his readers for his version of the appearances in Jerusalem and to remove any suggestion that Jesus would appear in Galilee. He alters the words spoken to the women who visit the tomb (italics added):

"But go, tell his disciples and Peter that *he is going ahead of you to Galilee;* there you will see him, just as he told you." (Mark 16:7, cf. 14:28)	"Remember how he told you, *while he was still in Galilee,* that the Son of Man must be handed over to sinners, and be crucified, and on the third day rise again." (Luke 24:6-7)

Furthermore, Luke must present the experience of Paul on the road to Damascus as something other than a resurrection appearance, because the resurrected Jesus had ascended and the Holy Spirit descended before Paul's con-

149

version (Acts 9:1-19; also 22:6-16; 26:12-18). The experience of Paul can be referred to as a "vision" (Acts 26:19), but it has more of the characteristics of a hearing than a seeing, a light-blinding audition than a vision. Central to the account are the familiar words from on high: "Saul, Saul, why do you persecute me?" (Acts 9:4; 22:7; 26:14). The Lukan presentation of the experience of Paul on the road to Damascus thereby stands over against Paul's own claim in 1 Corinthians that his conversion was an appearance of the resurrected Jesus of the same order as the earlier appearances of the resurrected Jesus to Cephas and the twelve.

In spite of these and other differences about the events surrounding the resurrection of Jesus, the five principal New Testament witnesses agree, or at least do not contradict, that *the disciples came to believe that Jesus had been resurrected from the dead by God because he had appeared to them and not because of the empty tomb.* The appearances constituted the primary evidence and the empty tomb, at best, supporting evidence. The Gospels contain outright denials that the disciples' resurrection belief was elicited by the women's reports about the empty tomb or by a firsthand examination of the empty tomb (Luke 24:11; John 20:1-10). The disciples' belief in the resurrection of Jesus presupposed on their parts a prior belief in the reality of God and probably some acceptance of the idea of a general resurrection at the end of history. They could not have "made sense" out of their experiences without these assumptions.

But after the death and burial of Jesus, was he actually resurrected from the dead by God or not? Did something happen to the dead Jesus as well as the downcast disciples? The traditional Christian answer, as attested by the Apostles' Creed, has been affirmative: "on the third day he rose from the dead." According to the New Testament, as we have just seen, this confession was first prompted by the appearances of the resurrected Jesus and confirmed by the empty tomb. But this confession stands at the beginning and not the end of theologizing about the resurrection of Jesus. A variety of theological positions have been staked out and debated.

One theological response to the question of Jesus' resurrection has been to exclude from consideration the question of what happened to the dead Jesus. Instead, this approach emphasizes the transformed lives and perspectives of Jesus' disciples in the days immediately following the crucifixion and burial. The empty tomb stories are considered to have been created within the early church for the purpose of dramatizing the objectivity of the resurrection.[6]

Another theological response to the question of Jesus' resurrection has included a defense of the historicity of the empty tomb and a description of the resurrection appearances as "objective visions" by which God communicated to the disciples that Jesus had been actually resurrected from the dead by God. It is sometimes said that if the tomb had not actually been empty, then the authorities antagonistic to Jesus would have publicly displayed his corpse to refute the disciples' claim that he had been resurrected from the dead. It is also said that the resurrection account of Paul carries the interpreter very close to the events surrounding the resurrection (1 Cor. 15:3-9) and that the description by Paul of his experience supports the idea of "objective visions" (1 Cor. 9:1; Gal. 1:15-16).[7]

Many historical portrayals of Jesus produced by the quest have concluded with negative replies to the question of the resurrection of Jesus. We have already noted some of these negative replies.

Perhaps the most common negative explanation for the resurrection belief of the disciples is what might be called the *hallucination theory.* The appearances of Jesus are explained as a series of "subjective visions" among his followers, which were possibly triggered by their anguished longing for his presence. The popularity of this view is understandable in an age enamored with depth psychology and psychoanalysis. This view at least takes seriously the appearances of Jesus, and not the empty tomb, as the primary source for the disciples' resurrection belief.

Another explanation for the origin of belief in the resurrection of Jesus is the *mistaken identity theory.* The appearances of the resurrected Jesus are considered as cases of mistaken identity whereby the distraught disciples imagine someone else to be Jesus. Hugh J. Schonfield appeals to this view in his exposé of the so-called Passover plot. This explanation finds some support in the episode in John involving the appearance of Jesus to Mary Magdalene near the tomb (John 20:11-18). Therein Mary mistakes the resurrected Jesus for the gardener before she realizes that it is actually Jesus. But the mistaken identity view says she was correct the first time: it *was* the gardener! Sometimes associated with this view is the idea that Mary and the disciples found the tomb empty because they visited the wrong tomb. The *wrong tomb theory* can also appeal to John and the account of the visitation to the tomb by Mary, Simon Peter, and the "beloved disciple" (John 20:1-10). Together these theories do account for both the appearance to Mary and the empty tomb.

The oldest negative explanation for the origin of resurrection belief is the *stolen body theory.* In Matthew itself there is the notation that within first-century Jewish circles the story circulated that the disciples had stolen Jesus' body (Matt. 28:11-15). Implied in this theory is the *deception theory* whereby the disciples simply fabricated the accounts of the appearances of the resurrected Jesus. Here is no mistaken identity but a conscious fraud. But together these theories do explain both the appearance traditions and the empty tomb traditions. Hermann Samuel Reimarus, at the very outset of the historical quest, claimed that the disciples stole Jesus' body and fraudulently claimed that he had appeared to them.

The Virgin Birth

In contrast to resurrection belief, the belief that Jesus was conceived by the Holy Spirit within his virgin mother was of little importance for the establishment and the proclamation of the early church. Without belief in the virgin birth, the church would still have emerged following the trauma of the crucifixion.

Outside the infancy narratives themselves, in Matthew and Luke, the New Testament is silent with regard to Jesus' conception by the Holy Spirit. This silence is particularly deafening in the sermons of Peter and Paul reported in the book of Acts (including Acts 2:14-40; 3:12-26; 13:16-41; 17:22-31). If these sermons owe a great deal to the creativity of the Lukan author, it is striking that one who records the virginal conception in his infancy account does not incorporate that belief into his formulation of early apostolic preaching. Or, if these sermons contain an ancient tradition of apostolic preaching, it is equally striking that the virginal conception is not a part of that tradition. This general silence about virginal conception is also maintained by Paul in his letters (cf. Gal. 4:4; Rom. 1:3-4) and by the authors of Mark and John. Nevertheless, two New Testament writers do narrate the events related to the virginal conception of Jesus. Outside the New Testament, the *Protevangelium (Infancy Gospel) of James*, with its overall theme of Mary's purity, emphasizes Mary's virginal status before, during, and after the birth of Jesus.[8]

Literary Evidence

Dependent upon Mark, but independent of each other, the Gospels of Matthew and Luke begin their narrations of the Jesus story with infancy accounts that include references to virginal conception and birth.[9]

The author of the Gospel of Matthew (chaps. 1–2) has prefaced his Markan source with a genealogy and a series of stories, each of which centers around an Old Testament quotation therein fulfilled: the birth of Jesus (1:23 = Isa. 7:14); the visit of the wise men to Bethlehem (2:6 = Mic. 5:2); the flight to Egypt (2:15 = Hos. 11:1); the massacre of the infants at Bethlehem (2:18 = Jer. 31:15); and the settlement at Nazareth (2:23 = ?).

Within this literary setting, immediately following the genealogy and introducing the narrative material, appears the story of Jesus' birth (1:18-25). This story presupposes that the virgin Mary has already conceived her child. The conflict involves Joseph's dismay over his betrothed's pregnancy and his intention to divorce her. The resolution of the conflict comes with Joseph's obedience to the divine will: he takes Mary as his wife and names her child "Jesus" (vss. 24-25). In many respects this is a story of naming. But this is also a story of adoption. Addressed by the angel as "son of David" (vs. 20), Joseph adopts the divinely conceived "Emmanuel" (vs. 23) into the Davidic line, the royal-messianic line. As is widely recognized by interpreters, the entire story serves as a commentary on verse 16 of the preceding genealogy: "And Jacob the father of Joseph the husband of Mary, of whom Jesus was born, who is called the Messiah." Within the Gospel of Matthew, therefore, the story that bears witness to the virginal conception reflects and supports the evangelist's interest in Jesus' genealogy—his origin.

Following his elegantly written prologue, the author of the Gospel of Luke (chaps. 1–2) has prefaced his Markan source with a series of stories: the annunciation of the birth of John; the annunciation of the birth of Jesus; the meeting between Elizabeth (John) and Mary (Jesus); the birth and infancy of John; the birth and infancy of Jesus; and the visit of Jesus to Jerusalem at age twelve. Whereas the Matthean stories cluster around quotations from Jewish Scripture, the Lukan stories are interspersed with Scripture-based hymns including the Magnificat (1:46-55), the Benedictus (1:67-79), and the Nunc Dimittis (2:29-32).

Within this narrative setting appears the brief story that reports the virginal conception (1:26-38). The Lukan account of the virginal conception is an annunciation story; conception has not yet occurred. The conflict within the story involves Mary's own dismay over the angelic appearance and the announcement that she would conceive even though she had no husband. The resolution of the conflict comes with her acceptance of the divine will for her. Like the Matthean story, this account includes both a reference to Joseph's Davidic lineage (vs. 27) and a command to name the child "Jesus" (vs. 31). Unlike the Matthean story, however, this episode is not linked to a genealogy (cf. 3:23-38). This Lukan story of the annunciation of Jesus' conception and birth is placed alongside a story of the conception and birth of John. Jesus' conception by the Holy Spirit establishes his solidarity with, but superiority to, John, who was simply filled with the Holy Spirit before his birth (1:15). Jesus' conception by the Holy Spirit makes him "the Son of the Most High" (vs. 32; also vs. 35). But John is simply "the prophet of the Most High" (1:76). Within the Gospel of Luke, therefore, the story that bears witness to the virginal conception supports the salvation-history interest of the evangelist.

The differences between the infancy accounts in Matthew and Luke are many and obvious. There are differences in the *overall* itinerary of Jesus' family. In Matthew there is movement from Bethlehem to Egypt back to the land of Israel, with final settlement in Nazareth of Galilee. In Luke there is movement from Nazareth of Galilee to Bethlehem to Jerusalem then back to Nazareth. Although Matthew implies that Joseph and Mary take up residence in Nazareth only after the birth of Jesus, Luke presents Nazareth as their home before and after the birth. Matthew portrays the threat of King Herod as initiating the movement of Joseph and Mary, but Luke reports the Roman census as the initiating factor. There are also differences in events and characters. In Matthew are the wise men and the slaughtered children; in Luke are the shepherds, Simeon, and Anna. The role of Joseph is highlighted in the Matthean narratives, while Mary occupies center stage in the Lukan stories.

As with the resurrection traditions, so in their infancy accounts: the authors of Matthew and Luke are drawing on special material to be designated M and L, not on Q.

Historical Reflections

Our literary survey leads inescapably to particular historical questions and to related theological issues. What events surrounded Jesus' birth and infancy? Was Jesus actually conceived by the Holy Spirit within Mary his virgin mother? If so, how did this very private occurrence become public information and eventually come to be written down in the Gospels? If not, how did the idea of virginal conception and birth originate within the early church? Scholars generally agree that Jesus was born while Herod was the Roman-appointed ruler of Palestine (Matt. 2:1; Luke 1:5). Accordingly, the birth of Jesus would have taken place before the death of Herod, which occurred early in the year 4 B.C.E.

A few scholars attempt to harmonize the sequences of events in the Matthean and Lukan infancy accounts in spite of their differences. Still other interpreters defend the historicity of such details as the guiding star (Matt. 2:2, 7, 9-10) and the census ordered by Caesar Augustus when Quirinius was Governor of Syria (Luke 2:1).

There is, however, the nearly universal recognition among interpreters that the infancy narratives in Matthew and Luke are written in the language of piety and poetry. As we have already noted, the author of the brief Matthean stories quotes a Scriptural text in each story, and the principal characters in the Lukan narratives periodically break forth in songs based on the Scriptures. But more than this, the details often recall persons and events from the history of Israel.

The saga of Israel and Moses is reflected in Matthew in such happenings as the slaughter of the children (Matt. 2:16; cf. Exod. 1:16, 22) and the exodus out of Egypt (Matt. 2:19-21). The identification of Jesus as "Nazorean" in Matthew may allude to the Davidic "branch" (Isa. 11:1; *nēzer* in Hebrew) or to the holy "Nazirite" (Judg. 13:5). The infancy stories in Luke draw on the story of the birth and growth of Samuel (cf. Luke 1:46-55 and 1 Sam. 2:1-10; Luke 2:40 and 1 Sam. 2:26). Like the Gospels they introduce, the infancy narratives are statements of faith. Here the problem of the historical Jesus is most problematic. Thus M. Eugene Boring can make this statement about a characteristic shared by most historical portrayals during the post-quest period in spite of their diversity: "The birth stories are generally considered unhistorical."[10]

But what about the virginal conception itself? Was Jesus actually conceived without male participation? The traditional Christian response, as attested by the Apostles' Creed, has been affirmative: yes, he "was conceived by the Holy

Spirit, born of the virgin Mary." This confession rests upon a rather remarkable agreement between two literarily independent and vastly different accounts of Jesus' infancy. Both Matthew and Luke agree that *Mary conceived of the Holy Spirit while a virgin betrothed to a man named Joseph.* Probably no single item in the Gospel records has occasioned more heated theological debate and acrimony than this. Few theologians still defend the virginal conception as biological fact, and most have been inclined to view virginal conception as a spiritual truth underscoring the closeness between Jesus and God.

Based on the Gospel records of Jesus' ministry, it is clear that Jesus did not appeal publicly to his virginal conception as the basis of his authority. Ultimately, the only way this private occurrence could have become public would have been through his parents. Indeed, there are those who suggest that the Matthean account, which emphasizes the role of Joseph, and the Lukan account, which focuses on Mary, are derived from Joseph and Mary respectively. But if Jesus was not conceived of the Holy Spirit, the origin of the idea of virginal conception and birth begs for an explanation. Over the years a number of proposals in this regard have been set forth.

Originating within the cultural and theological context of Judaism, the early church from its inception considered Jewish Scripture—the Old Testament—as its book. There was no expectation within Judaism that a messiah would be virginally conceived by a woman. But Jewish tradition, even the Hebrew Scriptures, has been used to account for the genesis of the virgin birth idea. Some scholars have pointed to texts which talk about the *Holy Spirit's abiding on a messianic figure* (Isa. 11:1-9). Other scholars appeal to the many dramatic *birth stories involving Israel's religious heroes* (Gen. 21:1-7; 25:19-26; 29:15–30:24; Judg. 13:1-25; 1 Sam. 1:19-20). In these narratives God is recognized as the source of fertility and sterility and is referred to as one who opens and closes wombs. Still other interpreters suggest the creative role of *the Greek translation of Isaiah 7:14* cited in Matthew 1:23: "Look, the virgin shall conceive and bear a son, and they shall name him Emmanuel." Whereas the Hebrew text refers to "a young woman" (*'almāh*), the Greek translation known as the Septuagint (symbolized by *LXX*) used the word *virgin (parthenos)*. Accordingly, the early church's use of these various passages in interpreting the Jesus story may have led to the emergence of virgin birth belief and to the creation of the Gospel stories that testify to this belief.

In its spread from Palestine into the Graeco-Roman world, the church and its thought inescapably became Hellenized. Some scholars have claimed that the Gospel accounts of Jesus' virginal conception and birth were in response to Greek culture and thought. Specifically, the Gospel stories of the virginal conception and birth of Jesus were said to have been shaped in imitation of *Hellenistic stories about gods who cohabited with mortal women* (cf. Gen. 6:1-4).

Within the early church, Jesus was confessed to be "Son of God." This

155

confession did not necessarily include, of course, the idea that Jesus was virginally conceived. For Paul, Jesus was "Son of God" in association with his being resurrected by God (Rom. 1:3-4) or his being sent by God (Gal. 4:4). The author of Mark, as we saw, stressed that Jesus was "Son of God" in relation to his obedient suffering and death (Mark 1:1; 15:39; et al.). Some scholars have suggested that this early *Christian confession of Jesus' divine sonship* resulted in the idea of virginal conception and led to the formulation of stories that illustrate and explain "how" Jesus became "Son of God."

The alternatives to Jesus' virginal conception, of course, are his conception by Joseph or by some other man. The genealogy of Jesus in Matthew traces Jesus' descent from Abraham and David by way of Joseph (Matt.1:1-17). One ancient manuscript, in Syriac, says rather directly: "Joseph, to whom was betrothed Mary the virgin, was the father of Jesus who is called the Messiah" (vs. 16). Scholarly arguments have been put forth for the probability of Jesus' paternity by Joseph.[11]

The Matthean infancy account itself, however, reports that Joseph initially suspected that Mary had conceived by another man, so that Joseph intended not to follow through with the marriage (Matt. 1:19). By the second century, stories were circulating in pagan circles claiming Jesus to be the illegitimate offspring of a Roman soldier named Panthera; and within rabbinic literature, Jesus was referred to as *Yeshu ben Pantera* ("Jesus the son of Pantera"). These ancient traditions of Jesus' paternity by a man named Panthera have been recently introduced to a broader public in the award-winning film *Jésus de Montréal* (1989), directed by Denys Arcand. The film tells the story of a controversial passion play written for a Catholic shrine in that Canadian city. In the film, the narrator of the passion play introduces Jesus as "the Jewish prophet *Yeshu ben Pantera*" and later refers to those ancient Jewish sources that label him "a false prophet, born of fornication." Based on a careful assessment of the evidence, scholarly arguments have also been put forth in support of the position that Jesus was in fact the offspring of a man other than Joseph, whether a Roman soldier or someone else.[12]

8

Titles of Honor

There was within the Palestinian Jewish tradition, including the Hebrew Scriptures, a variety of names and images. These names and images were used to designate Israel as the people of God and to identify particular social and religious roles within Israel: prophet, "son of David," priest, "one like a son of man," judge, "son of God," wise man, "messiah," scribe, "son of Aaron," servant, "righteous Branch," king, "man of God," and shepherd. Most of these expressions identified positions in Israel's past. But some were also used to designate a redeemer figure in Israel's future.

Jesus' followers, particularly after the resurrection experiences, confessed him to be the promised redeemer and bestowed upon him many traditional names and images as titles of honor. Like a magnet Jesus attracted such titles. They were eventually translated from Hebrew and Aramaic into Greek as the Christian message was carried from Palestine into the wider Mediterranean world. It has long been recognized that Jesus' own use, or avoidance, of honorific titles during his lifetime would cast light on the way he viewed himself and his mission. An appreciation of these titles, therefore, is an important aspect of understanding not only early Christian theology but also the historical Jesus.

Survey of the Evidence

The New Testament contains dozens of titles, names, and images for Jesus. We will briefly survey those that have played prominent roles in the historical quest: Christ (Messiah), Son (of God), Prophet, and Son of Man.[1]

157

Christ (Messiah)

Within Christianity, this title was destined to become a proper name in the phrase "Jesus Christ." But the English term "Christ," derived from the Greek *christos*, translates the Hebrew *māshîah* or messiah. Both the Greek and the Hebrew literally mean "anointed."

The term *messiah* was used in ancient Israel as a designation for the ruling king. Saul, the first king, was called messiah (1 Sam. 26:9; et al.). The subsequent rulers from the house of David who ruled in Jerusalem were also called messiah. This use is attested in the "royal psalms," which were probably sung in conjunction with the coronation and enthronement of the Davidic kings (Pss. 2:2; 89:51; et al.). Kings were called messiah because they had been anointed with oil (1 Sam. 10:1; 1 Kings 1:39). There was also the implication of a spiritual anointing with God's presence for special service. *Messiah* was a term, therefore, that could be used as a designation not only for kings but also for priests and prophets. Moreover, the great anonymous prophet of the Babylonian exile known as Second Isaiah referred to Cyrus the Persian ruler as messiah, for the latter had been chosen by God as the liberator of the Jewish captives (Isa. 45:1).

Even before the Babylonian exile there was occasional disillusionment with the reigning Davidic kings. Prophets such as Isaiah and Micah expressed hope for an ideal Davidic ruler who would perform God's will (Isa. 9:2-7; 11:1-9; Mic. 5:2-6). Later prophets such as Jeremiah and Ezekiel likewise anticipated the restoration of God's people under the leadership of a just and righteous Davidic ruler (Jer. 23:5-6; 33:14-18; Ezek. 34:23-24; 37:24-28).

By the first century, the term *messiah* itself was being used as part of the expectation that God was going to send a redeemer to deliver Israel from Roman oppression. Now the expression designated a future king of the house of David. As of old, the name *messiah* was also associated with other types of religious leaders. Specifically, there was the expectation that God was going to raise up a priestly redeemer descended from Aaron, the brother of Moses and first high priest. The members of the Qumran sect, for example, looked for two messianic figures: a high priest of Aaronic background and a king of Davidic lineage. In the scroll known as the Manual of Discipline, the Qumran sectarians refer to these two deliverers with the phrase "the messiah(s) of Aaron and Israel" (1QS 9:10-11). The term *messiah*, therefore, was used as an honorific title within Palestinian Judaism at the time of Jesus' ministry.

In the four Gospels, the title "Messiah," or Christ, occasionally appears on Jesus' lips. Sometimes the crowds and his opponents speculate about the possibility or impossibility of his being the Messiah. In the Gospel of John, Jesus even admits to the Samaritan woman that he is the Messiah (John 4:26). In the Gospel of Luke, he reads a messianic text from the book of Isaiah and

158

applies the passage to himself and his ministry (Luke 4:16-30). But Jesus does not openly and repeatedly use the Messiah title for himself.

Scholarly discussion about Jesus' relationship to this title usually centers around two episodes recorded in the Gospel of Mark: the confession of Peter near Caesarea Philippi (Mark 8:27-33 par.); and the interrogation by the high priest in Jerusalem (Mark 14:53-65 par.). In the former scene, Jesus asks: "Who do people say that I am?" Peter answers: "You are the Messiah." In the latter scene, the high priest asks: "Are you the Messiah, the Son of the Blessed One?" Jesus replies:

> "I am; and
> 'you will see the Son of Man
> seated at the right hand of the Power,'
> and 'coming with the clouds of heaven.'"

On the basis of these two scenes, many interpreters have perceived at least a qualified acceptance of the Messiah title by Jesus. But other scholars have not been so confident in drawing this historical conclusion from these texts. They quickly point out that the Synoptic evidence itself is ambiguous. In Mark, Jesus responds to the high priest's question with a straightforward: "I am." But both Matthew and Luke report a more evasive reply: "You say so." In Mark, Jesus offers no direct response to the confession of Peter. Only in Matthew does he acknowledge the confession with a blessing: "Blessed are you, Simon son of Jonah! For flesh and blood has not revealed this to you, but my Father in heaven" (Matt. 16:17).

Furthermore, some scholars using form critical analysis have detected beneath the Markan account of the episode at Caesarea Philippi an earlier version of the story in which Jesus actually rebuked Peter for bestowing the messiah title upon him. This pre-Markan version can be reconstructed as follows:

> And Jesus went on with his disciples to the villages of Caesarea Philippi; and on the way he asked his disciples, "Who do people say that I am?" And they answered him, "John the Baptist; and others, Elijah; and still others, one of the prophets." He asked them, "But who do you say that I am?" Peter answered him, "You are the Messiah." But turning and looking at his disciples, he rebuked Peter and said, "Get behind me, Satan! For you are setting your mind not on divine things but on human things." (cf. Mark 8:27-29, 33)

Form critics reconstruct this hypothetical pre-Markan account simply by removing from the Markan story those lines that are in keeping with the theological interest of the Gospel writer and that appear to be editorial additions. They remove the lines about the messianic secret (vs. 30) and the passion prediction (vss. 31-32).

However specific Gospel passages are interpreted, there is still very little evidence in the Gospels to support the idea that Jesus used the Messiah title as his chosen self-designation. At best he accepts it with qualifying comments. At worst he repudiates it. A supreme irony, consequently, emerges out of our investigation of the Messiah or Christ title. The title Jesus avoided during his lifetime became the name by which he has been known down through the ages: Jesus Christ.

Son (of God)

The title "Son," or "Son of God," was probably the most important honorific name for Jesus during the formative centuries of the church. According to the doctrine of the trinity, God was recognized as three in one: Father, Son, and Holy Spirit. The Father and the Son were said to be of the "same substance." There was also an idea of divine sonship in ancient Israel. But divine sonship was viewed more in terms of adoption than substance.

As attested by the Hebrew Scriptures, God as Father referred to Israel as Son. God had adopted Israel through the events related to the Exodus from Egypt (Exod. 4:22-23; Hos. 11:1). With the rise of monarchy, the king was also designated Son of God. His coronation or enthronement was the occasion on which he became adopted as Son of God (Ps. 2:7; 2 Sam. 7:14).

The reigning Davidic king was both Messiah and Son of God. It might be expected that the name Son would be used later to designate the coming royal messiah within Jewish eschatological thought. There is at least some evidence in the Dead Sea Scrolls that this was the case (4QFlor. 10–14).

Among the four Gospels, John repeatedly depicts Jesus with the name Son, or Son of God, on his lips as his self-designation (especially John 5:19-29). In John, of course, the divine sonship of Jesus is based on his preexistence as the eternal Word (John 1:1-18). The Synoptics also contain references to Jesus as Son or Son of God. The heavenly voice refers to him as Son both at his baptism and at his transfiguration (Mark 1:11 par.; 9:7 par.). But in the Synoptics the title is seldom found on Jesus' lips as a self-designation. There are, however, a couple of notable exceptions:

> "But about that day or hour no one knows, neither the angels in heaven, nor the Son, but only the Father." (Mark 13:32 par.)

> "All things have been handed over to me by my Father; and no one knows the Son except the Father, and no one knows the Father except the Son and anyone to whom the Son chooses to reveal him." (Matt. 11:27 = Luke 10:22)

The saying from Mark appears in the apocalyptic discourse. Some scholars have argued that the reference is not to the Son of God but to the apocalyptic

160

Son of Man. The other saying, a Q saying, has emphases characteristic of Jesus' speech in the Gospel of John. Some scholars have claimed that this is a Johannine saying that has somehow strayed into the Synoptic tradition.

Whether or not Jesus ever referred to himself as Son of God depends largely upon the interpreter's understanding of the discourses of Jesus in the Gospel of John. If these discourses stem from the creativity of the Gospel writer and his community, then they cannot be cited as evidence. There are scholars, however, who generally reject the Johannine discourses as primary evidence for the words of the historical Jesus but defend the authenticity of the Son of God sayings in the Synoptics. Their argument finds support in Jesus' undisputed address of God as *Abba*, "Father." It would have been natural, they reason, for Jesus, with his strong sense of God's Fatherhood, to have on occasion referred to himself as son. Their argument also finds support in rabbinic literature where rabbis, or holy men, are even addressed by the divine voice as "my son."

Nonetheless, based on the Synoptic tradition, there is slight evidence that Jesus used the Son of God title as his chosen self-designation.

Prophet

The designation of Jesus as prophet was of minimal importance for the church during its formative period. The name was not exalted enough to explain fully his relationship to God. Also, the category of eschatological prophet who would serve as a forerunner for the Messiah was reserved for John the Baptist as the forerunner of Jesus. But the term *prophet* had a long and honored history within Israel.

A prophet was one who spoke for God—one called by God to declare God's Word. Among the goodly company of prophets were reckoned such great figures as Isaiah, Jeremiah, and Ezekiel. By the first century, there had arisen the hope that God would send a prophet to Israel in the last days. Included in this expectation for an eschatological prophet were the ideas that he might be a prophet like Moses (Deut. 18:15, 18) or Elijah returned (Mal. 3:1; 4:5). The members of the Qumran sect not only anticipated the arrival of priestly and kingly messianic figures but also expected the appearance of a prophet like Moses (1QS 9:10-11; 4QTest.). It is possible that they even identified their own founder, the so-called Teacher of Righteousness, as this eschatological prophet.

Within the four Gospels, there is considerable discussion among the crowds about Jesus' being a prophet. In the familiar scene near Caesarea Philippi, Jesus asked: "Who do people say that I am?" The disciples replied: "John the Baptist ... Elijah ... one of the prophets" (Mark 8:27-28 par.). Jesus himself often refers to prophets of old and even identifies John the Baptist as the prophet Elijah (Matt. 11:7-19 = Luke 7:24-35).

There are also Synoptic sayings in which Jesus rather unpretentiously includes himself in the prophetic succession. In two passages, he views his rejection and death as extensions of the examples set by the prophets:

> "Prophets are not without honor, except in their hometown, and among their own kin, and in their own house." (Mark 6:4 par.; also John 4:44)

> "Yet today, tomorrow, and the next day I must be on my way, because it is impossible for a prophet to be killed outside of Jerusalem." (Luke 13:33; also Luke 13:34-35 = Matt. 23:37-39)

In another interesting saying, Jesus appeals to the prophet Jonah as a model for his own ministry (Matt. 12:38-42 = Luke 11:29-32). In the longer Matthean version of this Q saying, Jesus draws a parallel between the burial of Jonah in the belly of the whale for three days and three nights and his own burial in the earth. In the Lukan version, Jesus draws a parallel apparently between the preaching of repentance by Jonah and his own preaching. There is, therefore, some evidence that Jesus identified himself with the prophets of years past and as a prophet in his own ministry.

Son of Man

This phrase has been the subject of more continuing scholarly debate and intense critical analysis than any of the other titles for Jesus. The volume of literature on the subject signals both the complexity of the issues as well as the possible importance of the phrase for insight into the thought of the earliest church and even into the mind of Jesus himself. This phrase also presents a challenge for the English translator since the words in Hebrew *('ādām)*, Aramaic *('enāsh)*, and Greek *(anthrōpos)* traditionally translated "man" are generic words meaning "human," not the gender-specific category "male."

Within ancient Israel and postexilic Judaism, the phrase *son of man* was varied in meaning, initially in Hebrew and later in Aramaic. In Hebrew the expression *son of man (ben 'ādām)* was virtually a synonym for *man ('ādām)*, both collectively (meaning "human beings") and individually (referring to a particular "human being"). The psalmist bears witness to the collective use of the phrase (Ps. 8:4). The prophet Ezekiel testifies to the individualistic use, for he is repeatedly addressed by God as "son of man" (Ezek. 2:1, et al.). In most of these passages the phrase emphasizes human finitude and creatureliness by contrast to the power and glory of God. The NRSV translates the phrase in Psalm 8:4 as "mortals," in Ezekiel 2:1 vocatively as "O mortal."

In apocalyptic contexts, however, the expression *son of man* comes to function quite differently. In the book of Daniel, in the great night vision of four beasts, in Aramaic, the narrator refers to "one like a son of man" (*bar 'enāsh* Dan. 7:13). Here the phrase *son of man* is not yet a title; and the image itself is seemingly understood collectively. The narrator interprets the "one like a son of man" to represent "the saints," or "holy ones," who will receive the kingdom from God at the close of the present age of four beastly world empires (Dan. 7:17-18).

However, the phrase *son of man* is apparently used individualistically and as a title in a much discussed section of the book of Enoch (chaps. 37–71)—a book preserved in its entirety only in Ethiopic. The phrase apparently identifies the heavenly savior figure who will come to judge the world. Some scholars perceive in Enoch evidence for the expectation in pre-Christian Judaism for a transcendent redeemer figure designated by the title "Son of Man." Other scholars deny the pre-Christian origin of this portion of the book or deny that "son of man" is used in the book as a title.

In addition to these uses of *son of man* in ancient literature, the phrase was also used in first-century Galilean Aramaic—so it has been argued—as a substitute, or circumlocution, for the first person pronoun "I." This idiom was used by speakers in statements about themselves that were embarrassing or frightening in nature. The declaration "I am going to die," for example, could be expressed as, "The son of man (perhaps, *bar 'enāshā*) is going to die." It is against this complex historical and linguistic background that we must consider this name for Jesus in the Greek New Testament: "the Son of Man" (*ho huios tou anthrōpou*). The use and distribution of this name in the New Testament constitutes a remarkable literary phenomenon.

As a title for Jesus, the phrase *Son of Man* is virtually confined to the four canonical Gospels (cf. Acts 7:56; and Rev. 1:13; 14:14). Paul does not refer to Jesus by this name in any of his letters.

In the canonical Gospels, specifically the synoptic Gospels, the title "Son of Man" appears exclusively on the lips of Jesus (cf. John 12:34). Jesus appears to use this name above all names as the way of identifying himself and his mission. Foes and friends address Jesus by many names, including Christ, Son of God, and prophet. They do not call upon him as Son of Man.

In the synoptic Gospels, these so-called Son of Man sayings spoken by Jesus, apparently about himself, fall into three distinct categories. First, some sayings speak about the Son of Man apocalyptically in terms of his future coming in glory. Second, other sayings talk about the Son of Man in terms of his imminent suffering, death, and resurrection. Third, still other sayings depict the Son of Man in terms of such present activity on earth as his forgiveness of sins and his wandering style of ministry. The distinctions among these three categories are finely drawn. There is no single saying in which Jesus outlines the role of the Son of Man comprehensively from his present activity through his death and resurrection to his future return at the end of history. (See the chart JESUS' "SON OF MAN" SAYINGS on page 165.)

Our survey of the literary evidence for the Son of Man title, and the other titles of honor, leads us to an inescapable observation: *if Jesus had a preferred self-designation it was Son of Man.* But this observation also brings with it certain questions. Did Jesus in his teaching actually refer to the Son of Man? Did he use the name as his chosen self-designation? Or did he use it in other ways? Which Son of Man sayings are to be considered authentic? If Jesus did not use the name as his chosen self-designation, how can the prominence of the Son of Man sayings in the Gospels and their absence elsewhere be explained?

The "Son of Man" Sayings and Jesus

During the era of modern biblical criticism, innumerable answers have been given to the questions about the Son of Man sayings in the Gospels and their possible use by the historical Jesus. Each answer possesses its own subtle nuances and characteristics. At least five approaches to these questions have been proposed.

1. *The Son of Man sayings in all three categories are accepted as authentic.* This position appears in the writings of those scholars who portray Jesus as the suffering servant Messiah. Jesus did, according to them, adopt the Son of Man expression as his own special self-designation. Jesus was suspicious of the Messiah title because of its political overtones and thus used the Son of Man title to embrace all dimensions of his ministry and destiny. He used the Son of Man title to underscore his present activity on earth. This use was possibly a reflection of the Hebraic and Aramaic speech usages whereby *son of man* was a synonym for *humans* in their lowliness. Jesus also used the Son of Man title to anticipate his future exaltation or return on the clouds of heaven. This use paralleled the apocalyptic hope for a heavenly Son of Man who would serve as God's vice-regent at the last judgment. But Jesus, in addition, used the Son of Man title in association with his own expected crucifixion and resurrection. This use was uniquely his. He was influenced by the biblical image of the "Servant of the LORD" in the book of Isaiah, especially by the graphic portrayal of the suffering servant in chapter 53. One saying in particular seems to epitomize Jesus' creative bringing together of the Son of Man phrase and the idea of suffering servanthood:

"For the Son of Man came not to be served but to serve, and to give his life a ransom for many." (Mark 10:45 par.)

The approach that accepts the authenticity of Son of Man sayings in all three categories rests in part on the recognition that all three types are represented in Mark, the earliest Gospel. As in Mark, so Jesus in his historical ministry used the Son of Man title to refer to himself in his present work, his imminent suffering and death, and his future coming or vindication.

JESUS' "SON OF MAN" SAYINGS

	Present Work	Imminent Death and Resurrection	Future Coming
MARK	Mark 2:10 par. Mark 2:28 par.	*Mark 8:31 par. *Mark 9:9 par. *Mark 9:12 par. Mark 9:31 par. Mark 10:33 par. *Mark 10:45 par. Mark 14:21 par. *Mark 14:41 par.	Mark 8:38 par. Mark 13:26 par. Mark 14:62 par.
Q	+Matt. 5:11=Luke 6:22 Matt. 8:20=Luke 9:58 Matt. 11:19=Luke 7:34 Matt. 12:32=Luke 12:10 Matt. 12:40=Luke 11:30		+Matt. 10:32=Luke 12:8 +Matt. 19:28=Luke 22:30 Matt. 24:27=Luke 17:24 Matt. 24:37=Luke 17:26 Matt. 24:39=Luke 17:30 Matt. 24:44=Luke 12:40
M	#Matt. 16:13	#Matt. 26:2	Matt. 10:23 Matt. 13:37 Matt. 13:41 Matt. 24:30 Matt. 25:31
L	Luke 19:10	#Luke 22:48 #Luke 24:7	Luke 18:8 Luke 21:36
THOMAS	GThom. 86:1-2 cf. Matt. 8:20=Luke 9:58		

*Only two of the Gospels, Mark and Matthew or Mark and Luke, contain a "Son of Man" saying.

+Only one Gospel, Matthew or Luke, contains a "Son of Man" saying.

#The "Son of Man" reference may be redactional, from the author of Matthew or Luke, instead of from pre-Gospel tradition.

2. *Only the future apocalyptic Son of Man sayings are accepted as authentic.* Moreover, Jesus does not identify himself with the coming Son of Man when he speaks about that future figure. This view finds expression in the "new quest" writings of Günther Bornkamm, among others.

The reasoning that leads to this conclusion begins with those future Son of Man sayings in which Jesus seemingly distinguishes between himself in his earthly ministry and the coming Son of Man:

> "*Those who are ashamed of me* and of my words in this adulterous and sinful generation, *of them the Son of Man will also be ashamed* when he comes in the glory of his Father with the holy angels." (Mark 8:38 par.; also Matt. 10:32-33 = Luke 12:8-9; italics added)

Jesus did not say: "Those who are ashamed of me...of them I will also be ashamed." Nor did he say: "Those who are ashamed of the Son of Man...of them will the Son of Man be ashamed." But: "Those who are ashamed of me...of them will the Son of Man be ashamed." Jesus, therefore, adopted the apocalyptic idea that the "Son of Man" would serve as God's vice-regent at the last judgment in order to dramatize the decisive importance of his earthly ministry. He did not, however, identify himself as that coming apocalyptic figure.

The earliest Palestinian church, according to this approach, identified the resurrected Jesus as the exalted Son of Man after the resurrection experiences. Those believers remembered how Jesus had referred to the coming Son of Man during his earthly ministry. They logically and naturally equated the resurrected Jesus with that figure. They also freely placed the Son of Man name in sayings of Jesus that did not originally contain it (cf. Matt. 16:13 and Mark 8:27). Both the present and the suffering Son of Man sayings now preserved in the Gospels were created in their present form within the early church. They are inauthentic. Within this perspective, the so-called passion predictions are judged to be inauthentic (Mark 8:31 par.; 9:31 par.; 10:32-34 par.). These declarations not only contain the Son of Man title but reflect details about Jesus' fate that could only have been known after his trial, crucifixion, and resurrection.

This approach that accepts as authentic only future Son of Man sayings rests, in part, on the recognition that these sayings are attested in all four strands of Synoptic material: Mark, Q, M, and L. By contrast, the suffering Son of Man sayings are found nearly exclusively in Mark.

3. *None of the Son of Man sayings are accepted as authentic.* This view has received support from some representatives of the "new quest" and, in recent years, wider acceptance in scholarly circles.[2] Central to this view is a sharp focus on Jesus and his proclamation of the kingdom of God. The nearness of the kingdom for Jesus, according to this interpretation, did not allow time for his

departure and return as the exalted Son of Man. Nor did the finality of the kingdom for Jesus allow for another mediator such as the exalted Son of Man to stand between him and God. Even the future Son of Man sayings, therefore, are creations of the earliest Palestinian church. After the resurrection experiences, the followers of Jesus interpreted the resurrection in terms of Daniel 7:13. They proceeded to retroject the Son of Man name into other sayings of Jesus that dealt with his earthly activity and suffering.

The Son of Man title was not the means by which Jesus himself correlated all aspects of his ministry and destiny. As seen in the Gospel of Mark, it was the means by which the early church gradually correlated his earthly work, his death and resurrection, and his expected return in glory.

4. *The future Son of Man sayings based on Daniel 7:13 are inauthentic; but beneath other Son of man sayings may be authentic utterances of Jesus.* This view has been advanced by Geza Vermes,[3] and subsequently by others.[4] As we have seen, Vermes considers Jesus to have been a Galilean *Hasid*, or holy man. He claims that Jesus did refer to himself with the phrase *son of man*. But Jesus used the expression not as a title but as a circumlocution in keeping with idiomatic Galilean Aramaic. Out of modesty, for example, Jesus said: "But so that you may know that the Son of Man has authority on earth to forgive sins..." (Mark 2:10 par.). He meant: "I have authority on earth to forgive sins." Even the Son of Man sayings that speak about suffering, death, and resurrection possibly originated with Jesus himself. Here Jesus would have used circumlocution not out of modesty but out of a sense of foreboding. In their original form, however, these declarations referred only to his martyrdom and not to his vindication by resurrection. By contrast, the future Son of Man sayings were created by Jesus' followers after the resurrection by interpreting his resurrection and exaltation in the light of Daniel 7:13. Other scholars too have dismissed the future apocalyptic sayings as inauthentic, but have seen beneath other Son of Man sayings a generic use of the phrase by Jesus, corresponding to its meaning in Psalm 8:4. Thus when Jesus talked about the "son of man" lording over the Sabbath and the "son of man" having nowhere to lay his head, he was using the phrase neither as an honorific title nor as a circumlocution but as a general way of talking about humankind.

5. *All three kinds of Son of Man sayings may be authentic, but the future Son of Man sayings based on Daniel 7:13 refer to vindication and exaltation, not coming again at the end of the world.* With N. T. Wright, the ongoing discussion about the authenticity of Jesus' Son of Man sayings has come full circle.[5] He allows for the authenticity of all three kinds of Son of Man sayings, but with several interesting twists. Wright explicitly acknowledges that Jesus—as proposed by Vermes—may have used the phrase as a circumlocutory, or oblique, way of talking about his work on earth and his coming suffering. But Wright's overriding concern is to demonstrate how Jesus, in his retelling of Israel's story,

appropriated and used the book of Daniel, and Daniel 7:13, particularly in his apocalyptic discourse in Mark 13 par. Here Jesus draws on apocalyptic images from the book of Daniel, but not to talk about some coming redeemer figure nor about his own return at the end of the world. For first-century Jews, including Jesus, apocalyptic is simply a dramatic way of talking about coming events that will take place *within* history, not at the *end* of history. Thus for Jesus the eschatological prophet, the Messiah, "the son of man coming in clouds" refers to the announced vindication of his followers and himself when God uses the Romans to destroy the Temple and Jerusalem, as occurred in 70 C.E. The phrase "coming on clouds" refers not to a coming from heaven to earth but to a coming to God from earth.

At least these five main approaches to the Son of Man sayings have emerged in contemporary scholarship. As for the reason why the Son of Man title seldom occurs in the New Testament outside the words of Jesus himself, there is general agreement among those pursuing different approaches to the problem. The name originated in a Semitic language environment and was meaningless to persons entering the church from a Greek or Gentile background. Thus Paul in his letters and the Gospel writers in the literary framework of their writings generally avoid the title.

9

Kingdom Preaching (Eschatology)

The ministry of Jesus was itinerant, public, and verbal. Jesus may have used the villages of Capernaum in Galilee and Bethany in Judea as places of residence for a season. But he did not remain in one locale. His was a wandering, itinerant ministry. Jesus was accompanied on his travels by an inner core of followers, but he moved among the people. He was, therefore, unlike John the Baptist and the sectarians of Qumran insofar as he did not withdraw permanently to the Jordan River Valley nor to the wilderness beside the Dead Sea. He evidently avoided the larger Hellenized cities of Galilee such as Sepphoris and Tiberias, preferring the smaller towns and villages with predominantly Jewish populations. His was an open, public ministry. Immediate communication by Jesus on his travels required speaking, not writing. His was also a verbal ministry. Central to his message was the theme of the kingdom, usually expressed in the phrases *the kingdom of God* or *the kingdom of heaven*.[1]

Gospel Writers and Gospel Traditions

In the Gospel of John, Jesus refers to "the kingdom of God" only twice. Both references appear in his conversation with Nicodemus about being "born again" (John 3:3, 5; cf. 18:36). Thereafter he speaks of "eternal life" or simply "life." By contrast, in the Gospels of Matthew, Mark, and Luke, Jesus only rarely speaks about eternal life or life. Everywhere he announces the kingdom. The expressions "kingdom of God" and "kingdom of heaven" occur more than eighty times in the synoptic Gospels, including parallel passages.

The Centrality of the "Kingdom" Theme

Each of the Synoptic writers takes up and develops the "kingdom" theme in that Gospel's own distinctive presentation of the Jesus story. Mark, followed by Matthew, introduces Jesus' Galilean ministry with a brief summary statement of Jesus' message:

"The time is fulfilled, and the kingdom of God has come near; repent, and believe in the good news." (Mark 1:15)	"Repent, for the kingdom of heaven has come near." (Matt. 4:17; cf. 3:2; 10:7)

The wording and word order in each summary differ slightly. Mark uses his favorite word for the Christian message of salvation—"gospel," or "good news" *(euangelion)*. Mark's use of this word represents the common language of Christian mission among the Gentiles, as we see in Paul's letters. Matthew has his customary expression, *kingdom of heaven*. This avoidance of the divine name is appropriate for a Jewish-Christian community such as the church for which Matthew was probably written. But also, whereas Mark mentions the kingdom before repentance, Matthew reverses the order and places repentance before kingdom. In Mark, repentance seemingly represents a response to the kingdom's nearness. In Matthew, repentance becomes more of a condition to be met before the kingdom's arrival (cf. 5:20). The Markan emphasis would be welcome among Gentiles who had not previously known God. The Matthean emphasis would be more characteristic for persons of Jewish background. Both Mark and Matthew, however, identify the kingdom as the central theme of Jesus' message and ministry.

Luke introduces Jesus' public activity with an expanded account of his appearance in the synagogue at Nazareth (Luke 4:16-30). Luke does not, therefore, borrow for his narrative the Markan summary of Jesus' message. But he does report a statement by Jesus about the kingdom shortly after the episode at Nazareth. He also explains Jesus' postresurrection activity in terms of kingdom preaching, at the beginning of the book of Acts:

"I must proclaim the good news of the kingdom of God to the other cities also; for I was sent	After his suffering he presented himself alive to them by many convincing proofs, appearing to

for this purpose." (Luke 4:43)

them during forty days and speaking about the kingdom of God. (Acts 1:3)

All three Synoptic writers accordingly highlight the kingdom as the central theme of Jesus' message and ministry. But, of course, they found the theme in the traditions they inherited. Source-critical analysis reveals that the kingdom theme runs through all layers of the Synoptic tradition: Mark, Q, M, and L. More than a dozen of the 114 sayings in the *Gospel of Thomas* also contain one or more references to the kingdom, usually in an unqualified way as "the kingdom," sometimes as "the kingdom of the Father," and on occasion as "the kingdom of heaven." Many of these kingdom sayings in *Thomas* have no parallels in the Synoptics. Furthermore, in the Synoptics and in *Thomas* form critical analysis discloses that the kingdom theme appears in association with various kinds of traditions, stories, and sayings, but especially in parables and simple sayings.

For us to recognize the centrality of the theme for the Gospel writers and their traditions, however, still leaves for consideration the weightier questions of language, meaning, and time. In the Gospels, what is meant by the word *kingdom*? Does the word refer to a place or to an activity? Does the word function as a sign or as a symbol? What distinction, if any, is intended by the Gospel writers with their different turns of phrase for the kingdom, notably "the kingdom of God" and "the kingdom of heaven"? Is the kingdom announced by Jesus in the Gospels a future hope or a present reality? Both or neither?

The Language and Meaning of the "Kingdom"

The English word *kingdom* suggests space and place, a realm. The United Kingdom of England, Scotland, and Wales constitutes a political entity geographically surrounded by water. The Greek and Aramaic words for "kingdom," *basileia* and *malkûth*, can be used with reference to a political-geographical realm. But these words also convey the notion of activity—the activity of reigning or ruling.

The word *kingdom* in the Synoptic portrayal of Jesus is to be understood not spatially but dynamically, not as a place but as an activity. This represents an important insight of biblical scholarship. The message of Jesus, therefore, can be more accurately summarized as "the rule of God has come near," or "the rule of heaven has come near" (cf. Mark 1:15 and Matt. 4:17). This idea of God's rule is grounded ultimately in the Israelite view of God as king, as one who exercises sovereignty over history and over Israel as God's chosen people (Exod. 15:18; Ps. 145:1; et al.). God in the story of Israel's beginnings exerted rule over Israel prior to their occupation of their promised space. God ruled over Israel before the settlement of the land of Canaan. The kingdom of which Jesus speaks is also essentially an activity of God and not a place.

The word *kingdom* is a symbol.[2] That is, like a sign—even a billboard advertisement—it refers beyond itself. But its meaning is not exhausted in the way that a picture of a pair of jeans refers to denim jeans to be worn. As a symbol, *kingdom* is not exhausted by what might seem to be an obvious referent. In the Gospels and in Jesus' message, the notion of kingdom conjures up a variety of associations. The phrases *kingdom of God* and *kingdom of heaven*, for example, evoke the whole history of God's dealing with Israel. At the same time, the immediate social context of this language suggests a contrast between this kingdom and the kingdom of Rome. Thus recent commentators have even translated these expressions as "the Empire of God"[3] and "God's imperial rule."[4] Elisabeth Schüssler Fiorenza uses the collocation "*basileia*/commonweal/empire of G*d."[5]

In the Gospels, however, Jesus sometimes refers simply to "the kingdom" but, more often, he qualifies the term *kingdom* in one of two principal ways. In all four canonical Gospels, Jesus speaks about the "kingdom of God." But in Matthew, Jesus prefers the expression "kingdom of heaven." Although these two phrases are synonymous, and no theological distinction is intended, it is appropriate to spell out more systematically and in more detail the reasons for this generally accepted view.

First, the words *God* and *heaven* are interchanged in the same sayings of Jesus about the kingdom. The Gospel writers and their traditions thereby recognize the phrases *kingdom of God* and *kingdom of heaven* to be identical in meaning. Abundant examples are found in the triple tradition of Mark, Matthew, and Luke and in the double, or Q, tradition of Matthew and Luke (cf. Mark 10:14 par.; Matt. 5:3 = Luke 6:20). There are also Markan and Q sayings, in the Synoptics, that have parallels in the *Gospel of Thomas* where different kingdom phrases are used (cf. Mark 4:30 par. with GThom. 20:1; Matt. 5:3 = Luke 6:20 with GThom. 54).

Second, the word *heaven* sometimes serves as a substitute for *God* in other sayings of Jesus. This observation supports the position that the word *heaven* simply substitutes for *God* in the sayings of Jesus about the kingdom. Jesus reportedly asked the religious authorities in Jerusalem: "Did the baptism of John come from *heaven*, or was it of human origin?" (Mark 11:30 par., italics added). In Jesus' parable of the prodigal son, the penitent runaway says upon his return: "Father, I have sinned against *heaven* and before you" (Luke 15:18, 21, italics added).

Third, this avoidance of the divine name agrees with the Jewish practice of substituting another name for the sacred, four-letter name for God, YHWH. The practice of circumlocution began as a way to protect the commandment: "You shall not make wrongful use of the name of the LORD (YHWH) your God" (Exod. 20:7 and Deut. 5:11). Instances of substituting words other than *heaven* for *God* appear in the Gospels on the lips of others as well as on the lips of Jesus. The high priest asks: "Are you the Messiah, the Son of the *Blessed One?*" Jesus replies:

> "I am; and
> 'you will see the Son of Man
> seated at the right hand of the *Power,*'
> and 'coming with the clouds of heaven.'"
> (Mark 14:61-62 par., italics added)

Fourth, the Jewish-Christian background of Matthew and the Gentile orientations of Mark and Luke explain why the former Gospel favors kingdom of heaven and the latter Gospels use kingdom of God.

In the Gospels, therefore, Jesus means the same whatever the precise phrasing, whether he says "the kingdom of God," or "the kingdom of heaven," or quite simply "the kingdom." He means: the reign or rule of God! But a crucial question remains: is this rule of God a future hope or a present reality? Both or neither?

The Time of the "Kingdom"

The introductory summaries of Jesus' message in Mark and Matthew announce in Jesus' own words that the kingdom is future but "has come near" (Mark 1:15 and Matt. 4:17). The kingdom announced as future by Jesus remained future from the vantage point of the Synoptic writers toward the end of the first century. The kingdom had not yet arrived. History continued to run its course. But the authors of Mark, Matthew, and Luke variously perceived the nearness of that future kingdom. For Mark, the kingdom "has come near." For Matthew also, it "has come near," but less so than for Mark. For Luke, it is still expected but has not "come near."

Given the unfulfilled eschatological perspectives of the Synoptic authors, they have understandably incorporated into their Gospels teaching material that suggests *Jesus himself viewed the kingdom as future.*

There are several significant kingdom sayings that speak about the kingdom as *future.* In the Lord's Prayer, Jesus teaches his followers to invoke the kingdom's arrival: "Your kingdom come" (Matt. 6:10 = Luke 11:2). He also exhorts his followers to seek the kingdom: "But strive first for the kingdom of God and his righteousness, and all these things will be given to you as well" (Matt. 6:33 = Luke 12:31). On occasion he promises the arrival of the kingdom: "Truly I tell you, there are some standing here who will not taste death until they see that the kingdom of God has come with power" (Mark 9:1 par.). At the Last Supper, Jesus takes a vow in anticipation of the kingdom's arrival: "Truly I tell you, I will never again drink of the fruit of the vine until that day when I drink it new in the kingdom of God" (Mark 14:25 par.).

There are also kingdom sayings, including parables, that refer to a *future* judgment. Among the parables are those of the weeds and wheat (Matt. 13:24-30, 36-43), the fishnet (Matt. 13:47-50), the unmerciful servant (Matt. 18:23-34), the marriage feast (Matt. 22:2-10; cf. Luke 14:16-24), and the sheep and the goats (Matt. 25:31-46). A variety of images depict the fate of those judged both favorably and negatively. Judgment can be expressed in terms of inclusion at or exclusion from a banquet (Matt. 8:11-12 = Luke 13:28-29; Matt. 22:1-14). But negative judgment is often portrayed more dramatically. The luckless recipients may be rebuked verbally (Matt. 7:21-23), turned over to torturers (Matt. 18:34), thrown into a fiery furnace (Matt. 13:42, 50; 25:41), or cast into the outer darkness (Matt. 8:12; 22:13; 25:30). The one who exercises the final judgment is sometimes portrayed as a king (Matt. 18:23; 22:2; 25:31). The future Son of Man sayings also associate that transcendent figure with the last judgment (including Mark 13:26-27 par.).

Further evidence in the teaching of Jesus for the expectation of a *future* kingdom comes from the sayings and parables that appeal for their hearers to remain on constant guard since no one knows exactly when the kingdom or Son of Man will appear. Among the parables are those of the doorkeeper (Mark 13:34), the thief (Matt. 24:43 = Luke 12:39), the faithful and wise servant (Matt. 24:45-51 = Luke 12:42-48), and the ten maidens (Matt. 25:1-12).

Within the Synoptics, however, are also sayings and parables that suggest *Jesus viewed the kingdom as present already in his own ministry.* The sayings supporting this understanding are admittedly fewer in number than those supporting the view of the kingdom as still future. Furthermore, these sayings involve rather complicated problems of translation and interpretation. Three of these sayings require special comment.

The most startling statement about the kingdom as *present* appears in a brief narrative that has the marks of an abbreviated pronouncement story:

> Once Jesus was asked by the Pharisees when the kingdom of God was coming, and he answered, "The kingdom of God is not coming with things that can be observed; nor will they say, 'Look, here it is!' or 'There it is!' For in fact, the kingdom of God is among [*entos*] you." (Luke 17:20-21; cf. GThom 113:1-4)

The Greek preposition *entos* can be translated "within" (as in the King James Version). This translation implies a very individualistic and spiritual view of the kingdom's presence. But it is unlikely that the story intends to present Jesus as telling the Pharisees that the "kingdom of God is *within you*" (italics added). The translation "among" or "in the midst of," therefore, is more satisfactory and just as possible grammatically. Some interpreters, however, have denied that the contrast here is between the kingdom as future and the kingdom as present. They see a contrast between the future kingdom whose arrival can be calculated and the future kingdom that arrives suddenly without warning. Accordingly, they contend that the reply of Jesus means "*suddenly* the kingdom *will be* among you." But the translation "the kingdom of God is among you" is more faithful to the written text and probably conveys the intended meaning. The Pharisees approach Jesus with the traditional apocalyptic question about the time of the kingdom's arrival. Their question presupposes the apocalyptic conviction that the time of the kingdom's arrival can be calculated on the basis of external signs such as wars, famines, and earthquakes. Jesus' reply repudiates the notion of calculation. He also tells the Pharisees that their looking for the future kingdom results in their overlooking the kingdom present in him and his ministry.

Another saying about the kingdom as present appears in the Gospels of Matthew and Luke. These Gospel writers have inserted a Q saying into the Markan account of the Beelzebub controversy. Jesus declares:

> "But if it is by the Spirit of God ["finger of God," in Luke] that I cast out demons, then the kingdom of God has come [*ephthasen*] to you." (Matt. 12:28 = Luke 11:20)

Some interpreters claim that the Greek verb *ephthasen* here means "to draw near" rather than "to arrive." The translation "has come" reflects the latter meaning and is to be preferred. The parable of the strong man bound (Mark 3:27 par.; cf. GThom. 35:1-2), which immediately follows this saying in Matthew and Luke, suggests that these Gospel writers understood the verb to mean "has come." By casting out demons, Jesus has already—in his ministry—initiated the process of binding the "strong man," Satan.

Also, Luke reports that when the seventy disciples joyfully announce their successful control over demons, Jesus says: "I watched Satan fall from heaven like a flash of lightning" (Luke 10:18). Jesus refers here not to the primal fall of Satan but to the fall of Satan through the disciples' victory over the demonic hosts. The exorcisms by Jesus and his followers, therefore, represent the beginning of the end for the forces of evil. The expected future kingdom is already present in the ministry of Jesus.

There is still another important saying about the kingdom as present preserved in the Gospels of Matthew and Luke. In the Matthean form of this Q saying, Jesus says:

> "From the days of John the Baptist until now the kingdom of heaven has suffered violence, and the violent take it by force. For all the prophets and the law prophesied until John came." (Matt. 11:12-13 = Luke 16:16)

One thing is apparent in spite of a variety of issues raised by this statement. Jesus declares the law and the prophets to have been superseded by the kingdom present in and through his own ministry.

Thus the Synoptics contain evidence that Jesus viewed the kingdom of God as both future and present, not yet but already. A dialectical relationship between the future and the present appears in several kinds of teaching material. There are, as we have seen, future Son of Man sayings in which the basis for final judgment is one's present acceptance or rejection of Jesus and his message (Mark 8:38 par.). There are also paradoxical statements that announce a future reversal of one's present fortune and status. The first will be last, and the last first (Mark 10:31 par.). The humble will be exalted, and the exalted brought low (Matt. 18:4; 23:11-12; Luke 14:11; 18:14). The beatitudes express this principle of reversal; and two of them refer to the kingdom (Matt. 5:3 = Luke 6:20, GThom. 54; Matt. 5:10). Finally, there are those kingdom parables that sharply contrast an insignificant beginning with a great consummation. These so-called contrast parables include the parables of the mustard seed (Mark 4:30-32 par.; GThom. 20:1-4) and the leaven (Matt. 13:33 = Luke 13:20-21; GThom. 96:1-3). The kingdom of God does appear to have both a present and a future dimension in the teaching of Jesus as reported by the Gospel writers. But our review of the literary evidence leads us to consider the kingdom theme in the message of the historical Jesus.

Eschatology and Jesus

An occasional scholar has argued that Jesus historically preferred the expression *kingdom of heaven*, and not *kingdom of God*. Shirley Jackson Case, in his biography of Jesus, used his principle of suitability to reach this conclusion.[6] The phrase *kingdom of heaven* was common within Palestinian Judaism. Jesus was a Palestinian Jew. Therefore it was suitable for Jesus to prefer this expression. But most interpreters have concluded that Jesus used the phrase *kingdom of God*. Two obvious reasons support the majority conclusion. First, the Gospel evidence suggests that kingdom of heaven is redactional in Matthew and thereby characterizes the speech of the Matthean Jewish-Christian community. In the Synoptics, the phrase *kingdom of heaven* appears only in Matthew, and often in passages where Mark and Luke have *kingdom of God*. Furthermore, Matthew in a few passages also reads *kingdom of God* (Matt. 12:28; 19:24; 21:31, 43; and John 3:3, 5). And John, in the two rare references to the kingdom, uses the phrase *kingdom of God*, not *kingdom of heaven* (John 3:3, 5). Second, the phrase *kingdom of God* is understandable on Jesus' lips insofar as he otherwise addressed God in unconventional fashion. He addressed God with the intimate *'abbā'* ("Father") instead of the more formal *'ābînû* ("Our Father"). Consequently, *kingdom of heaven* represents the language of Matthew and *kingdom of God* recalls the actual speech of Jesus.

During the modern era of biblical criticism and the historical quest, at least five main ways of interpreting what *the kingdom of God* meant to Jesus have emerged. As implied in our previous discussions, two of these ways have come to represent the principal alternatives during the current period of Jesus research.

1. Jesus' kingdom preaching has been interpreted *spiritually/ethically*. This approach was especially characteristic of nineteenth-century theological liberalism but persists in much later writings about the historical Jesus.[7]

The kingdom of God is understood as the spiritual/ethical rule of God. That rule is spiritual in the heart of the individual, or truly "within you" (Luke 17:20-21). That rule is also ethical. The commandment of love of God and neighbor provides the substance for and the guiding principle of the kingdom (Mark 12:28-34 par.). Understood this way, the kingdom for Jesus was both *present and future*. Although the kingdom was present in his ministry among his disciples, it extended into the future through the work of the church in society at large. The kingdom parables of the mustard seed and the leaven within this perspective suggest not so much contrast as growth. These parables signal an evolutionary development as humankind responds to God through Jesus by building the kingdom on earth. The more apocalyptic aspects of Jesus' message are obviously de-emphasized or denied. On the one hand, it may be alleged that Jesus lapsed into traditional apocalyptic talk in the last dark days of his life (Mark 13 par.). On the other hand, it may be said that apocalyptic portions of his reported teaching derive not from him but from his more apocalyptically minded followers. But however explained, Jesus' apocalyptic speech was nonessential to his understanding of the kingdom even if he used such speech.

2. Jesus' kingdom preaching has also been interpreted in terms of a *futuristic eschatology*. This position was dramatically set forth by Albert Schweitzer in his attack on the liberal interpretation of the historical career of Jesus.[8]

The kingdom of God is understood as the supernatural rule of God at the end of history. The kingdom is not built by human effort but brought by God. Jesus' ministry, however, was closely related to the kingdom. Jesus had as his objective the preparation of his hearers for its advent in the near future, and he called for repentance and moral renewal. Nonetheless, the kingdom of God was wholly future from the standpoint of Jesus in his ministry. Some of Jesus' teachings admittedly seem to declare the presence of the kingdom; but they do not, according to this viewpoint. Jesus' exorcisms, for example, do not testify to the kingdom's arrival but simply represent tokens or signs of its nearness (Matt. 12:28 = Luke 11:20). The kingdom parables of the mustard seed and the leaven do not proclaim the insignificant beginnings of the kingdom during Jesus' ministry in anticipation of its complete manifestation later. These parables instead identify the present as the time of preparation and the future as the time of consummation. If Jesus had a "messianic consciousness," at least according to Schweitzer's interpretation, it was not a consciousness of his being the Messiah during his ministry. Instead, Jesus viewed himself as the

Messiah-to-be who would be glorified as the Son of Man/Messiah when the kingdom came with power. Within this perspective of futuristic eschatology, the apocalyptic aspects of Jesus' teachings are maximized.

3. Jesus' kingdom preaching has been further interpreted in terms of a *realized eschatology.* This view was initially advocated by C. H. Dodd in conscious opposition to the futuristic views of such interpreters as Albert Schweitzer.

The kingdom of God is understood as that rule of God that has already arrived in the ministry of Jesus, including his death and resurrection. Jesus, according to this interpretation, declared the kingdom to be *present* in himself, in the midst of his contemporaries (Luke 17:20-21). The parables of the mustard seed and the leaven do not proclaim the insignificant beginnings of the kingdom in Jesus' ministry in anticipation of its complete manifestation at the end. These parables instead identify the past as the time of preparation and the present as the time of consummation. All that was anticipated in Israel of old has been brought to fulfillment in the historic ministry of Jesus. Now is the rule of God! Jesus' teachings admittedly often contain apocalyptic images about the end of history. But Jesus has used these apocalyptic images to refer to his earthly ministry. Now is the harvest! Now is the judgment! Also talk by Jesus that seemingly identifies him as the Son of Man, not only in his earthly activity but at the end of history in accordance with Daniel 7:13, is just another way of talking about his victory over death. Jesus and his followers, therefore, do have a future. But their future is beyond history, beyond space and time. Within this perspective of realized eschatology, apocalyptic speech is not dismissed as nonessential, but it has been reinterpreted nonapocalyptically.

4. Jesus' kingdom preaching has been interpreted in terms of an *inaugurated eschatology.* This view shows indebtedness to the insights of both futuristic and realized eschatology. This view has among its proponents such scholars as Günther Bornkamm, but is by no means confined to representatives of the "new quest."

The kingdom of God is understood as that supernatural rule of God at the end of history. The apocalyptic nature of Jesus' preaching is clearly recognized. But the expected future rule of God has already dawned in and through Jesus' words and deeds, his activity and teaching. Inaugurated by Jesus, therefore, the kingdom had for him *both future and present dimensions.* The parables of the mustard seed and the leaven express this dialectical relationship between the not yet and the now. The future Son of Man sayings that distinguish between the coming Son of Man and Jesus in his ministry also express the interrelationship between the not yet and the now (Mark 8:38 par.). The kingdom proclaimed by Jesus reflected the two dimensions of future and present in keeping with the older liberal noneschatological interpretation. But from the perspective of inaugurated eschatology, the kingdom of God represents God's activity through Jesus and not human activity in response to Jesus.

5. During the most recent phase of the historical quest, Jesus' message of the kingdom of God has been understood in two divergent ways. On the one hand, there has been the reaffirmation of a *futuristic eschatology*. On the other hand, there has been the denial of a futuristic eschatology accompanied by an emphasis upon a *present eschatology*.

The first way of understanding Jesus' kingdom message carries forward the legacy, but does not simply replicate the work, of Albert Schweitzer. Like Schweitzer, the proponents of this view—notably E. P. Sanders, but also N. T. Wright, in his own way—understand the kingdom of God as announced by Jesus to have been imminently future. According to Sanders, Jesus expected this kingdom to be established through the direct intervention of God, not by human effort, and to involve the elimination of evil, the building of a new Temple, and the reassembling of Israel centered in Jerusalem under the leadership of Jesus and his disciples.[9] Although some sayings—such as those regarding the apocalyptic Son of Man—suggest that a cosmic event will introduce the coming kingdom, these sayings emphasize *how* the kingdom will come on earth and do not signal the end of the space-time universe. Those sayings that seem to declare the presence of the kingdom can be explained in others ways (Matt. 12:28 = Luke 11:20; Luke 17:20-21, GThom. 113:1-4). The kingdom parables of the mustard seed and the leaven would have been heard in Galilee as statements about the invisibility of the kingdom that was coming. In anticipation, Jesus simply asked his hearers to live right. Schweitzer's Jesus went to Jerusalem to take the sufferings of the end-time upon himself, with the certainty that he would be revealed as the Son of Man/Messiah. Sanders' Jesus also went to Jerusalem as the eschatological prophet with the expectation that God's kingdom would come and that God's will would be done on earth as in heaven. Just as Schweitzer's Jesus was wrong, so Sanders' Jesus was also mistaken.

This second way of understanding Jesus' kingdom message represents the polar opposite of the view set forth by Albert Schweitzer and many of his more recent successors. More than a decade ago, Marcus J. Borg presented what he called "a temperate case for a non-eschatological Jesus."[10] By "a non-eschatological Jesus," he meant a Jesus who did *not* expect the end of the world in his own generation.

Since then, Borg's noneschatological Jesus has become—in the work of many scholars—a Jesus who understood the kingdom of God to be wholly *present* in and through his own vision and program, through his own words and deeds. This Jesus is no eschatological prophet but a sage.

John Dominic Crossan is a representative of this point of view, although he still refers to Jesus' kingdom message as eschatological. In his view, Jesus' kingdom was not about an apocalyptic kingdom in the future but a sapiential kingdom here and now.[11] The word *sapiential*—from the Latin for "wisdom"—

describes that pragmatic approach to life expressed in such wisdom writings as the book of Proverbs and the Wisdom of Solomon. But Jesus was the purveyor and practitioner of a countercultural wisdom that challenged conventional values and behaviors. The parable of the mustard seed, for example, actually mocks the apocalyptic use of a great tree, such as the cedar, to symbolize God's coming kingdom. In the ancient world, mustard was viewed as an undesirable plant that grew uncontrollably in uncultivated areas—like kudzu in our southern states—and in cultivated areas attracted unwanted birds to nest in its shade.[12] Furthermore, according to Crossan, the only Son of Man saying that probably originated with Jesus was his saying "Foxes have holes, and birds of the air have nests; but the Son of Man has nowhere to lay his head" (Matt. 8:20 = Luke 9:58; GThom. 86:1-2). But here the phrase *son of man* was not a self-referential title but a generic way of talking about human beings, specifically about the poor and destitute. It was with them that Jesus practiced what Crossan called "a radical egalitarianism" and Schüssler Fiorenza labeled "a discipleship of equals." Thus she speaks of Jesus as a wisdom prophet. Robert W. Funk, who belongs to this interpretive tradition, can even say that Jesus' poetic vision of the kingdom of God was such that "he did not distinguish the past, present, and future as modes of time."[13] Thus the long history of discussion about the time of the kingdom's coming also includes an atemporal point of view.[14]

10

Torah Teaching (Ethics)

In his wandering ministry, Jesus proclaimed the rule of God and called his hearers to repentance. He also stated the implications of that rule for those who accepted his call. He talked about his claim on their lives and the will of God for their lives. He talked about their responsibility toward God, toward one another, and toward others. Jesus the preacher was at the same time a teacher. Like other scribes or rabbis of his day, Jesus often quoted and commented on the Torah, the commandments given by God through Moses to Israel. His exposition of the Torah often involved what we identify as ethical teachings. He made statements about what persons "ought" to do in relation to themselves, their possessions, and other persons. But the ethical teachings of Jesus, as we shall see, are by no means confined to an exposition of the Torah.

Gospel Writers and Gospel Traditions

In the Gospel of John, Jesus gives only one commandment of an ethical nature to his disciples. On the eve of his crucifixion he declares what he calls a "new commandment": "...that you love one another. Just as I have loved you, you also should love one another" (John 13:34; also 15:12). This commandment is "new." It neither reproduces nor explicitly expounds any of the old commandments of the Torah. By contrast, in the Gospels of Mark, Matthew, and Luke, Jesus quotes two love commandments from the Torah. He uses them as a summary of what the Torah requires.

Torah Summary

Each Synoptic writer tells a story in which Jesus singles out, by word or approval, two commandments in the Torah as paramount above all others: Deuteronomy 6:5 and Leviticus 19:18. In Mark, the story about the first commandment appears as an extended dialogue between Jesus and a scribe:

> One of the scribes came near and heard them disputing with one another, and seeing that he answered them well, he asked him, "Which commandment is the first of all?" Jesus answered, "The first is, 'Hear, O Israel: The Lord our God, the Lord is one; you shall love the Lord your God with all your heart, and with all your soul, and with all your mind, and with all your strength.' The second is this, 'You shall love your neighbor as yourself.' There is no other commandment greater than these." Then the scribe said to him, "You are right, Teacher; you have truly said that 'he is one, and besides him there is no other'; and 'to love him with all the heart, and with all the understanding, and with all the strength,' and 'to love one's neighbor as oneself,'—this is much more important than all whole burnt offerings and sacrifices." When Jesus saw that he answered wisely, he said to him, "You are not far from the kingdom of God." After that no one dared to ask him any question. (Mark 12:28-34 par.)

As with the "new commandment" in John, so here in Mark: *Jesus identifies love as the cardinal ethical category.* But there are important differences between the love commandment in John and the one in Mark.

First, in John, love is exclusively an ethical category, as Jesus commands his disciples to love one another. But in Mark, love is also descriptive of the individual's disposition toward God, in accordance with Deut. 6:5. Love of God and love of neighbor are brought together into the closest possible relationship. Love of God must express itself in love of neighbor; and love of neighbor will spring forth from love of God. Such love is also affirmed to be more important than burnt offerings and sacrifices.

Second, in John, the standard for ethical love is Jesus' own self-giving, sacrificial love. But in Mark, the standard for ethical love is love of oneself, in accordance with Lev. 19:18.

Third, in John, the love commandment is addressed to Jesus' own disciples and they are commanded to love one another and not outsiders, much less enemies. But in Mark, the love commandment has a broader appeal and requires love of "your neighbor"—again in accordance with Lev. 19:18. Within first-century Palestinian Judaism, the word *neighbor* would probably have had "fellow Jew" as its principal referent, although an adjacent commandment declares: "you shall love the alien as yourself" (Lev. 19:34). The Lukan version of this story reports that Jesus, upon request by the lawyer, defined the meaning of the term *neighbor* by telling the parable of the good Samaritan (Luke 10:30-35). Consequently, Jesus extended the meaning of *neighbor* to include outsiders, even enemies. Furthermore, the parable of the good Samaritan brings with it an implied definition of love. Love appears as an active concern for the well-being of the other person, as witnessed in the care extended by the Samaritan toward the injured traveler. Love appears to be neither a sentimental feeling nor even a liking for the other person.

Three Greek words are often used to delineate more sharply the character of Christian love. Christian love is described as *agapē*, self-giving or sacrificial love. This kind of love is compared with *philia*, mutual love or friendship, and *erōs*, romantic love or desire. Such a characterization of distinctively Christian love certainly receives support from the view of love enacted in the two love commandments in John and the Synoptics.[1]

The *Gospel of Thomas* also has a love commandment that recalls elements of both the Johannine and the Synoptic commandments: "Love your brother like your soul" (GThom. 25:1). The object of love, "your brother" has familial connotations like the "one another" in John. But the criterion of love, "like your soul," corresponds to the "as yourself" in the Synoptics.

Torah Commentary and Torah Controversy

Among the Synoptic writers, Matthew most self-consciously drapes Jesus in the mantle of a scribe. A major portion of his celebrated Sermon on the Mount constitutes a formal commentary on the Torah into which he has incorporated some of Jesus' most radical teachings (Matt. 5:17-48). Six statements of contrast by Jesus provide the structure for this commentary. Jesus introduces each contrasting statement with these familiar words: "You have heard that it was said . . . But I say to you . . ." (vss. 21, 27, 31, 33, 38, 43). The differences between the commandments in the Torah of Moses and the interpretation of Jesus can be summarized thus:

No murder (Exod. 20:13; Deut. 5:17)	No anger
No adultery (Exod. 20:14; Deut. 5:18)	No lust
Divorce allowed (Deut. 24:1)	Divorce—only for unchastity
No false swearing (Lev. 19:12)	No swearing
Eye for an eye (Exod. 21:24)	No resistance to evil
Love of neighbor (Lev. 19:18)	Love of enemy

In these so-called antitheses, *Jesus emphasizes the importance of inner attitude behind outward acts and extends the scope of outward acts of love to include even enemies.*[2]

Jesus in his interpretation of the Torah prohibits not only such deeds as murder and adultery. He also condemns the attitudes that produce these deeds—anger and lust.

Jesus reportedly allows for divorce on the sole ground of unchastity. Scholars generally acknowledge, however, that this allowance represents an addition by Matthew to Jesus' actual teaching on the subject (cf. Matt. 5:32; 19:9 with Mark 10:1-12 par.; 1 Cor. 7:10). In the Markan account, Jesus refuses to state any grounds for divorce. He suggests that Moses allows for divorce only as a concession to human sinfulness and prefers to talk about the purpose of marriage as given in the creation narrative from the book of Genesis.

Jesus further expresses the absoluteness of his claims on the individual by prohibiting both swearing and resistance to evil. To his statement on nonresistance to evil are appended those memorable injunctions about turning the other cheek, surrendering cloak as well as coat, going the second mile, and giving to anyone who begs.

The final antithesis by Jesus involves the commandment from Lev. 19:18 that Jesus, in Mark and Matthew, combines with Deut. 6:5 to form his love commandment. In Luke, Jesus expanded the meaning of *neighbor* to include one's enemy through his parable of the good Samaritan. But here he contrasts love of "enemy" with love of "neighbor"; and he commands love of enemies because God likewise makes the sun shine and the rain fall on the wicked and on the righteous (Matt. 5:45). This command to love enemies is itself a Q saying (Matt. 5:44 = Luke 6:27, 35).

Jesus appears in the Sermon on the Mount, therefore, as a teacher who systematically comments on the Torah. But in the Synoptics generally, he is clearly not just another teacher of the Torah. Jesus often finds himself embroiled in controversy with religious leaders because of his alleged failure to observe the Torah. In these controversy stories, Jesus further emphasizes the importance of inner attitude behind outward acts and also suggests that *acts of love take priority over narrowly understood religious requirements and customs.* Two of the main issues that set Jesus at odds with the religious leaders were those related to eating or dietary customs and to observance of the Sabbath.

Great emphasis was placed in Jesus' day on eating with the right people, eating in the right manner, and eating the right food because of a concern for ritual purity (see Lev. 17–26). Jesus caused dismay by his association at table fellowship with those referred to as "tax collectors and sinners." His defense of this practice rested ultimately on the character of God as one who loves and grants mercy. Jesus reportedly quoted the word of God from Hosea: "I desire mercy and not sacrifice" (Hos. 6:6 = Matt. 9:13; 12:7). He also dramatized the undeserved mercy of God in such parables as the two debtors (Luke 7:41-42), the lost sheep (Matt. 18:12-13 = Luke 15:3-6; GThom. 107:1-3), the lost coin (Luke 15:8-9), the prodigal son (Luke 15:11-32), and the laborers in the vineyard (Matt. 20:1-15). Jesus and his disciples were also accused of eating with unwashed hands. In defense, Jesus responded with a declaration remarkable for a culture that placed so much emphasis on the distinction between the clean and the unclean: "There is nothing outside a person that by going in can defile, but the things that come out are what defile" (Mark 7:15 par.). Later Jesus explained what defiles a person: "fornication, theft, murder, adultery, avarice, wickedness, deceit, licentiousness, envy, slander, pride, folly" (Mark 7:21-22 par.). This catalog served notice that for Jesus a person's inner disposition and outward words and deeds in relation to others were more important than religious ritual.

Great emphasis was also placed in Jesus' day on keeping the Sabbath holy (Exod. 20:8-11; Deut. 5:12-15). Jesus periodically violated the Sabbath in the eyes of his contemporaries by healing persons with various disabilities. On one occasion he and his disciples were accused of working on the Sabbath by plucking grain, or gleaning. Jesus defended his actions by an assortment of pronouncements. Perhaps the most penetrating of these pronouncements followed the incident involving the plucking of grain: "The sabbath was made for humankind, and not humankind for the sabbath" (Mark 2:27). This saying alludes to the story of creation in Genesis where God created humankind on the sixth day before resting on the seventh (Gen. 1:27; 2:2). Jesus thereby used the Torah itself to reinterpret the commandment to keep the day holy. Jesus subordinated the religious requirement of Sabbath observance to the principle of meeting human need, even incidental hunger. Jesus also invoked the principle of meeting human need to justify his healing on that day. He often argued from the lesser to the greater: since animals are cared for on the Sabbath, and humans are of greater value than animals, then humans should be cared for on the Sabbath (Mark 3:1-6 par.; Luke 13:10-17).

Jesus, however, not only defended his own actions, he also attacked verbally the upholders of the Torah: scribe and Pharisee (Mark 7:9-13 par.; Matt. 23:1-36 = Luke 11:37-52; 20:45-47). Given Jesus' reported concern for purity of heart and righteousness of behavior, it is not surprising that he discovered the religious leadership of his day sadly deficient on both counts. Inwardly they were "full of greed and self-indulgence" and outwardly "neglected the weightier matters of the law: justice and mercy and faith" (Matt. 23:25 = Luke 11:39; Matt. 23:23 = Luke 11:42).

Although Jesus, according to the Gospels, aroused the indignation of the religious leaders and even verbally attacked them, *he did not wholly reject the Torah or the religious system sanctioned by the Torah*. He attended the synagogue and participated in synagogue worship (Mark 1:21-28 par.; 6:1-6 par.; Luke 4:16-30; 13:10-17). He recognized the authority of the priest (Mark 1:40-45 par.). He also acknowledged the validity of sacrifice in the Temple and financial contributions for the Temple (Matt. 5:23-24; Mark 12:41-44 par.; Matt. 17:24-27). Jesus visited Jerusalem for such pilgrimage festivals as Passover (Mark 14:12-25 par.; and John 2:13; 5:1; 7:1-10; 11:55-57). He also supported the sincere practice of the three principal expressions of personal piety: almsgiving (Matt. 6:2-4), prayer (Matt. 6:5-8), and fasting (Matt. 6:16-18). Nonetheless, Jesus did appeal in his teaching and his behavior to the will of God that transcended the Torah and the religious system sanctioned by the Torah. This was the God whose kingdom, or rule, had drawn near through him and his ministry.

Beyond the Torah

The Synoptic writers identify the kingdom of God as the central theme of Jesus' message and ministry. They recognize that Jesus' Torah teaching presupposes his kingdom preaching. The account of the love commandment in Mark also indicates a connection between Jesus' proclamation of the kingdom and his exposition of the Torah. Jesus concluded his conversation with the scribe with these words: "You are not far from the kingdom of God" (Mark 12:28-34). This scribe in Mark may have been separated from the kingdom of God only by an act of repentance on his part, for elsewhere in Mark Jesus presents repentance as the appropriate response to his kingdom message (Mark 1:15). The Greek infinitive "to repent," *metanoein,* literally means "to change the mind." But the underlying Hebraic idea suggests a "change of direction." A positive response to Jesus and his preaching, therefore, may have drastic consequences for the individual—a reversal of direction, a break with the past, a reordering of values and priorities.

Some of Jesus' most shocking sayings represent a reversal of direction. Sometimes these sayings have the character of broad principles. At other times they are addressed to specific persons. Often they involve such rhetorical techniques as overstatement and dramatic speech. Most of these sayings have ethical implications. If taken literally, many of them appear to be what we would call unethical. They seemingly contradict some of Jesus' ethical pronouncements we have examined in relation to his Torah teaching. However dealt with, they cannot be ignored.

Jesus on various occasions and in different settings called upon his hearers to respond to him and his message by turning from—

adulthood to childhood
    from family harmony to family estrangement
        from family estrangement to a new family
            from wealth seeking to wealth abandonment
                from honored status to lowliness
                    from physical wholeness to mutilation
                        from comfort to suffering and death.

Jesus extolled the quality of childlikeness: "Truly, I tell you, whoever does not receive the kingdom of God as a little child will never enter it" (Mark 10:15 par.; cf. John 3:3, 5; and GThom. 22:1-3; 37:1-2; 46:2).

In talking about family relations, Jesus could use the language of hatred instead of love: "Whoever comes to me and does not hate father and mother, wife and children, brothers and sisters, yes, and even life itself, cannot be my disciple" (Luke 14:26 = Matt. 10:37; also Matt. 10:34-36 = Luke 12:51-53). Jesus said to the man with the implied family responsibility of burying his father: "Let the dead bury their own dead; but as for you, go and proclaim the kingdom of God" (Luke 9:59-60, 61-62 = Matt. 8:21-22).

Jesus not only called for separation from one's natural family, but he redefined family in terms of obedience to the will of God. When informed that his own family—mother, brothers, and sisters—wanted to see him, Jesus replied: "Whoever does the will of God is my brother and sister and mother" (Mark 3:31-35 par.; GThom. 99:1-3).

Jesus frequently warned about the dangers of wealth. He offered an emphatic either/or when he said: "You cannot serve God and wealth," or "mammon," an English rendering of an Aramaic word meaning "wealth" (Matt. 6:24 = Luke 16:13). He counseled against amassing treasures on earth and against anxiety about earthly matters (Matt. 6:19-21 = Luke 12:33-34; Matt. 6:25-34 = Luke 12:22-31). To the man with great possessions, Jesus declared: "You lack one thing; go, sell what you own, and give the money to the poor, and you will have treasure in heaven; then come, follow me" (Mark 10:17-31 par.).

Jesus also directed criticism, or extended advice, to those who sought positions of social prominence. He began his parable of the places at table with this line: "When you are invited by someone to a wedding banquet, do not sit down at the place of honor" (Luke 14:8-10). He called James and John to servanthood when they requested positions of honor beside him: "Whoever wishes to become great among you must be your servant, and whoever wishes to be first among you must be slave of all" (Mark 10:35-45 par.; cf. John 13:1-20).

As if loss of family, loss of wealth, and loss of status were not enough, Jesus could also talk in terms of self-inflicted injury: "If your hand causes you to stumble, cut it off.... And if your foot causes you to stumble, cut if off.... And if your eye causes you to stumble, tear it out. . . ." (Mark 9:43-48; also Matt. 5:29-30). But these were not the only extremities threatened. He concluded his discussion about divorce and marriage with this observation: "There are eunuchs who have made themselves eunuchs for the sake of the kingdom of heaven" (Matt. 19:10-12).

The ultimate price to be paid for following Jesus, of course, was life itself. "If any want to become my followers, let them deny themselves and take up their cross and follow me. For those who want to save their life will lose it, and those who lose their life for my sake, and for the sake of the gospel, will save it" (Mark 8:34-35 par.; also Mark 13:9-13 par.; Matt. 5:10-11 = Luke 6:22).

We began our discussion of Jesus' Torah teaching with the love commandment formulated on the basis of Deut. 6:5 and Lev. 19:18. In this love commandment, Jesus brought together the vertical love of God with the horizontal love of neighbor and the circular love of oneself. Jesus, in the midst of controversy over keeping the Torah, indicated repeatedly that the well-being of the neighbor and the well-being of oneself take priority over certain religious obligations. But in the repentance—or reversal—sayings just reviewed, the claims of the kingdom and the demands of discipleship often appear to point in the direction of alienation from others and abuse of oneself. There is a tension between the love of God, on the one hand, and the love of neighbor as oneself, on the other. Our survey of this literary evidence leads us to consider the ministry of the historical Jesus and the possible relationship therein between his kingdom preaching and his Torah teaching, between eschatology and ethics.

Ethics and Jesus

Jesus' ethical teachings confront the Christian believer with the question of the relationship between such uncompromising sayings as those preserved in the Sermon on the Mount and life in the contemporary world. Prohibitions against anger, lust, divorce, oaths, and retaliation, to say nothing of the command to love enemies, seem so impractical and impossible. The church over the centuries has concerned itself with the relevance of Jesus' ethical teachings. But scholars participating in the historical quest focus more sharply on the intention of Jesus in making these pronouncements and how they fit into his career. At least five ways of understanding Jesus' ethical teachings have emerged out of this quest. Each approach corresponds to one of the ways of interpreting what the kingdom of God meant to Jesus. Just as the most recent phase of Jesus research is characterized by two competing viewpoints about Jesus' eschatological outlook, so the latest phase is also characterized by two different claims about Jesus' ethical stance.

1. Jesus' ethical teachings have been interpreted as a *noneschatological ethic.* This approach typified nineteenth-century theological liberalism and many representatives of the "old quest." Jesus is often depicted as a teacher of true religion, or even a moralist.

There is here little appreciation for the apocalyptic nature of his kingdom preaching. In fact, his kingdom preaching is viewed in the light of his Torah teaching. The kingdom of God is that spiritual-ethical rule of God both present during the earthly ministry of Jesus and extending into the future through the work of the community he established. The love commandment constitutes the center and substance of Jesus' ministry (Mark 12:28-34 par.). The rule of God is spiritual insofar as people love God and ethical insofar as they love neighbor. Within this perspective, Jesus' basic objective was the transformation of the human heart, although he may have desired all society to be increasingly brought under the rule of God. He did not, therefore, intend to burden people with a new set of laws. His more radical teachings in the Sermon on the Mount had as their objective the transformation of the heart and are to be understood more figuratively than literally (Matt. 5:17-48).

2. Jesus' ethical teachings have been interpreted as an *ethic of preparation* within the context of a futuristic eschatology. Albert Schweitzer popularized this approach and described the ethic of Jesus as an "interim ethic."

Jesus is portrayed as an apocalyptist who proclaims the kingdom of God as future but imminent. In anticipation of the coming rule of God, Jesus calls his hearers to repentance or moral renewal. His ethical teachings, therefore, were intended by him for that brief interim between his proclamation of the kingdom and its arrival in power. Only those whose lives had been transformed would be fit for the kingdom and found acceptable at the coming judgment. Consequently, Jesus did intend for his more radical teachings to be followed. Perhaps a person could for a few weeks or months avoid anger, lust, divorce, oaths, and retaliation—and could even love enemies (Matt. 5:17-48; Mark 12:28-34 par.; Luke 10:30-35). This conviction that Jesus taught an ethic of preparation receives support from the word order of his message as summarized in Matthew: "Repent, the kingdom of heaven has come near" (Matt. 4:17; also 3:2). Repentance, or moral renewal, precedes the arrival of the kingdom of God.

3. Jesus' ethical teachings have also been interpreted as an *ethic of response* within the context of a realized eschatology. C. H. Dodd represents this viewpoint, but it is congenial to many other interpreters who understand the kingdom of God to have been present in some sense in the historic ministry of Jesus. They often describe the ethic of Jesus as a "kingdom ethic." Jesus the servant Messiah intended his ethical teachings for persons who had already placed themselves under the rule of God as proclaimed and realized through him. The rule of God cannot be reduced to an ethic but did include an ethical dimension. Jesus summarized the fundamental responsibility for persons living under the rule of God with his love commandment: love of God and love of neighbor as oneself, with the love of neighbor including the love of enemies (Mark 12:28-34 par.; Luke 10:30-35). Within the perspective of a realized eschatology in which the end of history was not viewed as imminent, Jesus intended his more radical sayings to serve as something of an ideal for persons living under the rule of God here and now (Matt. 5:17-48). These ethical statements of Jesus, like his parables, present dramatic pictures of the kind of action that might be appropriate under the rule of God. These statements rep-

resent examples, not laws. They provide standards by which human conduct under the rule of God might be judged and found wanting, on the one hand, and challenged to greater obedience, on the other.

4. Jesus' ethical teachings have been *interpreted existentially as eschatology.* This tendency, foreshadowed by Rudolf Bultmann, appears in the "new quest" writings of Günther Bornkamm within the context of an inaugurated eschatology.

Jesus of Nazareth proclaimed the kingdom of God as both future and present. There is here a clear recognition of the apocalyptic character of Jesus' kingdom preaching. But that future rule of God commonly expected at the end of history had begun through the words and deeds of Jesus in the present. Jesus' kingdom preaching, moreover, was paralleled by his Torah teaching. His Torah teaching included such ethical sayings as those pronouncements in the Sermon on the Mount (Matt. 5:17-48) and the love commandment (Mark 12:28-34 par.; Luke 10:30-35). Jesus intended by his ethical teachings, however, not to offer detailed directives for human conduct but to confront his hearers with the sovereign will of God. His kingdom preaching and his ethical teachings, therefore, share the same basic purpose: to make God immediately present. Whereas many spokesmen for the "old quest" interpreted Jesus' kingdom preaching in terms of his ethical teaching, Bornkamm as representative of the "new quest" tends to interpret Jesus' ethical teaching in terms of his kingdom preaching. Jesus' ethical teaching itself appears as eschatology.[3]

5. During the most recent phase of the historical quest, Jesus' ethical teaching—like his message of the kingdom of God—has been understood in two divergent ways. For those who have reaffirmed a futuristic eschatology, Jesus' ethic has again been interpreted, in various ways, as an ethic of preparation. So interpreted, Jesus' ethic has again been understood in relation to the *Torah.* But for many who emphasize a present eschatology, Jesus' ethic has been understood not in relation to the Torah but as an appropriation of the *Wisdom tradition.* Thus the real issue about Jesus' ethic during the present phase of the quest has to do with its basis: Torah? Or Wisdom?

The first approach presupposes Jesus' expectation that God will soon restore Israel. There is a great concern—particularly by E. P. Sanders—to demonstrate that Jesus, as a Jew, did not deviate from acceptable interpretations of the Torah nor from appropriate behaviors based on the Torah. Jesus' summary of the Torah, by which he joined together the love commandments from Deut. 6:5 and Lev. 19:18 (Mark 12:28-34 par.), corresponds to similar summaries formulated by his contemporaries. Although Jesus' radical teachings preserved in the Sermon on the Mount (Matt. 5:17-48) may reflect a kind of "perfectionism" that goes beyond the letter of the Torah, these teachings in no way abrogate the Torah. Jesus simply expected his disciples to observe high moral standards. But the dominant note throughout Jesus' teachings was not one of condemnation but one of compassion and mercy. Neither did Jesus teach his disciples to break the Sabbath and dietary laws. The stories and sayings in the Synoptics that involve conflict between Jesus and his contemporaries, particularly the Pharisees, reflect the disputes in the later church. Although Geza Vermes views Jesus as a charismatic rabbi or *Hasid*, not as an eschatological prophet, he also argues at length that Jesus in no way contradicted the Torah or attacked traditional Judaism.[4]

Some scholars who have adopted the eschatological prophet model but also made messianic claims for Jesus—notably N. T. Wright—have been less concerned to minimize the differences between Jesus' ethical teaching and practice and those of his Jewish contemporaries. But Wright still interprets Jesus' ethic in relation to the Torah and views Jesus' summary of the Torah in itself as unremarkable (Mark 12:28-34 par.). However, Jesus' focus on love, as part of his overall eschatological program, becomes a basis for his redefining those markers that had separated Israel from the nations: Sabbath, food, nation, and Temple. Differences over these issues did spark controversy between Jesus and his fellow Jews. His radical teachings in the Sermon on the Mount, for instance, included instructions to his followers not to participate in resistance movements against the Romans (Matt. 5:17-48). Jesus himself replaces Torah as well as Temple.

By contrast, the other approach to Jesus' ethic that has emerged in recent years rests on the conclusion that Jesus historically did not comment in any formal way on the Torah. Neither the summary of the Torah (Mark 12:28-34 par.) nor the commentary on the Torah (Matt. 5:17-48) was formulated by the historical Jesus. Jesus was not a scribe but a sage whose kingdom message and ethic expressed themselves in parables and aphorisms. His teaching may even reflect some kind of indebtedness to the Cynics. Eschatology and ethics, therefore, represent a false distinction. The kingdom of God was present in and through the vision of reality and mode of existence shared by Jesus with his followers. Jesus' sapiential eschatology, as John Dominic Crossan calls it, was ethics. Although the category of sage represents only one dimension of Jesus' ministry for Marcus Borg, he describes Jesus' ethic in broad terms as a "politics of compassion" over against the reigning "politics of holiness." Jesus challenged the conventional understandings of family, wealth, honor, and religion. He did so in and through those startling sayings that were described earlier in this chapter as going beyond the Torah.[5] The summary of the Torah based on Deut. 6:5 and Lev. 19:18 may not come from Jesus. The formalized commentary on the Torah represented by the antitheses may not come from Jesus. However, the radical commands like "love your enemies" (Matt. 5:44 = Luke 6:27, 35)—a Q saying—are consistent with his teaching as a subversive sage.

191

11

Parables

The parable represented the most characteristic form of Jesus' speech. He used the parable as a vehicle for his proclamation of the kingdom of God since this involved not only relations to God but relations to oneself and to others. In this respect Jesus differed from later scribes, or rabbis, who used the parable as a means of expounding the Torah. But many of Jesus' parables did have at least an indirect relationship to the Torah. He used parables to proclaim an understanding and experience of God that on occasion seemingly led him to act contrary to religious custom, at least in matters of Sabbath observance and ritual purity. He also used parables to defend himself and his behavior against those who accused him of violating the commandments. Thus the parables of Jesus reflect not only an eschatological but an ethical dimension.

Gospel Writers and Gospel Traditions

In the Gospel of John, Jesus speaks in long and often repetitious discourses. These discourses contain a variety of literary images, including those of water and bread (chaps. 4 and 6), shepherd and sheep (chap. 10), vine and branches (chap. 15). But the Gospel of John does not contain a single parable.

Among the canonical Gospels, therefore, the parables of Jesus are preserved exclusively in the synoptic Gospels of Mark, Matthew, and Luke. But the *Gospel of Thomas* also has several parables. Some of these parables parallel those in the Synoptics; others were previously unknown. Scholars have generally agreed on forty or so Synoptic sayings of Jesus that can be classified as parables. The exact numbers differ according to their definitions of *parable* and their applications of their definitions to the Gospel evidence. We have classified as parables forty-five of Jesus' sayings in the Synoptics and sixteen of his sayings in the *Gospel of Thomas*, thirteen of which have parallels in the Synoptics. (See the chart JESUS' PARABLES on pages 194-95.)

A Definition of "Parable"

The parable as a literary form has been variously defined. The limitation of all such definitions as they relate to the parables of Jesus should be recognized. But the parables of Jesus can be defined as *figures of speech that make comparisons between commonplace objects, events, persons, and that transcendent reality symbolized by the phrase* the kingdom of God. An examination of this definition will enable us to identify the main features of the parables from the vantage point of contemporary scholarship. The parables of Jesus make a comparison. The very idea of comparison underlies the English word *parable*. In the Gospels, the English "parable" usually translates the Greek *parabolē*. The Greek term had been previously used within Judaism to translate the Hebrew *māshāl*. The basic meaning of both expressions is that of comparison.

The parables of Jesus have as their subject matter objects, events, and persons that are rather commonplace. The parables are so down to earth—the earth of first-century Galilee. They no doubt preserve the experiences of Jesus as he grew into adulthood in and around Nazareth. Much material in the parables comes from nature: vineyards; fig trees; mustard seed; wheat and weeds; fish and sheep. Some material comes from activity characteristic of a modest household or a small town: the leavening of bread; the sowing of seed; the search for a lost coin; a wedding and its festivities; children playing in the marketplace; a son leaving home for a life of his own; a man going on a journey. Still other material refers to social roles well-known in ancient Palestine: the judge; the tax collector and the Pharisee; the rich man and the beggar; the priest, the Levite, and a Samaritan.

The parables of Jesus, however, refer beyond themselves to that transcendent reality symbolized by the phrase *the kingdom of God*. Jesus introduces many of his parables with statements or questions. "The kingdom of God is as if...." "With what can we compare the kingdom of God?" Jesus often concludes his parables with comments that explain their meaning. "So...." "Just so, I tell you...." "Let anyone with ears listen!"

Consequently, the parables of Jesus do involve a comparison between the everyday and the transcendent, the earthly and the heavenly. But the parables are figures of speech. As such, the parables are closely related to those foundational images that involve a comparison, the simile and the metaphor. The *simile* makes a comparison between one object and another object by linking the one to the other with the words *as* or *like*. Jesus used similes: "See, I am sending you out like

JESUS' PARABLES

MARK

Cloth and Wineskins (Mark 2:21-22 par.)	Sower (Mark 4:3-8 par.)	Wicked Tenants (Mark 12:1-9 par.)
Divided Kingdom (Mark 3:24-26 par.)	Seed Growing Secretly (Mark 4:26-29)	Budding Fig Tree (Mark 13:28 par.)
Strong Man Bound (Mark 3:27 par.)	Mustard Seed (Mark 4:30-32 par.)	Doorkeeper (Mark 13:34-36 par.)

Q

Two Builders (Matt. 7:24-27=Luke 6:47-49)	Lost Sheep (Matt. 8:12-13=Luke 15:3-6)
Playing Children (Matt. 11:16-17=Luke 7:31-32)	Thief (Matt. 24:43=Luke 12:39)
Unclean Spirit (Matt. 12:43-45=Luke 11:24-26)	Faithful and Wise Servant (Matt. 24:45-51= Luke 12:42-48)
Leaven (Matt. 13:33=Luke 13:20-21)	

M

Weeds and Wheat (Matt. 13:24-30)	Unmerciful Servant (Matt. 18:23-34)	Wedding Garment (Matt. 22:11-13)
Hidden Treasure (Matt. 13:44)	Laborers in Vineyard (Matt. 20:1-15)	Ten Maidens (Matt. 25:1-12)
Pearl (Matt. 13:45-46)	Two Sons (Matt. 21:28-30)	Talents (Matt. 25:14-30)
Fishnet (Matt. 13:47-48)	Marriage Feast (Matt. 22:2-10)	Sheep and Goats (Matt. 25:31-46)

L

Two Debtors (Luke 7:41-42)	Great Banquet (Luke 14:16-24)	Rich Man and Lazarus (Luke 16:19-31)
Good Samaritan (Luke 10:30-35)	Tower Builder (Luke 14:28-30)	Farmer and His Servant (Luke 17:7-10)
Friend at Midnight (Luke 11:5-8)	Warring King (Luke 14:31-32)	Unjust Judge (Luke 18:2-5)
Rich Farmer (Luke 12:16-20)	Lost Coin (Luke 15:8-9)	Pharisee and Tax Collector (Luke 18:10-13)
Barren Fig Tree (Luke 13:6-9)	Prodigal Son (Luke 15:11-32)	Pounds (Luke 19:12-27)
Places at Table (Luke 14:8-10)	Unjust Steward (Luke 16:1-8)	

JESUS' PARABLES

THOMAS

Fishnet (GThom. 8:1-4; cf. Matt. 13:47-48)	Weeds and Wheat (GThom. 57:1-4 cf. Matt. 13:24-30)	Leaven (GThom. 96:1-3; cf. Matt. 13:33=Luke 13:20-21)
Sower (GThom. 9:1-5; cf. Mark 4:3-8 par.)	Rich Farmer (GThom. 63:1-4; cf. Luke 12:16-20)	Empty Jar (GThom. 97:1-4)
Mustard Seed (GThom. 20:1-4; cf. Mark 4:30-32 par.)	Feast (GThom. 64:1-11; cf. Luke 14:16-24)	Assassin (GThom. 98:1-3)
Children in Field (GThom. 21:2-4)	Wicked Tenants (GThom. 65:1-8; cf. Mark 12:1-9 par.)	Lost Sheep (GThom. 107:1-3; cf. Matt. 18:12-13= Luke 15:3-6)
Harvest (GThom. 21:4; cf. Mark 4:26-29)	Pearl (GThom. 76:1-3; cf. Matt. 13:45-46)	Hidden Treasure (GThom. 109:1-3; cf. Matt. 13:44)
Strong Man Bound (GThom. 35:1-2, cf. Mark 3:27 par.)		

sheep into the midst of wolves" (Matt. 10:16 = Luke 10:3). The disciples of Jesus are *as*, or *like*, sheep. The *metaphor* makes a comparison by substituting one object for another. Jesus also talked in metaphors: "I was sent only to the lost sheep of the house of Israel" (Matt. 15:24; also 10:5-6). The common folk *are* sheep. The expansion of a simple image or singular comparison into a narrative results in what has usually been called a *parable*. Jesus declared a parable about a lost sheep that was found: "If a shepherd has a hundred sheep, and one of them has gone astray, does he not leave the ninety-nine on the mountains and go in search of the one that went astray? And if he finds it, truly I tell you, he rejoices over it more than over the ninety-nine that never went astray" (Matt. 18:12-13 = Luke 15:3-6; GThom. 107:1-3). According to Matthew, Jesus derived from the parable a lesson about God's desire that all little ones be saved: "So it is not the will of your Father in heaven that one of these little ones should be lost" (Matt. 18:14).

The parable as an expanded simile or metaphor is also to be distinguished from the allegory. Like the parable, the allegory is a narrative that involves a comparison. But with allegory, all details have individualized and interrelated symbolic importance. Jesus in Matthew did not interpret the parable of the lost sheep allegorically. If he had, he could have explained the meaning of the details in this manner:

> shepherd = God or Jesus himself
> hundred sheep = all God's people
> ninety-nine sheep = religious folk
> one lost sheep = sinner
> mountains = places of worship

Essentially, however, the parables of Jesus are not allegories. Or, to state the contrast differently, *the parable tends to make a single point whereas the allegory makes many points*. The nonallegorical nature of the parables represents one of the assured insights of biblical scholarship over the past century. At the same time, it must be acknowledged that many of the parables lend themselves to allegorical interpretations, even when viewed within the setting of Jesus' historical ministry. Within Jewish tradition, God and God's chosen leaders were often referred to as shepherds; and God's people were often identified as sheep (cf. Mark 6:34; Ezek. 34; Zech. 13; Ps. 23). Those persons who actually heard Jesus declare the parable of the lost sheep could have responded by thinking along the allegorical lines suggested above.

Research into the parables has also led some scholars to classify them into three main types. First, there is the *similitude*. The similitude as a brief narrative involves at the everyday level that which is usual, regular, and expected. A shepherd looks for his lost sheep (Matt. 18:12-13 = Luke 15:3-6; GThom. 107:1-3). The tiny mustard seed grows into such a large plant that birds nest in its branches (Mark 4:30-32 par.; GThom. 20:1-4). Yeast hidden in flour leavens all that dough (Matt. 13:33 = Luke 13:20-21; GThom. 96:1-3). Seed scattered on the ground grows of its own accord without assistance from the man who sowed it (Mark 4:26-29). Second, there is the *story parable*. The story parable as a longer narrative focuses not on the general but the specific. It narrates a specific incident which often includes action contrary to that normally expected. A householder pays his vineyard workers equal pay for unequal work (Matt. 20:1-15). A father celebrates the homecoming of his wayward son with great feasting (Luke 15:11-32). Finally, there is the *example story*. These narratives tell about persons whose conduct should be imitated or avoided. They tell about such characters as the compassionate Samaritan (Luke 10:30-35), the humble tax collector (Luke 18:10-13), the rich man who hoarded his wealth (Luke 12:16-20; GThom. 63:1-4), and the rich man who ignored poor Lazarus (Luke 16:19-31).

Use of the Parables

Scholars are quite confident that the parables generally provide trustworthy evidence for the message and ministry of the historical Jesus. They distinguish, of course, between the use of the parables by the Gospel writers and their use by Jesus himself. They are sensitive to the varied adaptations of the parables within the early church all along the path of oral and written transmission. Several kinds of adaptation of the parables are evident within the Gospels themselves.

One kind of adaptation of the parables involves their placement in the Gospels. All parables have been placed in their present Gospel settings to serve the interests of the Gospel writers. Consequently, the use of the parables by the Gospel writers may to a greater or lesser degree correspond to their use by Jesus himself.

The authors of Matthew and Luke, for example, have incorporated the parable of the lost sheep (Matt. 18:12-13 = Luke 15:3-6) into very different narrative contexts. Matthew reports that Jesus addresses the parable to his own disciples; and he places the parable in the midst of his discourse on church authority and discipline (chap. 18). He thereby uses the parable to encourage reconciliation among church members. But Luke reports that Jesus addresses the same parable to the Pharisees and scribes in defense of his association with sinners or religious outcasts, and he places the parable in the midst of his extensive travel account (chaps. 9–19). He thereby uses the parable to foreshadow the mission of the church to Gentiles or outsiders. Luke in all likelihood has captured more precisely than Matthew the use of the parable by Jesus himself. The parable of the lost sheep represents one of several parables apparently employed by Jesus both to proclaim the universal reach of God's mercy and to defend his own expression of that mercy to the religious outcasts of his day (cf. Luke 15:8-9, 11-32).

The author of Mark, to take another example, has placed the parable of the doorkeeper (Mark 13:34) near the conclusion of his apocalyptic discourse (chap. 13). He uses the parable to challenge his community to maintain constant watchfulness for the second coming of Jesus. The reference in this parable to a man's going on a journey and his returning at an unknown hour allows for its interpretation as a "parousia" parable (cf. Matt. 25:1-12). But the parable may have been used by Jesus not to counsel readiness for his own return but to counsel readiness for the kingdom's arrival—in the future, or within the personal experiences of his hearers then and there.

Another kind of adaptation of the parables involves the addition of brief explanatory or hortatory statements. These additional comments may serve the theological interest of the Gospel writers but often miss the original point of the parable or at least shift the emphasis. The author of Matthew, for example, places this word of Jesus immediately after the parable of the laborers in the vineyard (Matt. 20:1-15): "So the last will be first, and the first will be last" (Matt. 20:16; cf. Mark 10:31 par.; Luke 13:30). The parable itself declares not that the last will replace the first but that the last will be treated as equals to the first. Within the setting of Jesus' ministry, this story would have been for him a proclamation of God's universal mercy and a defense of his ministry to religious outcasts. But Matthew has used the parable as part of his own polemic against nonbelieving Jews. For Matthew and his Jewish-Christian community, the parable of the laborers in the vineyard declares that nonbelieving Jews have been replaced in God's plan by believers, both Jews and Gentiles.

Another kind of adaptation of the parables involves a thoroughgoing allegorical interpretation placed alongside certain parables. The Synoptic writers portray Jesus himself as interpreting at least three parables in an allegorical manner: the parables of the sower (Mark 4:3-8 par. and 4:14-20; cf. GThom 9:1-5), the weeds and the wheat (Matt. 13:24-30 and 13:37-43; cf. GThom. 57:1-4), and the net (Matt. 13:47-48 and 13:49; cf. GThom. 8:1-4). The *Gospel of Thomas*, however, preserves versions of these three parables without allegorical interpretations.

Many scholars consider the allegorical interpretations of these parables to be the creations of the early church and not the words of the historical Jesus. They base this conclusion on a careful analysis of the language used in the allegorical passages. Furthermore, the parables themselves are understandable within the setting of Jesus' ministry apart from their allegorical interpretations. The parable of the sower offers assurance that the kingdom of God will come in spite of all obstacles. This message of assurance would have been appropriate for Jesus to declare to his discouraged disciples (cf. Mark 4:26-29, 30-32 par.; Matt. 13:33 = Luke 13:20-21). The parable of the weeds and wheat and the parable of the net call for the patient acceptance of the intermingling of the righteous and the unrighteous in the present age. This message of patient acceptance would have been appropriate for Jesus to declare to such followers as those who wanted to take God's judgment into their own hands.

A final kind of adaptation of the parables involves possible alterations of detail within the parables themselves. Two parables in the Gospels, for instance, appear to be allegories of God's way with the world through God's own Son. These are the parables of the wicked tenants (Mark 12:1-11 par.; cf. GThom. 65:1-8) and the marriage feast (Matt. 22:2-10; cf. Luke 14:16-24 and GThom. 64:1-11). God's way with the world as presented in these parables includes: God's sending a Son to historic Israel; Israel's rejection of God's Son; and God's subsequent punishment of Israel, or the Jews, and then turning to others, the Gentiles. A number of scholars consider these two parables to be formulations by the early church in their present allegorical forms. But even skeptical interpreters often admit the possibility that authentic parables of Jesus underlie them.

Purpose of the Parables

One mark of an effective teacher, or author of a book, is that person's ability to explain the lesson in readily understandable terms. The viewpoint has often been expressed that Jesus himself adopted the parable form in order to make clear his kingdom message to his hearers. Accordingly, the Synoptic writers are said to have incorporated parables into their Gospels to make their messages about him more understandable to their readers. But a puzzling passage in the Gospel of Mark seemingly challenges and denies this viewpoint.

The author of Mark presents Jesus' parable of the sower and shortly thereafter Jesus' allegorical interpretation of that parable. Between the parable and its interpretation, the author comments on the purpose behind Jesus' use of the parable form (Mark 4:10-12; cf. 4:33-34):

> When he was alone, those who were around him along with the twelve asked him about the parables. And he said to them, "To you has been given the secret of the kingdom of God, but for those outside, everything comes in parables [*parabolais*]; in order that [*hina*]
>
> > 'they may indeed look, but not perceive,
> > and may indeed listen, but not understand;
> > so that they may not [*mēpote*] turn again and be forgiven.' "

In this scene, Jesus has drawn a sharp line of demarcation. On the one hand, there are those around him to whom has been revealed "the secret of the kingdom of God." On the other hand, there are those outsiders who neither perceive nor understand. In words recalling Isaiah 6:9-10, Jesus states that the purpose of the parables is to conceal his message from outsiders—lest they accept it! Thus he identifies the parables as means of concealment, not revelation. The parables obfuscate. They do not communicate. They become means of revelation and communication for those around Jesus only as he further explains the parables to them.

An occasional interpreter has viewed Jesus as the founder of a secret society. Morton Smith referred to Jesus as "the magician," as we have seen. These interpreters find primary evidence for their understanding of Jesus in the preceding Markan passage. They consider Jesus' parables to be esoteric teaching intended by him to confuse outsiders and to enlighten only those members of the society who receive additional instruction.

Many scholars, however, are convinced that Jesus intended for his kingdom message to be understood by the general public. They find it difficult, therefore, to accept as historical the words of Jesus as reported in Mark 4:10-12. They deal with these words about the parables in one of two ways. Either they deny that Jesus uttered them, or they deny that Jesus meant what the words seem to say.

Those scholars who deny that Jesus spoke the words in Mark 4:10-12 suggest that the words were formulated within the early church. Some claim that the words were formulated to support the general theme of "messianic secrecy" so prominent in Mark, however that theme be understood. Thus the author of Mark views Jesus' teaching in parables as one way Jesus kept his messiahship secret. Others who deny that Jesus spoke the words in Mark claim that the words were formulated to explain "why" Jesus' own people did not universally accept his message and subsequently rejected the gospel about Jesus. Thus, according to this interpretation, the author of Mark views Jesus' teaching in parables as a way Jesus himself fulfilled the prophecy in Isaiah that the people would see and not perceive, hear and not understand. In other words, the author of Mark is dealing with the same issue Paul concerned himself with in his letter to the church at Rome (Rom. 9–11). Paul reasons that God brought a hardening upon Israel only until the full number of Gentiles had entered in; and then all Israel would be saved. Paul quoted extensively the Scriptures, or Old Testament, to buttress his argument.

Those scholars who deny that Jesus meant what the words seem to say try to explain what he actually said about the parables. Using various arguments, some claim that the Markan text in Greek rests in part on a mistranslation of the underlying Aramaic. They allege, for example, that the Greek *parabolē* translates the ambiguous Aramaic word *mathlā*, which here means "riddle." Furthermore, underlying the Greek *hina* ("in order that") may be an Aramaic form that also means "who." Finally, beneath the Greek *mēpote* ("lest") may be an Aramaic expression that means "unless." So reconstructed, Jesus' words to his followers were these (cf. Mark 4:11-12):

> "To you has been given the secret of the kingdom of God, but for those outside everything comes in riddles, who look but do not perceive, and listen but do not understand, unless they turn again, and be forgiven."

Jesus' words, therefore, were not originally a comment on the purpose of the parables but an observation on the generally negative response to them. Or, as has been proposed, Jesus' words may have been spoken by him originally not as a comment specifically on the parables but as an observation on the generally negative response to his entire ministry in Galilee.

Whatever sense the interpreter makes of the words of Jesus reported in Mark 4:11-12, however, it is also necessary to reflect on the purpose of the parables in the light of his broader ministry as sketched in the synoptic Gospels. That ministry was both inclusive and exclusive.

Jesus' proclamation of the "kingdom of God" and his call for "repentance" were addressed to everyone. It was precisely his reaching across traditional barriers that led to controversy with the religious leaders over matters of Torah observance. His universal call for repentance was a summons to a radical reversal of one's life. He expressed this reversal in highly dramatic sayings. Hate father and mother! Pluck out the eye! Sell possessions! Become a servant! Take up a cross! But each of these outward acts would have required a prior inward reversal of mind, of will, and of experience. The *parables* were well suited for such a subtle subversion of the self. With images drawn from everyday life in Galilee, and with characters and happenings familiar to Jesus and his hearers, the *parables* on the surface threatened no one. But if hearers really heard, they were suddenly challenged. They were attracted, or they were repelled. They experienced the crisis of the kingdom, the rule of God.

On occasion, Jesus' call for repentance expressed itself as command: "Follow me!" His inclusive ministry, therefore, was also exclusive. There were those whose reversal of life resulted in their literally following him. The parables were also well suited for ongoing reflection and self-examination. Those who were attracted and not repelled continued to act out, to understand, and to experience "the secret of the kingdom of God."

Jesus no doubt adopted the parable form in order to make his message of the kingdom of God understandable to his hearers. He wanted to communicate, not to obfuscate. But it appears that the *fundamental purpose of the parables was to transform peoples' lives through and under the rule of God.* As we shall see, the parables were well suited for this difficult task. This conclusion is based not only on the Gospel evidence but on how the parables and Jesus have been interpreted.

Parables and Jesus

The study of the parables of Jesus has moved forward in five stages during the modern era of biblical criticism and the historical quest. The insights of one stage have often been carried forward into the next, but each stage has had its own distinctive focus.

1. The parables were interpreted *allegorically.* This approach to the parables generally prevailed at the beginning of the modern era. The tendency to treat the parables as allegories, already evident in the Gospels themselves, had been amplified within the later church. Probably no allegorist has received more attention than Origen of Alexandria (died ca. 251). Modern scholars often perceive in him and his work useful examples of how *not* to interpret the parables.[1] He allegorized the parable of the good Samaritan (Luke 10:30-35) as follows:

traveling man = Adam\
Jerusalem = heaven\
Jericho = world\
robbers = devil and henchmen\
wounds = effects of sin\
priest = law\
Levite = prophets\
Samaritan = Jesus Christ\
beast = body of Jesus Christ\
inn = church\
two denarii = knowledge of Father and Son\
return of Samaritan = second coming of Jesus Christ

For the allegorist, the parables serve an instructional purpose. In the case of Origen, the lesson he taught was his own (or the church's) theology. This theology may have validity in itself. But it has obviously been superimposed on the parable of the Good Samaritan and has very little to do with the intention of Jesus in declaring it.

2. The parables were demonstrated to be essentially *nonallegorical* in nature. The pivotal figure in the modern study of the parables was Adolf Jülicher, who wrote near the end of the nineteenth century.[2] He distinguished between allegory and parable. He identified parable as an extended simile. As similes, parables still serve an instructional purpose. But now the lesson taught by each parable involves not many points but one major point. Details in a parable have no independent symbolic importance. The parable of the good Samaritan contains references to places ("Jerusalem" and "Jericho") and persons ("priest," "Levite," and "Samaritan"). Such items simply contribute to the demonstration of the central point. For Jülicher, this parable had to do with self-sacrificial love: "The self-sacrificial act of love is of the highest value in the eyes of God and men; no privilege of position or birth can take its place."[3] Jülicher wrote within the theological framework of the reigning liberal theology during the period of the "old quest." Thus he considered the parables to be making very general religious and moral points.

3. The original forms of the parables were sought, and they were interpreted *within the context of Jesus' eschatological proclamation* of the kingdom of God. C. H. Dodd[4] and Joachim Jeremias[5] made important contributions to the field of parable research. Both Dodd and Jeremias were interested in the parables as evidence for Jesus' message and ministry and continued the quest for Jesus throughout the period of "no quest" and beyond. Each recognized the eschatological character of Jesus' proclamation and interpreted the parables accordingly. Dodd found support in the parables for his "realized eschatology." Jeremias allowed for more of a tension between the present and the future by describing his position as "eschatology in the process of being realized."

Jeremias in particular claimed considerable success in recovering the oldest forms of the parables by pruning away secondary additions. In this undertaking, he even availed himself of the *Gospel of Thomas*, which had found its way into scholarly circles in the late 1950s. Jeremias also examined the tiniest details in the parables in the light of first-century Palestinian customs and life. Consequently, with the earliest forms of the parables identified and the details clarified, he speculated in controlled fashion on the likely setting of each parable in Jesus' historical ministry. In a memorable phrase, Jeremias referred to the parables as "weapons of warfare"[6] since many of them seem to reflect a situation of conflict between Jesus and his opponents. Like Jülicher before him, Jeremias continued to emphasize that the parables were essentially similes and made a single point. But for Jeremias the point was not so broad but more specific, less moralistic and more eschatological. To him the parable of the good Samaritan gave dramatic precision to the quality of life brought by the kingdom of God. He classified this parable under the heading of "realized discipleship" and said: "In this parable Jesus tells his questioner that while the 'friend' is certainly, in the first place, his fellow-countryman, yet the meaning of the term is not limited to that."[7] Thus the parable of the good Samaritan served an instructional purpose.

4. Since the 1960s, the parables have increasingly been appreciated and analyzed from several angles as artistic or *literary works*. This approach was anticipated by Dan O. Via in a 1967 publication, the title of which suggested that a new turn in parable study was at hand: *The Parables: Their Literary and Existential Dimension.*[8] Via was seeking an interpretation of the parables that did not reduce their meanings to single points nor confine their meanings to their original literary and historical contexts. He came to see the parables as "aesthetic objects," with their own narrative worlds and peopled by very human characters.

At the center of this literary approach to the parables lies the claim that parables are to be understood primarily as metaphors, not similes. This claim is made with the recognition that the parables are often presented in the Gospels as similes: "The kingdom of God is like...." But the importance of this claim for an appreciation of the parables derives from the different ways the simile and the metaphor relate to the mind and the imagination. A simile, in making a comparison, refers explicitly to both objects being compared. Jesus said to his disciples: "I am sending you out like sheep." He thereby compares "you" with "sheep." We know who is being compared with sheep because we are told. But the metaphor, in making a comparison, refers explicitly to only one of the objects being compared. Jesus said to the Gentile woman: "I was sent only to the lost sheep." He thereby compares something with sheep, but we are not told what. We are challenged to make the comparison for ourselves based upon prior knowledge or other clues. The simile, therefore, is more instructive than the metaphor; and the metaphor makes more of a demand on the imagination than the simile. If the parables are essentially metaphors, this has important implications. One implication is that the parables invite the hearer to participation in their stories. Another implication is that the parables have as their fundamental purpose not the imparting of information but the inducement of transformation—transformation of thinking and transformation of the self. Still another implication is that the parables, although not allegories, may make several points depending on their use and the perspectives of their hearers.

Via concluded his analysis of the parables with observations about the uneasy relationship between the literary form of Gospel, into which the parables have been placed, and the parables themselves. The Gospels represent confessions of faith in Jesus as the Christ whereas parables as aesthetic objects indirectly invite their hearers to participate in Jesus' own vision of what it meant to live authentically. Among scholars who have taken the literary path to the parables are John Dominic Crossan and Robert W. Funk, both of whom have contributed greatly to recent discussions about Jesus.

Crossan, early on in 1973, considered the parables within the context of Jesus' kingdom preaching.[9] As metaphors, they solicit the involvement of their hearers and become the medium for an experience of the rule of God. Crossan does not view the parable of the good Samaritan as an example story, contrary to most modern interpreters and even contrary to the author of the Lukan Gospel. Crossan considers the use of the parable in Luke to be secondary and denies that its original point was about helping a neighbor in need. Instead, he calls the parable a "parable of reversal." In such a parable, the images are used to contradict normal understandings so that the world of the hearer is turned upside down. Regarding this parable, he says: "The whole thrust of the story demands that one say what cannot be said, what is a contradiction in terms: Good + Samaritan."[10] Thus the metaphorical point made by Jesus with the parable was that the rule of God also turns the world of the hearer upside down: "The hearer struggling with the contradictory dualism of Good/Samaritan is actually experiencing in and through this the inbreaking of the Kingdom."[11]

Funk, some years ago, also denied that the parable of "Good Sam," as he now calls it, represented an example story and claimed that it was a metaphor.[12] Funk has returned to this parable more recently and said that on Jesus' lips it was "probably intended to introduce the listener to the contours of the world as Jesus saw it under the direct rule of the God he called Father."[13] He then imagines the varied responses that Jesus' performance of the parable would have evoked from its original hearers even as its plot was unfolding.

5. Over the past three decades, this literary approach to the parables has produced a number of significant parable studies.[14] But during this period, another literary form has been elevated, by some, to a position of prominence alongside the parable as a distinctive speech form of the historical Jesus: *the aphorism.*

Unlike parables, but like proverbs, aphorisms are brief and pithy sayings. Proverbs and aphorisms are also statements without accompanying explanations or warrants. It is understandable that proverbs are not accompanied by an explanation because proverbs have been polished by the wisdom of the ages. For example, Jesus reportedly says: "so do not worry about tomorrow, for tomorrow will bring worries of its own" (Matt. 6:34*a*); and "Today's trouble is enough for today" (Matt. 6:34*b*). These admonitions express self-evident truth. By contrast, aphorisms beg for explanations. Their wisdom, if recognized as such, contradicts conventional wisdom. In response to a man who expressed the need to go home and bury his father, Jesus said: "Let the dead bury their own dead" (Matt 8:22 = Luke 9:60). This statement runs counter to the social expectation that parents be honored by receiving a proper burial.

Therefore, in spite of their formal differences, aphorisms and parables function in similar ways. They engage the mind and challenge conventional ways of viewing life. A well-known aphorism that coheres with the parable of the good Samaritan (Luke 10:30-35) is Jesus' pointed directive: "Love your enemies" (Matt. 5:44 = Luke 6:27). This memorable statement cuts across the social grain and startles the hearer with its paradoxical joining of two terms: love + enemies.

A decade after his 1973 study of the parables, John Dominic Crossan published a study of the aphorisms. This monograph was identified as the very first book-length treatment of Jesus' sayings that focused exclusively on the aphoristic tradition. Crossan limited his investigation to material in Mark and Q, but he isolated and discussed 133 aphorisms.[15]

The emergence of the literary approach to the parables and the recognition of aphorisms as comparably distinctive speech forms have been foundational for those historical reconstructions of Jesus that model him as a sage, a wisdom teacher, or even a Cynic. According to many scholars who have taken this route, Sayings Gospel Q and the *Gospel of Thomas* become the most valued sources for the historical Jesus because their parables and aphorisms take us closest to the voice and mind of Jesus. The apocalyptic eschatological sayings are considered secondary creations by the church; and the Gospel narratives become a later framework for the contrary eschatological and wisdom sayings traditions.

12

Miracles

Jesus used the parable form in his kingdom preaching and in relation to his Torah teaching. But he was known by his contemporaries not only for his words but for his deeds. Integral to his ministry appear to have been acts of exorcising the demon-possessed, curing the sick, resuscitating the dead, and controlling nature. Jesus the preacher and teacher was at the same time a miracle worker.

Gospel Writers and Gospel Traditions

In the Gospel of John, Jesus centers his public ministry around a series of seven miraculous happenings. These seven miracles, or signs, provide evidence for those who claim that a Signs Gospel underlies the Gospel of John as we now know it. The synoptic Gospels of Mark, Matthew, and Luke also report miraculous activity by Jesus. Unlike John, however, the Synoptics contain a number of exorcisms and an important debate between Jesus and his opponents about their meaning. (See the chart JESUS' MIRACLES.)

A Definition of "Miracle"

The concept of miracle has produced a great amount of discussion among philosophers.[1] Commonly defined, a miracle is *an event contrary to the known laws of nature.* According to this definition, however, there is no concept of miracle

JESUS' MIRACLES

MARK

Capernaum Demoniac
(Mark 1:21-18 par.)
Simon's Mother-in-Law
(Mark 1:29-31 par.)
Leper
(Mark 1:40-45 par.)
Paralytic
(Mark 2:1-12 par.)
Man with Withered Hand
(Mark 3:1-6 par.)
Stilling of Storm
(Mark 4:35-41 par.)
Gerasene Demoniac
(Mark 5:1-20 par.)
Raising of Jairus' Daughter
(Mark 5:21-24a, 35-43 par.)
Woman with Flow of Blood
(Mark 5:24b-34 par.)

Feeding of Five Thousand
(Mark 6:30-44 par.)
Walking on Sea of Galilee
(Mark 6:45-52 par.)
Gentile Woman's Daughter
(Mark 7:24-30 par.)
Deaf and Mute Man
(Mark 7:31-37 par.)
Feeding of Four Thousand
(Mark 8:1-10 par.)
Blind Man of Bethsaida
(Mark 8:22-26)
Epileptic Boy
(Mark 9:14-29 par.)
Blind Bartimaeus
(Mark 10:46-52 par.)
Cursing of Figtree
(Mark 11:12-14, 20-25 par.)

Q

Centurion's Servant
(Matt. 8:5-13=Luke 7:1-10)

L

Catch of Fish
(Luke 5:1-11)
Raising of Widow's Son
(Luke 7:11-17)
Healings Before John's Disciples
(Luke 7:21)
Crippled Woman
(Luke 13:10-17)

Man with Dropsy
(Luke 14:1-6)
Ten Lepers
(Luke 17:11-19)
Ear of High Priest's Servant
(Luke 22:51)

JOHN

Water into Wine
(John 2:1-11)
Official's Son
(John 4:46-54)
Lame Man
(John 5:1-18)
Feeding of Five Thousand
(John 6:1-14)

Walking on Sea of Galilee
(John 6:16-21)
Blind Man
(John 9:1-41)
Raising of Lazarus
(John 11:1-44)

within the biblical traditions, for therein appears no notion of nature as a closed system of law. As God's creation, the world even in its ordinariness testifies to its creator. God sends and withholds the rain and storm. God opens and closes the womb. Nonetheless, the biblical accounts—including the Gospels—do refer to happenings that, from a modern viewpoint, have often been judged to be contrary to the laws of nature. These happenings were out of the ordinary even within an ancient perspective. The Gospels contain something of a technical vocabulary for these miraculous or extraordinary events.

The author of John uses the word *sign (sēmeion)* to designate those acts whereby Jesus cured the afflicted, resuscitated the dead, and controlled nature (John 2:11; 4:54; 6:14; 20:30-31). The word itself does not necessarily suggest an act contrary to natural law although the King James Version sometimes translates the word *sēmeion* in John as "miracle." The word suggests an event that points beyond itself. In John, the "signs" of Jesus are those actions through which he is revealed to be the Christ, the Son of God. This word has a counterpart in the Old Testament. There "sign" *('ôth)* sometimes appears alongside "wonder" *(môphēth)* as a name for those extraordinary happenings performed by God at the time of the Exodus from Egypt (Exod. 7:3; Ps. 105:27). But the word *sign ('ôth)* can also be used to describe the Sabbath as a holy day (Exod. 31:13, 17). Thus both the usual and the unusual serve as pointers to God—for those with eyes to see.

Within the synoptic Gospels, the word *sign (sēmeion)* has a very negative connotation. "Signs" are what Jesus' opponents demand of him and what Jesus refuses to perform, namely, unequivocal demonstrations that he is of God (Mark 8:11-13; Matt. 12:38-42 = Luke 11:29-32; Matt. 16:1-4; Luke 11:16).

The more common expression for Jesus' acts of exorcism and cures in the Synoptics is *mighty work (dunamis*—literally "might," "power," or "dynamite"). This word appears both in the narratives by the Gospel writers and in the sayings of Jesus himself (Mark 6:1-6 par.; 9:39; Matt. 11:20-24 = Luke 10:13-15). But the expression *mighty work* does not necessarily mean an act contrary to natural law. Again the King James Version sometimes translates the word *dunamis* in the Synoptics as "miracle"; but the word itself suggests an event through which the power of God has been manifested. Indeed, "Power" *(dunamis)* can be used as a circumlocution for God and for the Spirit of God (Mark 14:62 par.; Luke 24:49; Acts 1:8). Not surprisingly, the expression *mighty work* has a counterpart in the Old Testament. There, in poetic passages, "mighty doings" *(g'bûrôth)* serves as a sweeping way of describing God's activity on behalf of Israel throughout their history together (Pss. 106:2, 8; 145:4, 12; 150:2).

The Gospel words *sign* and *mighty work* do not, therefore, necessarily suggest events contrary to natural law. But these words are used by the Gospel writers to designate the actions of Jesus that were considered extraordinary in his day and miraculous retrospectively from our day.

The Synoptic writers, however, do not usually use a general word to designate Jesus' miraculous activity. In periodic summary statements, they prefer to describe Jesus' healing the sick and casting out demons quite simply in those terms: "And he cured many who were sick with various diseases, and cast out many demons" (Mark 1:32-34 par.; 1:39 par.; 3:7-12 par.; 6:7-13 par.). The Gospels of Matthew and Luke also contain other sayings of Jesus in which he summarizes his own exorcising and healing activity in the same way: "Listen, I am casting out demons and performing cures today and tomorrow, and on the third day I finish my work" (Luke 13:32-33; Matt. 11:4-6 = Luke 7:22-23). Jesus in his own summary statements mentions not only exorcisms and healings but also dead raisings. Neither the Synoptic writers in their narrative summaries nor Jesus in his sayings, however, refer to his so-called nature miracles. There is no mention of nature miracles outside these miracle stories themselves.

Miracle Stories

Jesus reportedly cast out demons, healed the infirm, raised the dead, and controlled nature. But *the kinds of deeds performed by Jesus in the Gospel miracle stories were only extraordinary and not unique when viewed within the broader cultural context of the ancient world.* Ancient literature abounds in stories about persons who distinguished themselves by performing various extraordinary feats. These stories represent diverse backgrounds: Graeco-Roman, Christian, and Jewish.[2]

The Gospel miracle stories, of course, achieved their present form in a Graeco-Roman environment. There are also preserved Graeco-Roman stories of extraordinary happenings. At Epidaurus in southern Greece was the greatest of shrines to Asclepius, the god of healing. Excavations have unearthed thanksgiving tablets containing inscriptions about persons who were delivered by Asclepius from a multitude of ailments including blindness, lameness, and a five-year pregnancy. One of the most celebrated miracle workers in the Mediterranean world was a vagabond philosopher named Apollonius of Tyana. Probably born while Jesus was alive, he was immortalized in a third-century biography. His deeds included the casting out of demons and the resuscitation of the dead. Even the Roman Emperor Vespasian on one occasion in Alexandria reportedly healed a crippled man and restored sight to another.

The Gospel miracle stories were shaped by Christian storytellers in the interest of the Christian message of salvation through Jesus Christ. There are other Christian miracle stories preserved in the New Testament. Such early Christian leaders as Peter and Paul enabled the lame to walk (Acts 3 and 14). Paul apparently refers to his own miracle working among the Corinthians when he writes: "The signs of a true apostle were performed among you with utmost patience, signs and wonders and mighty works" (2 Cor. 12:12).

Palestine was the geographical setting for the happenings narrated in the Gospel miracle stories. There are accounts in Jewish sources of rabbis remembered not only for their exposition of the Torah but for their extraordinary deeds. Hanina ben Dosa, a Galilean rabbi who lived in the first century, was remembered for curing the ill sons of other, more famous rabbis of that period such as Johanan ben Zakkai and Gamaliel. Another rabbi, Honi the Circle-Drawer, who lived a century earlier, was remembered for his rainmaking.

Jesus in the synagogue at Nazareth refers to the prophets Elijah and Elisha as models for his own ministry according to the account in Luke (chap. 4). He alluded to ancient Israelite miracle stories recorded in Scripture, the Old Testament. In Israel there were no miracle workers greater than these two prophets. They healed the sick, brought the dead to life, and performed dazzling feats with inanimate objects (see especially 1 Kings 17 and 2 Kings 4–6). But, of course, stupendous feats were as old as Israel. At the time of the Exodus not only did Moses and Aaron mediate the ten plagues with which God afflicted Egypt but Pharaoh's magicians were able to match the initial two plagues. They, too, turned the waters of the Nile into blood and called up a swarm of frogs (Exod. 7–8).

The mighty acts performed by Jesus in the Gospel miracle stories, therefore, were no different in kind than acts allegedly performed by others. And in the Gospels, *Jesus himself even acknowledged that some of his contemporaries had powers similar to his.* These miracle workers acknowledged by Jesus included his own disciples whom he sent out to heal and to cast out demons (Mark 6:7-13 par.; Luke 10:1-20). They also included potential friends (Mark 9:38-41 par.) and probable enemies (Matt. 12:27 = Luke 11:19).

To recognize similarities between the Gospel miracle stories and other miracle stories, however, is not to suggest that all ancient miracle accounts present the happenings therein in identical ways. The theological perspective presupposed by the Jewish and Christian stories certainly differs from the perspectives of the Graeco-Roman accounts. For the Jew and the Christian, the extraordinary happenings pointed beyond themselves to the transcendent God, the Creator, and the power of God was expressed through them. They were indeed "signs" and "mighty works." Furthermore, in the Gospel miracle stories the healing activity of Jesus was characterized by several distinctive features.

First, the Gospel accounts may have been narrated with an intention of glorifying Jesus, but Jesus in these accounts avoids self-glorification. Jesus commands demons and persons healed to remain silent about him and his work (Mark 1:34 par.; 3:12 par.; et al.). This theme of "messianic secrecy" to which we have often referred was expanded and highlighted by the author of Mark. But the miracle stories lent themselves to such treatment (Mark 1:44 par.; 5:37 par.).

Second, the Gospel accounts present Jesus' healing activity as his response to perceived human need. He usually healed in response to a specific request. His acts, therefore, become expressions of "pity" (Mark 1:41), "compassion" (Mark 6:34; 8:2 par.; Matt. 20:34; Luke 7:13), and "mercy" (Mark 5:19).

Third, in the Gospel accounts, Jesus effects healing usually by means of command or simple touch, although there is occasional mention of his using spit and clay (Mark 7:33; 8:23; also John 9:6, 11). He seldom physically manipulates the person in need of healing, and he avoids magical potions. The retention of Aramaic expressions in a couple of Markan stories does give the outward appearance of magical formulas (Mark 5:41; 7:34). But Jesus seemingly refrains from incantations and lengthy ritual.

Finally, the Gospel accounts emphasize "faith" as a prerequisite for Jesus' healings. For Paul and John, "faith"—or "belief"—represents *trust in* Jesus as the Christ. But in the Synoptics, faith is linked quite specifically to Jesus' ability to heal. Faith represents *confidence that* the healing power of God flows through him. As confidence, faith may characterize the attitude of those needing to be healed. Thus the woman with an issue of blood (Mark 5:34 par.), blind Bartimaeus (Mark 10:52 par.), and the Samaritan leper (Luke 17:19) had faith. But faith may also characterize those interceding with Jesus on behalf of someone else. Thus faith also belonged to the four men carrying a paralytic (Mark 2:5 par.), Jairus whose daughter was ill (Mark 5:36 par.), the father with the possessed son (Mark 9:23-24 par.), the Roman centurion with the paralyzed servant (Matt. 8:10 = Luke 7:9), and the Canaanite woman with the possessed daughter (Matt. 15:28). This faith as confidence that Jesus can heal represents the faith that can move mountains. But this faith must express itself in a request or in a prayer to become effective (Mark 9:29; 11:20-25 par.; Matt. 17:20 = Luke 17:5-6). Understandably, therefore, the disciples' failure to pray made it impossible for them to cast out a demon (Mark 9:14-29 par.). Also understandably, the lack of faith at Nazareth even limited Jesus' ability to perform mighty works there (Mark 6:1-6 par.). In the Gospel miracle stories, "faith" is integral to the healing process. The church today continues to describe certain healings in the name of Jesus as "faith healings." The Gospel evidence for the miracle-working affinity of Jesus is not confined to the miracle stories proper. There are in the Gospels several important sayings by which Jesus himself comments on that activity.

Miracle Sayings

Two complexes of material deserve special attention when discussing the miracle sayings of Jesus. One concerns the so-called Beelzebub controversy; the other a question asked by John the Baptist.

211

The author of Mark reports the Beelzebub controversy within the broader setting of the Galilean ministry (Mark 3:19-27 par.). According to this passage, *the
issue during Jesus' ministry was not whether he actually performed mighty works but the
meaning of those works.* Scribes from Jerusalem readily acknowledged that Jesus
cast out demons. But they saw in his exorcisms evidence that he was doing the
work of Beelzebub, or Satan. The issue, therefore, was not *what* Jesus did but the
meaning of what he did. With his twin parables of the divided kingdom and the
strong man bound, Jesus refuted the claim of the scribes that his exorcisms were
the work of Satan. He affirmed that his exorcisms were in opposition to Satan
and implied that they were the work of God. That which is implied in the Markan
story is spelled out openly in Matthew and Luke. Matthew and Luke have inserted into the Markan material, between the two parables, these words of Jesus:
"But if it is by the Spirit of God ["finger of God," in Luke] that I cast out demons,
then the kingdom of God has come to you" (Matt. 12:28 = Luke 11:20).

Thus Jesus declared that he cast out demons on behalf of God and God's
kingdom. We considered these words earlier as an indication that Jesus
announced the rule of God as already present in his historical ministry. To him
the eschatological binding of Satan at the end of history had already been inaugurated within history through his exorcising activity. These words are certainly important for his understanding of his exorcisms; but they may also be
important for his understanding of other acts of healing. Physical ailments
were also viewed in his day as caused by Satan (cf. Luke 13:10-17). But there
are other words of Jesus that disclose more directly his understanding of his
physical cures and his dead raisings.

The authors of Matthew and Luke report a question asked Jesus by John
the Baptist during the course of Jesus' Galilean ministry (Matt. 11:2-6 = Luke
7:18-23). John sent two of his own disciples and asked Jesus: "Are you the
one who is to come, or are we to wait for another?" Jesus replied: "Go and tell
John what you hear and see: the blind receive their sight, the lame walk, lepers are cleansed, the deaf hear, the dead are raised, and the poor have good
news brought to them."

John asked Jesus a question about messiahship; but Jesus responded with
references to his healing activity. Jesus' words recall such passages from the
prophets as Isaiah 29:18-19; 35:5-6; 61:1. These prophetic texts refer to the
healings that will occur when the new age of God dawns. Like the exorcisms,
therefore, the other healings are placed within an eschatological perspective by
Jesus himself.

Jesus' words in response to the accusation of the scribes and the question of
John make no mention of his so-called nature miracles. But his understanding
of his exorcisms, physical cures, and dead raisings seems clear: *Jesus understood
his mighty works to signify the inbreaking of the rule of God.* His mighty works were
eschatological signs. The synoptic Gospels confront their readers with a bit of

212

irony. The religious leaders asked Jesus for "signs" that he was of God, but he refused. Jesus performed "mighty works," and the religious leaders failed to grasp their "sign"-ificance.

But what was really going on during Jesus' historical ministry? Did he actually perform the miracles attributed to him in the Gospels? This question of "fact" shifts the discussion to a different level.

Miracles and Jesus

The question of miracle has been a topic for lively discussion throughout the modern period of biblical criticism and the historical quest. The modern era actually began with two approaches to the miracles of Jesus, which were opposites when consistently followed. But these antithetical positions were joined by other approaches that transcended them while often reflecting an indebtedness to them.

1. The miracles of Jesus were dismissed. The miracles could not have occurred as reported in the Gospels because they appear to contradict the laws of nature. This reasoning characterized *rationalism*. Those interpreters who followed this approach dealt with the miracles in one of two ways. Either they ignored the miracles or they explained them away as purely natural events.

Thomas Jefferson followed the first alternative by ignoring the miracles. In 1820, after many years of hesitation, Thomas Jefferson finally produced what he called *The Life and Morals of Jesus of Nazareth extracted textually from the Gospels in Greek, Latin, French & English*.[3] This small volume, later published as *The Jefferson Bible*, consisted of excerpts from the four canonical Gospels, printed in four languages in parallel columns. The volume narrated the life of Jesus from birth to burial. Jefferson had gone through the Gospels and literally "cut out" all references to supernatural events. He removed the virgin birth, the miracles, and the resurrection. The Jesus that emerged, therefore, was a moral philosopher whose greatest wisdom appeared in such teachings as those preserved in the Sermon on the Mount, in Matthew 5–7.

Contemporaries of Jefferson and their successors pursued the second alternative by explaining them as natural occurrences. Over the years, they have proposed various and often ingenious explanations for what really happened behind the miracle stories. The exorcisms of Jesus have usually been explained as occasions of psychological catharsis, since demon-possession was the way ancient folk understood mental illness. The healings of Jesus have been subjected to different interpretations. Those persons who were healed of functional disorders such as paralysis, blindness, and deafness may also have experienced a psychological catharsis that resulted in a physical cure. The recovery from ailments like fever in the presence of Jesus may have been coincidence. The resuscitation of the dead by Jesus may actually have involved persons who were not dead but in a coma. At least the raisings of Jairus' daughter and the widow of Nain's son allow for such a possibility (Mark 5:21-24, 35-43 par.; Luke 7:11-17). The nature miracles by Jesus have also been explained naturally. In feeding the multitudes, Jesus did not really multiply the fish and the loaves of bread (Mark 6:30-44 par.; 8:1-10 par.; John 6:1-14). He set an example of sharing his food that was followed by others in the crowd until all were satisfied. Neither did Jesus really walk on the water of the Sea of Galilee (Mark 6:45-52 par.; John 6:16-21). He walked along the shore or on a sand bar. Nor did Jesus really still the storm by his word of command (Mark 4:35-41 par.). The subsiding of the storm was pure coincidence.

So the miracles have been naturalized. These interpretations, and others quite similar, have often been set forth without any denial that God was working through natural processes. Many interpreters viewed the exorcisms and many physical healings as expressions of psychological catharsis but also affirmed that these cures stemmed from the healing power of God that flowed through Jesus.

2. The miracles of Jesus were defended. The miracles must have occurred because the Gospels claim that Jesus the Son of God did them. This reasoning characterized *supernaturalism*. But the interpreters who adopted this approach also advanced different arguments in defending the miracles.

There were those who emphatically distinguished between "natural events" and "supernatural events." The former kinds of happenings follow prescribed laws built into the natural order, while the latter interrupt those otherwise universal laws of nature. According to this view, God was ultimately the author of both kinds of events. If God established the laws of nature, then God can momentarily suspend those laws. This was what happened with the miracles of Jesus. The exorcisms and cures, the raisings of the dead and the control over nature, were indeed contrary to natural law. They were genuine miracles worked by God through Jesus as Son, or worked by Jesus as Son of God.

But other interpreters defended the miracles by making certain qualifications about them. Such an interpreter was David Smith, whose biography of Jesus was earlier reviewed.[4] One line of reasoning used in defense of the miracles involved the idea of accommodation. This was the idea that God, by becoming human in Jesus his Son, had accommodated himself to our humanity, specifically to some ancient beliefs now known to be invalid. Thus Jesus did not really believe in demons but simply accommodated himself to that ancient belief in order to effect his exorcisms. The exorcisms of Jesus were occasions of psychological catharsis. Still another line of reasoning used in defense of the miracles involved the idea of acceleration, an idea anticipated centuries earlier by Augustine. This was the conviction that the miracles were not contrary to natural law but represented an acceleration of the natural process. This interpretation had its greatest appeal in relation to the healings of Jesus both psychological and physical. Since there are laws that guide the healing process of mind and body, the healings of Jesus represented the acceleration of those natural laws so that wholeness occurred instantaneously. This interpretation was also applied to some of the nature miracles. Since there are laws that direct the production of fish, bread, and wine, the multiplication of the fish and bread (Mark 6:30-44 par.; 8:1-10 par.; John 6:1-14) and the changing of water into wine (John 2:1-11) represented the acceleration of natural processes.

The rationalistic and supernaturalistic approaches to the miracles of Jesus can stand over against each other in opposition. But there are representative expressions of each approach that bring them closer together, as was obvious in the preceding discussion. Many contemporary writings on Jesus continue to reflect the legacy of rationalism and supernaturalism.

3. As long ago as the early nineteenth century, a bold attempt was made to move the discussion of the life of Jesus and the miracles beyond the polarities of rationalism and supernaturalism. This effort was undertaken by David Friedrich Strauss.[5] We mentioned his writing on Jesus in our survey of the "old quest." Strauss considered as indefensible both the attempts to explain all miracles as natural occurrences and the efforts to establish their historicity on supernatural grounds. He advocated what he called a *mythological* approach. Strauss acknowledged the possibility of natural healings underlying some of the Gospel stories of miraculous healings. But to him the significance of these stories lay elsewhere. He called for an appreciation of the Gospel miracle stories as narratives composed by early Christians to express their faith in Jesus as the Messiah sent in fulfillment of the promises made to Israel. The Gospel stories of Jesus' feeding the multitudes (Mark 6:30-44 par.; 8:1-10 par.; John 6:1-14), for example, were said to have been modeled on Old Testament accounts of miraculous nourishment. Influential in this regard were stories about the multiplication of foodstuffs by Elijah and Elisha (1 Kings 17; 2 Kings 4) and about the manna and the quail at the time of Moses (Exod. 16; Num. 11).

Strauss, therefore, reformulated the whole question of miracle. Both the rationalists and the supernaturalists concerned themselves with the historical question of what actually happened behind the Gospel miracle stories during the life of Jesus. But he was concerned more with the literary question of what the miracle stories meant to those early Christians who shaped them in the interest of their own confessions of faith. His recognition that Old Testament models such as Moses, Elijah, and Elisha played an important role in the formulation of the Gospel miracle stories represents a lasting contribution.

4. An intellectual successor to D. F. Strauss was Rudolf Bultmann, whose name has appeared with some frequency in our surveys of Gospel criticism and the Jesus quest.

As a form critic, Bultmann recognized the creative role played by the early church in shaping the oral traditions about Jesus. He came to represent a "no quest" point of view with regard to the historical Jesus.

Like Strauss, Bultmann sought a way beyond rationalism and supernaturalism and adopted the category of myth as central to his method for moving beyond those options. Also like Strauss, he was interested in what miracle stories meant to the early Christian community. Furthermore, Bultmann readily acknowledged that Jesus performed deeds considered miraculous by that community and Jesus himself.[6] But for Bultmann, Jesus' miracles were expressions of an outdated mythological worldview—a worldview in which deeds were attributed to supernatural divine causation.

However, Bultmann the Christian theologian and preacher was concerned with what the Christian message, including miracles, meant for twentieth-century believers like himself who no longer thought mythologically but thought scientifically. Thus he developed his proposal that the New Testament be *demythologized through existential interpretation.*[7]

Interpreters approached the Gospels not with the question of what happened historically back then, but with the question of what the text communicated about God and human existence here and now, in a way that natural law was not violated. Accordingly, even the nature miracle stories could address modern believers. In a sermon on the so-called miraculous catch of fish (Luke 5:1-10), Bultmann called the story "a work of pious fiction."[8] The truth of the story lay in the words spoken by Peter to Jesus, "Go away from me, Lord, for I am a sinful man" (vs. 8), and in Peter's decision to follow him. Here for Bultmann is true miracle for twentieth-century believers: God's transformation of human life in response to the Christian message of and about Jesus. Bultmann has no interest in what may have happened historically in the life of Jesus to generate the story.

Bultmann's own students initiated the "new quest" for the historical Jesus. But they—like their mentor—were interested primarily in Jesus' words. Even a cursory comparison between Bultmann's *Jesus and the Word* (1926; English trans. 1934) and Günther Bornkamm's *Jesus of Nazareth* (1956; English trans. 1960) discloses this to be the case. Both volumes have expansive chapters that deal with "the kingdom of God" and "the will of God."

5. Much has happened in recent decades to carry the discussion of miracles beyond rationalism and supernaturalism and to complement ongoing philosophical discussions about the possibility of miracles. There have been the refinements of the disciplines of source, form, and redaction criticisms as well as the appropriation of social-scientific models for understanding healings and exorcisms. There have been significant shifts in the historical quest for Jesus. An approach to the miracles has emerged out of these developments that in its own way occupies a mediating position beyond rationalism and supernaturalism. This approach does not bracket out what may lie behind the Gospel miracle stories nor interpret them existentially. Perhaps this approach, variously followed during the "post-quest" period, can best be described as *historical.*

Foundational to this historical approach is, on the one hand, a refusal to dismiss dogmatically the miracles of Jesus as having no basis in his historical career and, on the other hand, a refusal to accept dogmatically the miracle stories at face value. Several observations provide a framework for understanding the role and status of miracles in many writings from the "post-quest" period.

First, Jesus was historically an exorcist and a healer. This statement receives virtually unanimous affirmation by Jesus scholars, however the dynamics of his healings and exorcisms be understood. Jesus' "mighty works" were integral to his message and ministry. Strong support for this judgment comes from the criterion of multiple attestation when applied to forms as well as sources. Sayings and stories refer to Jesus' exorcising and healing activity. These sayings and stories represent traditions identified as Mark, Q, L, and John. Significant specialized studies on Jesus the exorcist[9] and Jesus the healer[10] have appeared.

Second, the "mighty works" of Jesus are to be understood in relation to his "kingdom" activity, however the time and nature of the kingdom be understood, whether as future, present, or both; whether apocalyptically, nonapocalyptically, or sapientially. In this assessment, Jesus' reported sayings about exorcisms and healings play significant roles (Matt. 12:28 = Luke 11:20; Matt. 11:2-6 = Luke 7:18-23).

Third, it is virtually impossible to establish the historical probability for the details in the miracle stories as presented in the Gospels and difficult to recover the events underlying them. But the stories of Jesus' exorcisms and healings represent the kinds of acts he performed and the kinds of situations in which he found himself. But there have been significant analyses of the broad tradition of Jesus' miracles on a case-by-case basis—especially the exorcisms and healings—in an attempt to recover some kind of historical core or foundation. The older, readable study by R. H. Fuller[11] has been complemented by the more detailed analyses by John P. Meier[12] and the Jesus Seminar.[13]

Among the Markan stories that Meier or the Jesus Seminar—not necessarily both—conclude have some basis in events in the life of Jesus are: the healing of Peter's mother-in-law (Mark 1:29-31 par.); the leper (Mark 1:40-45 par.); the paralytic (Mark 2:1-12 par.); the Gerasene demoniac (Mark 5:1-20 par.); the raising of Jairus' daughter (Mark 5:21-24*a*, 35-43 par.); the woman with a flow of blood (Mark 5:24*b*-34 par.); the possessed boy (Mark 9:14-29 par.); and blind Bartimaeus (Mark 10:46-52 par.).

Fourth, and last, the nature miracles continue to present special problems. Not the least of the problems is their absence in Jesus' summaries of his miraculous activity. Neither Meier nor the Jesus Seminar, for example, finds historical bases for the Markan sea stories of Jesus' stilling of the storm (Mark 4:35-41 par.) and walking on the water (Mark 6:45-52 par.). Both Meier and the Jesus Seminar consider the Lukan story of the catch of fish (Luke 5:1-10) to have originated as a resurrection appearance story and to be related in the pre-Gospel tradition to the Johannine story of Jesus' appearance beside the lake (John 21:1-14).

13

Arrest, Trial, and Crucifixion

Paul, in writing to the believers at Corinth, reminded them of the gospel he first preached to them: "For I decided to know nothing among you except Jesus Christ, and him crucified" (1 Cor. 2:2). Paul remembers how Jesus died but provides few details about the circumstances surrounding his death. For these details, we rely primarily on the passion narratives in the canonical Gospels.

Passion Narratives and Passion Traditions

The passion narratives represent the portion of the Jesus story about which there is the greatest agreement among the canonical Gospels. Each Gospel follows a similar sequence of events from the closing days and hours of Jesus' life:

Presence in Jerusalem at Passover time
Conspiracy by Jewish authorities
Betrayal by Judas
Last Supper with disciples on evening of arrest
Arrest that night by Jewish authorities accompanied by Judas
  —scuffle and severance of ear of the high priest's servant

Appearance at night before Jewish authorities
— denial by Peter in high priest's courtyard
Appearance next morning before Roman Governor Pontius Pilate
— release of Barabbas
Crucifixion on Roman cross as "King of the Jews"
Burial by Joseph of Arimathea

These are the similarities among the Gospel passion narratives that led form critics to conclude that the passion of Jesus was the first portion of his story to be told consecutively. Many scholars have attempted to reconstruct the earlier written or oral passion account that underlies our present Gospels.[1]

Raymond E. Brown's encyclopedic, scene-by-scene commentary on the passion narratives focuses primarily on the ways the Gospel writers treat the passion story, and he disavows any interest in reconstructing a pre-Markan passion account. But along the way, he makes suggestions about the content of the passion traditions underlying the accounts.[2]

In recent years, however, the claim has been made that the *Gospel of Peter* provides the basis for reconstructing an early passion-resurrection narrative that served as a source for the accounts in all four canonical Gospels. John Dominic Crossan, who has provided the most detailed argument for this position, has referred to this formative account as the Cross Gospel.[3]

All this talk about similarities among the Gospel passion narratives, about pre-Markan passion accounts and traditions, and about the Cross Gospel must not, however, lead the interpreter to a false conclusion. The interpreter must not think that only a short step lies between the passion narratives in the Gospels and sound historical conclusions about what transpired during the last hours of Jesus' life. *There are features about the Gospel passion narratives that render the historian's task more difficult than initially supposed.* We will consider three such features.

First, there is a *theological tendency* in the Gospel passion narratives that makes it difficult at points to distinguish between the church's interpretation of what happened and what did happen during the last hours of Jesus' life. Specifically, *there is the tendency to view all the happenings as fulfillment of Scripture.* Direct quotations from and allusions to the prophets and the psalms abound. The psalms of lamentation, such as Psalm 22, play a very important role.

The Gospel writers occasionally introduce passages from the Jewish Scriptures with formulas of fulfillment. Matthew uses one of his characteristic fulfillment quotations in connection with Judas' return of the thirty pieces of silver to the Jewish authorities and their subsequent purchase of a potter's field (Matt. 27:9-10 = Zech. 11:12-13; also Jer. 18:1-3; 32:6-15). John introduces into his passion narrative three formula quotations to establish that even actions by the Roman soldier at the crucifixion fulfilled the Scriptures. The soldiers divided the garments of Jesus into four parts and decided to cast lots for his seamless tunic (John 19:24 = Ps. 22:18; cf. Mark 15:24 par.). They did not break the legs of Jesus (John 19:36 = Exod. 12:46). But one soldier thrust a spear into his side (John 19:37 = Zech. 12:10).

In addition to explicit quotations of the Scriptures, the Gospel writers record traditions that echo various Scriptural texts in more subtle ways. The events that recall Scriptural passages include: the washing of hands by Pontius Pilate (Matt. 27:24 = Deut. 21:6-9); the crucifixion of Jesus (Mark 15:24 par.; John 19:23 = Ps. 22:16); the offering of vinegar to Jesus (Mark 15:36 par.; John 19:28-30 = Ps. 69:21); the spitting at Jesus while he is being beaten (Mark 14:65 par.; 15:19 par. = Isa. 50:6); the wagging of heads in derision by those who pass the cross (Mark 15:29-30 par. = Ps. 22:7); the words of mockery hurled at him on the cross by the religious leaders (Matt. 27:43 = Ps. 22:8); and the gazing on the cross by his acquaintances from afar (Luke 23:49 = Ps. 38:11).

Furthermore, the words of Jesus are shaped by the Scriptures in the passion narratives more than any other portion of the Gospels. Jesus, too, can refer to specific passages that find fulfillment in the events surrounding him. The events that Jesus identified as the fulfillment of Scripture included the betrayal of Judas (Mark 14:21 par. = Ps. 41:9), the scattering of his disciples (Mark 14:27 par. = Zech. 13:7), and the purchase of swords by his disciples with the subsequent disturbance at his arrest (Luke 22:37 = Isa. 53:12). Jesus sometimes quoted the Scriptures without identifying his words as a quotation. He did this in his reply to the women of Jerusalem who followed him along the way to his crucifixion (Luke 23:30 = Hos. 10:8). His words over the bread and wine at the Last Supper apparently allude to a number of Scriptural precursors (Mark 14:22-25 par.; Exod. 24:8; Jer. 31:31; Zech. 9:11) .

There is also a close relationship between the Scriptures and the seven sayings spoken by Jesus while hanging on the cross. The liturgy of the church in our day refers to these sayings as the seven last words of Jesus. The traditional Good Friday service centers around them. But no single Gospel contains all seven. Mark reports only one saying; and Matthew follows Mark. Luke reports three additional sayings. John records still three more. These seven sayings in a traditional liturgical order are:

> "Father, forgive them; for they do not know what they are doing." (Luke 23:34)
> "Truly I tell you, today you will be with me in Paradise." (Luke 23:43)
> "Woman, here is your son. . . . Here is your mother." (John 19:26-27)
> "My God, my God, why have you forsaken me?" (Mark 15:34 and Matt. 27:46 = Ps. 22:1; cf. GPet. 5:5)
> "I am thirsty." (John 19:28; cf. Ps. 69:21)
> "It is finished." (John 19:30)
> "Father, into your hands I commend my spirit." (Luke 23:46 = Ps. 31:5)

Three of these last sayings of Jesus have direct connections with the Scriptures, so that the Gospels themselves portray Jesus as dying with the words of the Scriptures on his lips and in his mind. So the passion accounts reflect the tendency to view all events related to the death of Jesus as the fulfillment of Scripture.

This tendency has led John Dominic Crossan to describe the passion accounts as 80 percent "prophecy historicized" and 20 percent "history remembered."[4] That is, the passion narratives—including his hypothetical Cross Gospel—do not just appeal to the Scriptures to explain events that happened but consist of events that have been created out of specific Scriptural texts. After the trauma of Jesus' death, his followers searched the Scriptures to understand what had happened and turned prophecies into events. So, for example, the reference in Psalm 22:18 to the division of clothing, and the casting of lots for the garments of one near death, became the basis for the scene in which Roman soldiers divide Jesus' clothing and cast lots for his robe, or tunic (John 19:23-25).

By contrast, Raymond E. Brown expresses greater confidence than Crossan that the passion narratives rest upon a solid historical foundation. Nonetheless, he too recognizes the difficulty in moving from the Gospel texts to historical events; and his own expansive commentary repeatedly demonstrates how great the difficulty is.[5]

But there is still another feature of the passion narratives that makes it difficult to distinguish between the church's interpretation of what happened and what did happen during the final hours of Jesus' life. These narratives exhibit an *apologetic tendency to shift the responsibility for Jesus' execution from the Roman authorities to the Jewish authorities.* Central to this political apologetic is the characterization of Pontius Pilate in his dealings with the Jewish authorities, with Jesus, and with Barabbas.

In Mark, Pilate suspects the Jewish leaders of envy and only reluctantly delivers Jesus over to be crucified while releasing Barabbas (Mark 15:10, 14-15). Matthew essentially repeats the Markan presentation but with two significant additions. He adds that Pilate's wife, as the result of a dream, intercedes on behalf of Jesus, "that innocent man" (Matt. 27:18-19). He also adds the scene in which Pilate washes his hands of Jesus' blood and the Jewish people accept the responsibility for it: "His blood be on us and on our children!" (Matt. 27:24-25). Luke also makes an important addition to his account. He adds the scene in which Pilate sends Jesus to Herod Antipas for judgment. Whereas in Matthew, Pilate declares himself innocent of Jesus' blood, now in Luke he three times pronounces Jesus innocent of any crime and announces that Herod shares this view (Luke 23:4, 14-15, 22). In John, Pilate also openly declares Jesus to be innocent of any crime (John 18:38; 19:4, 6). The four Gospels, therefore, characterize Pontius Pilate as one with a sensitive conscience but with weakness of will in his relations with the Jewish authorities. Pilate does not want to order the execution of Jesus, but he does.

Outside the Gospel passion narratives, however, appears a strikingly different characterization of Pontius Pilate. Josephus, the Jewish historian with pro-Roman sympathies, depicts Pilate as being very strong-willed in his relations with the Jewish leaders and the populace and quite willing to resort to force. Josephus reports three incidents during the rule of Pilate that involved him in considerable controversy.[6] He sent Roman troops into Jerusalem bearing standards with images of Caesar in defiance of the Jewish prohibition against images. He also confiscated money out of the sacred treasury in the Temple in order to build aqueducts. When crowds gathered to protest, he disguised troops as civilians and upon signal had them attack, thereby killing a number of persons. Finally, he sent soldiers to search out and destroy a band of Samaritans suspected of preparing for a rebellion. This portrayal of Pilate as a ruthless person, interestingly enough, receives support in the Gospels themselves, but outside passion narratives. In the Gospel of Luke, Jesus refers to an occasion when Pilate killed certain Galilean pilgrims who had come to Jerusalem to worship in the Temple (Luke 13:1-5). So the canonical passion accounts in a number of ways tend to shift the responsibility for Jesus' crucifixion from the Romans, from Pontius Pilate, to the Jewish authorities.

The *Gospel of Peter* is even more blatant than the canonical Gospels in blaming "the Jews" collectively for the death of Jesus. The opening lines of what remains of this Gospel depicts "the Jews," including Herod, as refusing to wash their hands of the Jesus matter. Herod himself presides over the proceedings, with Pilate a bystander, and Herod turns Jesus over to the people themselves who proceed to mock him and crucify him.

This political apologetic in the passion narratives not only makes it difficult for the historian to move from literary sources to historical reconstruction but becomes a source for the anti-Semitism that has marked much of western history and the history of the church.[7]

There is, however, still a third feature of the Gospel passion narratives that complicates the historian's task. *The passion narratives present very different, sometimes contradictory, perspectives on specific issues related to the death of Jesus.*

Historical Issues

The Gospels offer similar outlines of the events leading up to the death of Jesus. But they differ among themselves about particular issues. The issues about which they present some disagreement include the date of his death, the Jewish and Roman legal proceedings prior to his death, and his own interpretation of his death.

The Date

According to the Jewish calendar, the seven-day week was climaxed by the Sabbath, the day of rest. Each twenty-four-hour day began at sundown so that the darkness plus the light equaled one day. Passover, the annual spring festival that commemorated the Exodus from Egypt under Moses, could fall on any day of the week in a given year. The Passover celebration itself centered around two events. In the afternoon of the fourteenth day of the month called Nisan, lambs were ritually slain in the Temple at Jerusalem. That evening after sundown, Nisan 15, the Passover meal was eaten in small groups at selected places around the city of Jerusalem. The meal included roasted lamb, unleavened bread, and bitter herbs; wine was drunk at prescribed intervals (cf. Exod. 12). The liturgy at the table involved the remembrance of God's deliverance of Israel from past bondage and the prayer for God's continued good favor toward Israel .

The Gospels agree that Jesus' last supper was held (by our reckoning) on a Thursday evening and that he was crucified on Friday the following day. Friday, of course, was the day of preparation for the Sabbath that began at sundown. But the Gospels disagree about the relationship between these events and the Passover celebration. According to the Synoptics, Jesus' last meal on Thursday evening was a Passover meal (Mark 14:12-16 par.) and his crucifixion on Friday occurred on Passover day. The meal and the execution took place on Nisan 15. But according to John, the supper on Thursday evening was not a Passover meal because his crucifixion on Friday occurred on the day of preparation for Passover (John 18:28; 19:14, 31, 42). The meal and the execution took place on Nisan 14. In John, therefore, Jesus died on the cross at the time the Passover lambs were being slaughtered in the Temple.

There are at least four ways of handling the apparently conflicting data relative to the time of the Last Supper and crucifixion. Representative scholars have adopted each of these possibilities.

1. The *Synoptic dating* has been adopted. The Last Supper was a Passover meal and the crucifixion occurred on Passover day, Nisan 15. From this perspective, the dating of John was theologically motivated. John changed the dating of the crucifixion to the day of preparation for Passover because he desired to have Jesus' death coincide with the slaughter of the Passover lambs (cf. John 1:29, 36).

The case for the Synoptic dating rests to a large extent on details in the passion accounts that are in keeping with the Passover celebration. Joachim Jeremias was a staunch advocate of this view.[8] He cited several incidental items in the stories of the Last Supper that point to its character as a Passover meal: Jesus hosted the supper in Jerusalem as required for a Passover meal and did not withdraw to Bethany as he had done earlier in the week. After the supper, he remained within the extended city limits of Jerusalem (in Gethsemane on the Mount of Olives) as also required for a Passover meal. The supper was eaten at night like Passover meals and not in the late afternoon as customary with daily meals. The dish into which the disciples dipped with Jesus was probably that which contained the sauce for the unleavened bread and the bitter herbs. The comparison made by Jesus between the wine and his blood suggests the use of red wine as characteristic of a Passover meal. White or black wines were more common for daily use. The supper concluded with singing. This probably involved the singing of the Hallel, the six psalms of thanksgiving sung at Passover (Pss. 113–118).

The supporters of the Synoptic dating must explain the absence of any reference to the Passover lamb in the stories of the Last Supper, if it was a Passover meal. Some interpreters claim that those who told the stories simply omitted such a reference because of their primary interest in those elements central for the church's sacrament of the Lord's Supper—the bread and the wine. Other interpreters suggest that Jesus himself may have intentionally omitted the Passover lamb because he was presenting himself as a substitute. But this absence of any reference to the Passover lamb, among other reasons, has led still other interpreters to reject the Synoptic dating in favor of another alternative.

2. The *Johannine dating* has been adopted. The Last Supper was not a Passover meal, and the crucifixion occurred on the day of preparation for Passover, Nisan 14. From this perspective, the Synoptic dating was theologically motivated. The Synoptic writers and their predecessors wished to connect more closely the sacramental meal of the church with the commemorative meal of Judaism—the Lord's Supper with the Passover supper.

The principal case for the Johannine dating rests on details in the passion narratives that make improbable the Synoptic dating of the crucifixion on Passover day, Nisan 15. Passover as a holy day was considered a Sabbath and its holiness was protected by traditional Sabbath restrictions. Several incidents related to the crucifixion are difficult to understand as having happened on a Sabbath, and thus on Passover. These incidents include Jewish participation in the legal proceedings against Jesus, the crucifixion itself, the travel of Simon of Cyrene "from the country" (Mark 15:21 par.), the purchase of the "linen cloth" by Joseph of Arimathea (Mark 15:46 par.), and the burial of Jesus' body.

Shirley Jackson Case decided against the Synoptic dating and for the Johannine dating of the crucifixion, and thus the Last Supper, based on his principle of suitability.[9] The Synoptic dating would be less suitable and the Johannine dating more suitable for the Palestinian Jewish setting. Both Raymond E. Brown and John Dominic Crossan also favor the Johannine dating. Brown notes how Paul in the earliest written account of the Last Supper makes no mention of it as a Passover meal (1 Cor. 11:23-32), which supports its not having been a Passover meal.[10] Crossan points to the *Gospel of Peter* and the underlying Cross Gospel, which claim that Jesus' crucifixion occurred on the day of preparation for Passover, not on Passover day (GPet. 2:5).[11]

Other scholars faced with the differences in dating between the Synoptics and John have followed still other alternatives.

3. *Both the Synoptic and the Johannine datings* have been adopted. In spite of the apparent contradictions in chronology between the synoptic Gospels and the Gospel of John, some scholars have tried to harmonize them. Central to many harmonizing efforts is the acceptance of the dating in John as the dating for the Last Supper and crucifixion according to the "official" calendar prevalent in Jerusalem. Jesus, therefore, observed his final meal and suffered execution on the day of preparation for Passover, Nisan 14.

Sometimes these harmonizations include the claim that Jesus on the evening of Nisan 14 nonetheless celebrated his last supper as a Passover meal a day early, knowing that his arrest was imminent, as proposed by C. H. Dodd.[12] But at other times these harmonizations claim that Jesus celebrated it as a Passover meal according to a different "unofficial" calendar, such as the calendar used at Qumran.[13] But whatever the reason given for Jesus' having celebrated it as a Passover meal, the Synoptic presentation of that supper as a Passover meal is thereby explained. Both the Synoptic and the Johannine accounts, therefore, preserve something of the truth about the time of Jesus' final hours. But there are yet other scholars faced with the differences between these accounts who pursue the final alternative.

4. *Neither the Synoptic nor the Johannine dating* is adopted. Günther Bornkamm recognized theological motives behind the Markan and the Johannine dating. He was content to say that Jesus was arrested, tried, and executed at Passover time.[14]

The Trial(s)

The administration of justice in Roman Judea at the time of Jesus was centered in the Emperor's appointed governor, the prefect, such as Pontius Pilate (26–36 C.E.). In typical Roman fashion, he shared the responsibility for law enforcement with local authorities. The most important governing body for first-century Judaism was the Sanhedrin, or Council, in Jerusalem. This seventy or seventy-one member council under the leadership of the high priest, such as Caiaphas (26–36 C.E.), could convene as a law court. Today no Roman documents exist that clearly delineate the judicial arrangement between the Roman governors and the Jewish Sanhedrin. Whether or not the Sanhedrin retained the authority to pass final judgment in cases involving the death penalty has been much debated. Also today no Jewish documents exist that provide certain information about the judicial regulations and procedures of the Sanhedrin at the time of Jesus. The Mishnah, that collection of laws written toward the beginning of the third century, does contain a tractate, or section, called "The Sanhedrin," but its applicability to the first-century situation has been debated.

Uncertainties about the relationship between the Gospel accounts and about the customary legal practices in Roman Judea, therefore, constitute a major problem for any historian who intends to reconstruct the trial of Jesus. But another major problem comes from the Gospels themselves. The Gospels agree on the broad framework within which the legal proceedings against Jesus took place. They agree that the Jewish authorities conspired against him and had him arrested, but that the Romans executed him on political charges as "King of the Jews." But the Gospels also disagree among themselves on a number of significant points.

The Gospels disagree on the exact nature of the legal proceedings against Jesus by the Jewish authorities. Mark, followed by Matthew, reports that Jesus on the night of his arrest is taken before the high priest and the Sanhedrin. A *formal trial* takes place with testimony by witnesses, the interrogation of Jesus himself, an accusation of blasphemy by the high priest, and a condemnation unto death by those present. The next morning, the Sanhedrin meets again before handing Jesus over to Pontius Pilate (Mark 14:53–15:1 and Matt. 26:57–27:2). Neither Luke nor John, however, mentions a formal trial of Jesus before the Sanhedrin. In Luke, Jesus on the night of his arrest is taken to the high priest's house, but there is no reference to his having met with the high priest and no gathering of the Sanhedrin. When the Sanhedrin does meet the next morning, the meeting has more the character of an *inquiry* than a trial (Luke 22:54–23:1). In John, and only in John, Jesus is taken after his arrest to Caiaphas only after a prior appearance before Annas—Caiaphas's father-in-law, a former high priest himself. A *conversation* occurs between Jesus and Annas. But there is no gathering of the Sanhedrin that night or the next morning (John 18:12-28).

The Gospels also disagree on the charges brought against Jesus by the Jewish authorities at the trial before Pontius Pilate. Mark and Matthew do not report the accusations made by the Jewish authorities before Pilate although they had stressed Jesus' blasphemy before the high priest and the Sanhedrin. Luke and John do report the charges made against Jesus—but very different charges. Luke says that the Jewish authorities bring *political* charges before Pilate: "We found this man perverting our nation, forbidding us to pay taxes to the emperor, and saying that he himself is the Messiah, a king" (Luke 23:2; also vs. 5). John says that the Jewish authorities bring *religious* charges before Pilate: "We have a law, and according to that law he ought to die because he has claimed to be the Son of God" (John 19:7).

Finally, the Gospels disagree on the reason the Jewish authorities took their case before Pontius Pilate instead of taking final action against Jesus. In Mark and Matthew, the Sanhedrin condemns him as deserving death for blasphemy. But neither Gospel contains an explanation of why that body did not follow through with his execution, which presumably would have been by stoning. In Luke, the Jewish leaders make accusations of a political nature against Jesus before Pilate. The implication may be that the Jewish leaders brought the case before Pilate because they all along considered Jesus' offenses to be essentially political and not religious. But in John, there does appear to be an explicit reason why the Jewish authorities took their case before Pilate. Those authorities reportedly remind Pilate: "We are not permitted to put anyone to death" (John 18:31). Accordingly, the Jewish leaders did not execute Jesus because under Roman rule they did not have the authority.

The trial of Jesus continues to be the subject for detailed investigation and speculation. In attempting to unravel the threads in the mystery of the legal actions taken against Jesus, interpreters voice opinions with subtleties appropriate for a complicated historical issue. Haim Cohn, a Justice of the Supreme Court of the modern state of Israel, once reviewed the evidence for the legal proceedings against Jesus with sometimes astonishing results.[15] He even claimed that Caiaphas supported Jesus' action in the Temple and convened the Sanhedrin to develop strategy to win acquittal for Jesus before Pontius Pilate. Obviously the ploy failed. Various interpretations with many nuances have been proposed regarding the legal actions taken against Jesus; but three principal alternatives have emerged.

1. Jesus was subjected to *two trials*, a *Jewish trial* directed by Caiaphas before the Sanhedrin and a *Roman trial* convened by Pontius Pilate. This traditional, and still common, position results from what amounts to a harmonizing of the four Gospel accounts but with prominence given to the Markan and the Matthean accounts.

Although Raymond E. Brown tends to view Jesus' appearance before Caiaphas—after Jesus' arrest—as an interrogation instead of formal trial, he does consider historical events to underlie the Gospel presentations of a Jewish trial and a Roman trial.[16] N. T. Wright is also reluctant to refer to Jesus' appearance before the Jewish authorities as a trial and prefers instead to speak about "Jewish hearing(s)," but in the final analysis he upholds the basic historicity of at least two formal gatherings, one Jewish and the other Roman.[17]

Jesus was arrested by representatives of the Jewish authorities and taken before the Sanhedrin for trial. Witnesses were heard but did not agree with one another in their testimony. The high priest then asked Jesus about his messianic pretensions or aspirations. For whatever precise reasons, Jesus' reply was viewed as blasphemy. He was condemned as worthy of death. The

Romans, however, had reserved for themselves the right of final judgment in capital cases, so Jesus also had to stand trial before Pilate. In order to obtain a death sentence for Jesus from Pilate, the Jewish leaders had to present their case in political terms. Specifically, he was taken to Pilate as one pretending to be Messiah or "King of the Jews." Pilate had reservations about Jesus' guilt and possibly thought him innocent. But he finally gave in to the pressure of the Jewish leaders and the cries of the aroused crowds. He released Barabbas and sentenced Jesus to death by crucifixion. On a Roman cross, therefore, Jesus died as King of the Jews. From this perspective, the statement in the Gospel of John that the Jewish authorities could not put a person to death is judged to be historically accurate.

2. Jesus was subjected to only *one trial*—the *Roman trial* before Pontius Pilate. This position has been argued, with variations, by Paul Winter[18] and William R. Wilson.[19] It rests upon the dismissal of the Markan account of the Jewish trial as nonhistorical. It also gives special weight to the Lukan account of the trial that concentrates on the political charges brought against Jesus by the Jewish authorities before Pilate.

Jesus was arrested by a company of persons sent by the Jewish leaders. But the leaders subjected him to interrogation and not to a formal trial. The purpose of the questioning by the high priest was to formulate a case against him as an insurrectionist and a political threat. The next day, Pontius Pilate sat in judgment over Jesus' case as well as the case against Barabbas. The followers of Barabbas cried out for him to be released. In response, Pilate let Barabbas go. But he accepted the political accusations against Jesus and sentenced him to death by crucifixion. From this perspective, the question of the power of Jewish leaders to execute a person is irrelevant for the case of Jesus. They all along perceived him to be a political threat and intended to prosecute him as such before Pilate. This idea that Jesus was viewed as a political threat by the Jewish authorities opens up the possibility that their conspiracy against Jesus involved the Romans from the beginning. That Caiaphas and Pontius Pilate ruled simultaneously for ten years suggests some degree of cooperation and mutual respect. There is also a brief notation in the Gospels that Roman soldiers were included in the company that arrested Jesus (John 18:3; cf. 11:45-53).

3. *Jesus had no trial.* This is the position advocated by John Dominic Crossan.[20] Crossan considers Jesus' action in the Temple to be the crime that led to his arrest. His followers fled and would not have known exactly what happened thereafter. What did happen was Jesus' crucifixion. Given the nature of power arrangements between the Roman patrons and the Jewish clients, between Pilate and Caiaphas, Crossan sees no need to postulate a trial or trials. Neither trial account rests upon history remembered. Both trial accounts represent prophecy historicized.

The Death

That Jesus died on a Roman cross is indisputable. But how did he understand his death? This question has generated considerable discussion. The historical quest itself began with the claim by Hermann Samuel Reimarus that to Jesus, death was unexpected and tragic. In the course of our own quest, we have encountered many different answers to this question. A significant number of scholars have claimed that any answer lies beyond the reach of historical scholarship.

All four Gospels, however, say that Jesus used his final meal with his followers as an occasion to interpret by deed and by word the meaning of his impending death. In John, Jesus washes his disciples' feet in anticipation of his supreme act of self-giving love on the cross (John 13:1-20). In the Synoptics, Jesus uses bread and wine as symbols for his body and blood (Mark 14:22-25 par.; 1 Cor. 11:23-32). Mark describes the scene in these words:

> While they were eating, he took a loaf of bread, and after blessing it he broke it, gave it to them, and said, *"Take; this is my body."* Then he took a cup, and after giving thanks he gave it to them, and all of them drank from it. He said to them, *"This is my blood of the covenant, which is poured out for many.* Truly I tell you, I will never again drink of the fruit of the vine until that day when I drink it new in the kingdom of God."

The distinction is customarily made between Jesus' words of interpretation (in italics above) and the concluding eschatological saying about the "kingdom of God." Scholars have debated whether the words of institution and the eschatological saying can be used as evidence for Jesus' understanding of his death.

By the principle of dissimilarity, of course, the words over the bread and wine cannot be established as authentic. They are not only similar to but identical with the teaching and sacramental practice of the church. But some scholars, such as Günther Bornkamm, who suspend judgment about the words of interpretation nonetheless accept as historical the saying about the kingdom of God.[21] The dissimilarity of this saying to the teaching and sacramental practice of the early church is indicated by its omission from Paul's account of the institution of the Lord's Supper. The eschatological hope of the Pauline and other early Christian communities was expressed not in terms of the coming kingdom but in terms of the parousia, the second coming, of the Lord Jesus Christ.

Other scholars, however, have been less willing to push to one side the words of interpretation over the bread and wine. They confidently draw upon these words as evidence of how Jesus viewed his approaching death. Working back from the Greek texts of the Gospels, they have even attempted to reconstruct the earlier Aramaic forms of the bread and wine sayings.

The amount of textual evidence they have to work with is greater than immediately apparent. There is Mark's account of what Jesus said over the bread and wine, which has parallels, with differences in wording, in both Matthew and Luke. There is also Paul's account of what Jesus said, again with differences in wording. But there is available still more evidence. Luke itself, at least in some ancient Greek manuscripts of that Gospel, reports words of Jesus over the bread and wine not found in Mark. The King James Version and the New Revised Standard Version include these words in their text of Luke (22:19*b*-20). The Revised Standard Version and the New English Bible, however, exclude these words and print them as footnotes. Also, the second-century Christian advocate for the faith known as Justin Martyr reports Jesus' words in greatly abbreviated form: "This is my body. . . . This is my blood."

Swiss scholar Eduard Schweizer acknowledged indebtedness to the scholarship of Joachim Jeremias and listed three possibilities for the Aramaic forms of Jesus' words of interpretation over the bread and wine:[22]

1. Jesus said: "This is my body.... This cup is the new covenant in my blood." The phrase "new covenant" appears in the Pauline text and in the longer version of the Lukan text. If Jesus uttered these words during the Last Supper, then he understood his death primarily in terms of *covenant-making.* The new covenant was established by the shedding of blood and with a sacred meal just as the old covenant was ratified through Moses by the shedding of blood and with a sacred meal (Exod. 24:1-8).

2. Jesus said: "Take; this is my body.... This is my blood which is poured out for many." The phrase "for many" appears in the Markan and the Matthean texts. If Jesus uttered these words during the Last Supper, then he understood his death primarily in terms of *substitutionary atonement.* The idea of suffering for others is reflected in the "Suffering Servant" passages of Isaiah (especially Isa. 52:13–53:12) that some interpreters consider to underlie Jesus' sayings about the suffering "Son of Man" (Mark 8:31 par.; et al.).

3. Jesus said neither of the above. It has been suggested on occasion that the words of institution presented by Justin Martyr represent the oldest form of what Jesus said at his final meal: "This is my body" and "This is my blood." If Jesus uttered these words over the bread and wine, then he understood his death quite simply as *martyrdom.* This understanding would be in keeping with those other sayings of Jesus where he places himself and his ministry in the succession of those prophets who suffered for their faithfulness to God (Mark 6:4 par.; Luke 13:32-33; Luke 13:34-35 = Matt. 23:37-39).

The ideas of new covenant, substitutionary atonement, and martyrdom do not necessarily contradict or exclude one another. If Jesus did use bread and wine to interpret his approaching death on the cross, he incorporated his death into his ministry of word and deed. For him, according to this view, his death was neither unexpected nor tragic. He died in obedience to God and on behalf of others.

The later church obviously viewed the different reports of Jesus' words at the Last Supper as supportive of one another. In the New Testament, the church included the different writings containing these reports of what Jesus said on the night he was betrayed. In its liturgy for the sacrament of the Lord's Supper, the church still harmonizes Jesus' words. The historical Jesus becomes the contemporary Christ of faith for believers who recite these words within the context of worship:

> On the night in which he gave himself up for us,
>> he took bread, gave thanks to you, broke the bread,
>> gave it to his disciples, and said:
> *"Take, eat; this is my body which is given for you.*
> *Do this in remembrance of me."*

> When the supper was over, he took the cup,
>> gave thanks to you, gave it to his disciples, and said:
> *"Drink from this, all of you;*
>> *this is my blood of the new covenant,*
>> *poured out for you and for many*
>>> *for the forgiveness of sins.*
> *Do this, as often as you drink it,*
>> *in remembrance of me."*[23] (italics added)

231

Notes

Introduction: Who Is Jesus?

1. W. Barnes Tatum, *Jesus at the Movies: A Guide to the First Hundred Years* (Santa Rosa, Calif.: Polebridge Press, 1997).

2. Jaroslav Pelikan, *Jesus Through the Centuries: His Place in the History of Culture* (New Haven: Yale University Press, 1985).

3. Walter Rauschenbusch, *A Theology for the Social Gospel* (1917; reprint, Nashville: Abingdon Press, 1978).

4. Charles M. Sheldon, *In His Steps* (1897; Nashville: Broadman and Holman Publishers, 1995).

5. Nikos Kazantzakis, *The Last Temptation of Christ*, trans. P. A. Bien (New York: Simon & Schuster, 1960).

6. Kazantzakis, *The Saviors of God: Spiritual Exercises*, trans. Kimon Friar (New York: Simon & Schuster, 1960), 106.

7. The lecture by Clarence Jordan, "Jesus the Rebel," on cassette tape (Americus, Ga.: Koinonia Partners, n.d.).

8. Albert B. Cleage Jr., *The Black Messiah* (New York: Sheed and Ward, 1968).

9. For writings by Harvey Cox with similar themes, see: "God and the Hippies," *Playboy* (January 1968); *The Feast of Fools: A Theological Essay on Festivity and Fantasy* (Cambridge: Harvard University Press, 1969).

Chapter 1: Gospel Origins

1. Eusebius, *The Ecclesiastical History*, trans. Kirsopp Lake and J. E. L. Oulton, 2 vols., The Loeb Classical Library (Cambridge: Harvard University Press, 1926, 1932), III.xxxix.15.

2. Ibid., III.xxxix.16.

3. Ibid., III.xxxix.4.

4. *New Testament Apocrypha*, ed. Edgar Hennecke and Wilhelm Schneemelcher, English translation ed. R. McL. Wilson (Philadelphia: Westminster Press, 1963–1964), 1:43.

5. *Early Christian Fathers*, ed. Cyril C. Richardson, The Library of Christian Classics, vol. 1 (Philadelphia: Westminster Press, 1953), 370.

6. Ibid., 382.

7. *The Other Gospels: Non-Canonical Gospel Texts*, ed. Ron Cameron (Philadelphia: Westminster, 1982); *The Complete Gospels: Annotated Scholars Version*, rev. ed., ed. Robert J. Miller (Santa Rosa, Calif.: Polebridge Press, 1994); Bart D. Ehrman, *The New Testament and Other Early Christian Literature* (New York-Oxford: Oxford University Press, 1998).

8. Eusebius, *Ecclesiastical History*, VI.xiv.5-7.

9. Philip Schaff, ed., *A Select Library of the Nicene and Post-Nicene Fathers of the Christian Church* (1888; reprint, Grand Rapids: Eerdmans, 1991), 6:78-80.

10. For this alternative contemporary view, see the writings of Burton L. Mack: *The Myth of Innocence: Mark and Christian Origins*, Foundations and Facets (Philadelphia: Fortress Press, 1988); *Who Wrote the New Testament? The Making of the Christian Myth* (San Francisco: HarperSanFrancisco, 1989); *The Lost Gospel: The Book of Q and Christian Origins* (San Francisco: HarperSanFrancisco, 1993).

Chapter 2: Gospel Criticism

1. Theodore G. Tappert, ed., *Selected Writings of Martin Luther,* vol. 4 (Philadelphia: Fortress Press, 1967), 398.

2. William R. Farmer, *The Synoptic Problem: A Critical Analysis* (1964; reprint, Dillsboro, N.C.: Western North Carolina Press, 1976).

3. H. J. Holtzmann, *Die synoptischen Evangelien: Ihr Ursprung und geschichtlicher Charakter (The Synoptic Gospels: Their Origin and Historical Character)* (Leipzig: Engelmann, 1863).

4. B. H. Streeter, *The Four Gospels* (London: Macmillan, 1924).

5. K. L. Schmidt, *Der Rahmen der Geschichte Jesu: Literaturkritische Untersuchungen zur ältesten Jesusüberlieferung (The Framework of the Story of Jesus: Literary-Critical Investigations on the Oldest Jesus Tradition)* (Berlin: Trowitzsch, 1919).

6. Martin Dibelius, *From Tradition to Gospel,* trans. Bertram Lee Woolf (New York: Charles Scribner's Sons, 1935).

7. Rudolf Bultmann, *The History of the Synoptic Tradition,* trans. John Marsh, rev. ed. (New York: Harper & Row, 1976).

8. Consult C. H. Dodd, *The Apostolic Preaching and Its Developments* (New York: Harper & Brothers, 1936).

9. Vincent Taylor, *The Formation of the Gospel Tradition* (London: Macmillan, 1935).

10. Norman Perrin, *What Is Redaction Criticism?* Guides to Biblical Scholarship (Philadelphia: Fortress Press, 1969).

11. Günther Bornkamm, "The Stilling of the Storm," in *Tradition and Interpretation in Matthew,* trans. Percy Scott, New Testament Library (Philadelphia: Westminster Press, 1963), 52-57.

12. Willi Marxsen, *Mark the Evangelist: Studies on the Redaction History of the Gospel,* trans. James Boyce et al. (Nashville: Abingdon Press, 1969).

13. Hans Conzelmann, *The Theology of St. Luke,* trans. Geoffrey Buswell (New York: Harper & Row, 1960).

14. For an overview of these two approaches, see the collection of articles in *Gospel Interpretation: Narrative-Critical & Social-Scientific Approaches,* ed. Jack Dean Kingsbury (Harrisburg, Pa.: Trinity International Press, 1997).

15. Mark Allan Powell, *What Is Narrative Criticism?* Guides to Biblical Scholarship (Minneapolis: Fortress Press, 1990),

16. Werner H. Kelber, *Mark's Story of Jesus* (Philadelphia: Fortress Press, 1979).

17. David Rhoads and Donald Michie, *Mark as Story: An Introduction to the Narrative*

of a Gospel (Philadelphia: Fortress Press, 1982); Jack Dean Kingsbury, *Matthew as Story,* 2nd ed. (Philadelphia: Fortress Press, 1988); Robert C. Tannehill, *The Narrative Unity of Luke-Acts: A Literary Interpretation,* 2 vols. (Philadelphia: Fortress Press, 1986, 1990); R. Alan Culpepper, *Anatomy of the Fourth Gospel: A Study in Literary Design,* Foundations and Facets (Philadelphia: Fortress Press, 1983).

18. John H. Elliott, *What Is Social-Scientific Criticism?* Guides to Biblical Scholarship (Minneapolis: Fortress Press, 1993).

19. See, for example: Shirley Jackson Case, *Jesus: A New Biography* (Chicago: University of Chicago Press, 1927); and Shailer Mathews, *Jesus on Social Institutions* (New York: Macmillan, 1928).

20. Gerd Theissen, *Sociology of Early Palestinian Christianity,* trans. John Bowden (Philadelphia: Fortress Press, 1978).

21. Bruce J. Malina, *The New Testament World: Insights from Cultural Anthropology,* rev. ed. (Louisville: Westminster/John Knox Press, 1993), *Christian Origins and Cultural Anthropology: Practical Models for Biblical Interpretation* (Atlanta: John Knox Press, 1986), *Windows on the World of Jesus: Time Travel to Ancient Judea* (Louisville: Westminster/John Knox Press, 1993).

22. Bruce J. Malina and Richard L. Rohrbaugh, *Social-Science Commentary on the Synoptic Gospels* (Minneapolis: Fortress Press, 1992).

23. P. Gardner-Smith, *Saint John and the Synoptic Gospels* (Cambridge: Cambridge University Press, 1938).

24. D. Moody Smith, *John Among the Gospels: The Relationship in Twentieth-Century Research* (Minneapolis: Fortress Press, 1992).

25. See, for example, Robert T. Fortna, *The Fourth Gospel and Its Predecessor: From Narrative Source to Present Gospel* (Philadelphia: Fortress Press, 1988).

Chapter 3: Gospel Portrayals

1. Charles Talbert, *What Is a Gospel? The Genre of the Canonical Gospels* (Philadelphia: Fortress Press, 1977), 16; also R. A. Burridge, *What Are the Gospels? A Comparison with Graeco-Roman Biography* (Cambridge: Cambridge University Press, 1992).

2. Helmut Koester, *Ancient Christian Gospels: Their History and Development* (Philadelphia: Trinity Press International, 1990), 46.

3. Burton Mack, *The Myth of Innocence: Mark and Christian Origins* (Philadelphia: Fortress Press, 1988), 315ff.

4. B. W. Bacon, *Studies in Matthew* (New York: Henry Holt, 1930).

5. Jack Dean Kingsbury, *Matthew: Structure, Christology, Kingdom* (Philadelphia: Fortress Press, 1975), 7-11.

6. W. D. Davies, *The Setting of the Sermon on the Mount* (Cambridge: University Press, 1964).

7. Anthony J. Saldarini, *Matthew's Christian-Jewish Community,* Chicago Studies in the History of Judaism (Chicago-London: University of Chicago Press, 1994), 7-9.

8. Raymond E. Brown, *The Birth of the Messiah: A Commentary on the Infancy Narratives in the Gospels of Matthew and Luke,* rev. ed. (Garden City, N.Y.: Doubleday, 1993), 241-43.

9. W. Barnes Tatum, "The Epoch of Israel: Luke 1–2 and the Theological Plan of Luke-Acts." *New Testament Studies* 13 (1967): 184-95.

10. Philip Francis Esler, *Community and Gospel in Luke-Acts: The Social and Political Motivations of Lucan Theology* (Cambridge: Cambridge University Press, 1987), 24-45. For the application of social-scientific models to Luke-Acts, see: Jerome H. Neyrey, ed. *The Social World of Luke-Acts: Models for Interpretation* (Peabody, Mass.: Hendricksen Publishers, 1991).

11. Rudolf Bultmann, *The Gospel of John: A Commentary*, German original, 1941; trans. G. R. Beasley-Murray (Philadelphia: Westminster Press, 1971).

12. J. Louis Martyn, *The Gospel of John in Christian History: Essays for Interpreters* (New York: Paulist Press, 1978); also see his *History and Theology in the Fourth Gospel*, rev. ed. (Nashville: Abingdon Press, 1979).

13. Raymond E. Brown, *The Community of the Beloved Disciple: The Life, Loves, and Hates of an Individual Church in New Testament Times* (New York: Paulist Press, 1979).

14. Urban C. von Wahlde, "Community in Conflict: The History and Social Context of the Johannine Community," in *Gospel Interpretation*, 222-33.

15. The thesis of Leon Morris, "The Fourth Gospel and History," *Jesus of Nazareth: Saviour and Lord*, ed. Carl F. H. Henry (Grand Rapids: Eerdmans, 1966), 123-32.

16. The texts and background information on these other Gospels can be found in *The Complete Gospels: Annotated Scholars Version*, ed. Robert J. Miller (Santa Rosa, Calif.: Polebridge Press, 1994), and John S. Kloppenborg et al., *Q Thomas Reader: The Gospels Before the Gospels* (Sonoma, Calif.: Polebridge Press, 1990).

17. Morton Smith, *The Secret Gospel: The Discovery and Interpretation of the Secret Gospel According to Mark* (New York: Harper and Row, 1973).

18. *The Nag Hammadi Library in English*, ed. James M. Robinson, 4th ed. (New York: E. J. Brill, 1996).

19. John Dominic Crossan, *The Cross That Spoke: The Origins of the Passion Narrative* (San Francisco: Harper & Row, 1988).

20. Quotations from the *Gospel of Thomas* are taken from Kloppenborg et al., *Q Thomas Reader.*

21. Stephen J. Patterson, *The Gospel of Thomas and Jesus: Thomas Christianity, Social Radicalism, and the Quest of the Historical Jesus* (Sonoma, Calif.: Polebridge Press, 1992).

22. See Leif E. Vaage, *Galilean Upstarts: Jesus' First Followers According to Q* (Valley Forge, Pa.: Trinity Press International, 1994).

23. John S. Kloppenborg, *The Formation of Q: Trajectories in Ancient Wisdom Collections* (Philadelphia: Fortress Press, 1987), 92. The verses in parentheses are disputed by some scholars relative to their position in the order of Q (16:16) or their presence in Q (12:13-14, 16-21). Also see Kloppenborg's *Q Parallels: Synopsis, Critical Notes, and Concordance*, Foundations and Facets (Sonoma, Calif.: Polebridge Press, 1988). For a recent overview and assessment of Kloppenborg's work by someone who ended up writing a compositional history of Q contrary to his original intentions, see Dale C. Allison Jr., *The Jesus Tradition in Q* (Harrisburg, Pa.: Trinity Press International, 1997).

Chapter 4: Historical Problem

1. Marcus J. Borg, "Portraits of Jesus," in *The Search for Jesus: Modern Scholarship Looks at the Gospels*, ed. Hershel Shanks (Washington, D.C.: Biblical Archaeology Society, 1994), 86.

2. John P. Meier, *A Marginal Jew: Rethinking the Historical Jesus*, 2 vols. (New York: Doubleday, 1991, 1994), 1:21-40; but compare Luke Timothy Johnson, *The Real Jesus: The Misguided Quest for the Historical Jesus and the Truth of the Traditional Gospels* (San Francisco: HarperSanFrancisco, 1996), 141-66.

3. C. Stephen Evans, *The Historical Christ and the Jesus of Faith: The Incarnational Narrative as History* (Oxford: Clarendon Press, 1996).

Chapter 5: Historical Search

1. John Calvin, *A Harmony of the Gospels of Matthew, Mark, and Luke*, trans. A. W. Morrison, 3 vols. (Grand Rapids: Eerdmans, 1972).

2. *Reimarus: Fragments*, ed. Charles H. Talbert, trans. Ralph S. Fraser, Lives of Jesus Series (Philadelphia: Fortress Press, 1970).

3. Ibid., 150.

4. Ibid., 151.

5. David Friedrich Strauss, *Life of Jesus Critically Examined*, ed. Peter C. Hodgson, trans. George Eliot, Lives of Jesus Series (Philadelphia: Fortress Press, 1972).

6. Ernest Renan, *Life of Jesus*, Modern Library (New York: Random House, 1927, 1955).

7. Albert Schweitzer, *The Quest of the Historical Jesus*, trans. W. Montgomery (1910; reprint, New York: Macmillan, 1968).

8. Ibid., 398.

9. Ibid., 401.

10. Ibid., 358-59.

11. Ibid., 389.

12. This turn-of-the-century skepticism has become associated especially with William Wrede. His work on the gospels led him to the conclusion that the "messianic secrecy" motif that runs through Mark did *not* go back to the historical Jesus who believed that he was the Messiah but maintained secrecy about his messianic identity. Instead the "messianic secrecy" motif originated within the early church to explain why Jesus was not recognized as Messiah during his lifetime. See Wrede's *Das Messiasgeheimnis in den Evangelien [The Messianic Secret in the Gospels]* Göttingen: Vandenhoeck & Ruprecht, 1901).

13. Rudolf Bultmann, *Jesus and the Word*, trans. Louise Pettibone Smith and Erminie Huntress Lantero (New York: Charles Scribner's Sons, 1934, 1958). A significant precursor of Bultmann and the "no quest" point of view was Martin Kähler, *The So-Called Historical Jesus and the Historic, Biblical Christ*, trans. and ed. Carl E. Braaten (German original, 1896; Philadelphia: Fortress Press, 1964).

14. Ernst Käsemann, *Essays on New Testament Themes*, trans. W. J. Montague, Studies in Biblical Theology (London: SCM Press, 1964), 15-47.

15. Ibid., 45.

16. Ibid., 45-46.

17. Ibid., 46.

18. Günther Bornkamm, *Jesus of Nazareth*, trans. Irene McLuskey and Fraser McLuskey with James M. Robinson (New York: Harper & Brothers, 1960).

19. James M. Robinson, *A New Quest of the Historical Jesus*, Studies in Biblical Theology (London: SCM Press, 1959).

20. The phrase *third quest* with reference to Jesus research originated with British scholar N. T. Wright. See: Stephen C. Neill and N. Thomas Wright, *The Interpretation of the New Testament, 1861–1986* (Oxford: Oxford University Press, 1988); "Jesus, Quest for the Historical" in *The Anchor Bible Dictionary*. Wright, however, uses the phrase not to designate a chronological period but the kind of Jesus research practiced by E. P. Sanders and himself, among others. Accordingly, the third quest carries on the tradition of Albert Schweitzer and views Jesus within the context of Jewish eschatological tradition. Thus Wright sharply distinguishes between those scholars who follow the third quest and those who continue the "new quest," such as Robert W. Funk, John Dominic Crossan, and the Jesus Seminar. Funk, in his recent monograph on Jesus, also distinguishes his task from that of the "third questers" whose work he sees as an apology for Christian orthodoxy. Thus he prefers to identify his approach and interests as the "renewed quest." See Robert W. Funk, *Honest to Jesus: Jesus for a New Millennium* (San Francisco: HarperSanFrancisco, 1996), 57-76. Others, however, have adopted the phrase "third quest" to designate more broadly the latest period of Jesus research. See, for example, M. Eugene Boring, "The 'Third Quest' and the Apostolic Faith," in *Gospel Interpretation: Narrative-Critical and Social-Scientific Approaches*, ed. Jack Dean Kingsbury (Harrisburg, Pa.: Trinity International Press, 1997), 237-52; and Ben Witherington III, *The Jesus Quest: The Third Search for the Jew of Nazareth*, 2nd ed. (Downers Grove, Ill.: InterVarsity Press, 1997). We have chosen the phrase *post-quest* to identify a distinguishing characteristic of the current phase of Jesus research as acknowledged by a cross-section of Jesus scholars: its theological neutrality.

21. E. P. Sanders, *Jesus and Judaism* (Philadelphia: Fortress Press, 1985), 2.

22. Robert W. Funk et al., *The Parables of Jesus: A Report of the Jesus Seminar* (Sonoma, Calif.: Polebridge Press, 1988), xii.

23. John Dominic Crossan, ed., *Sayings Parallels: A Workbook for the Jesus Tradition* (Philadelphia: Fortress Press, 1986).

24. Robert W. Funk, Roy W. Hoover, and The Jesus Seminar, *The Five Gospels: The Search for the Authentic Words of Jesus* (New York: Macmillan, 1993); and Robert W. Funk and The Jesus Seminar, *The Acts of Jesus: The Search for the Authentic Deeds of Jesus* (San Francisco: HarperSanFrancisco, 1998).

25. Walter P. Weaver, "Forward: Reflections on the Continuing Quest for Jesus," in *Images of Jesus Today*, ed. James H. Charlesworth and Walter P. Weaver, Faith & Scholarship Colloquies 3, Florida Southern College (Valley Forge, Pa.: Trinity Press International, 1994), xiv.

26. Boring, "Third Quest," 241.

27. Dennis Duling shared this phrase with me in a telephone conversation and later on a handout for his course at Canisius College: RST 305, Life and Teaching of Jesus (Spring 1998).

28. John P. Meier, *A Marginal Jew: Rethinking the Historical Jesus*, 2 vols. (New York: Doubleday, 1991, 1994), 1:1-2.

29. Sanders, *Jesus and Judaism*; James H. Charlesworth, *Jesus Within Judaism: New Light from Exciting Archaeological Discoveries*, The Anchor Bible Reference Library (New York: Doubleday, 1988); John Dominic Crossan, *The Historical Jesus: The Life of a Mediterranean Jewish Peasant* (San Francisco: HarperSanFrancisco, 1991); Geza Vermes, *Jesus the Jew: A Historian's Reading of the Gospels* (London: William Collins Sons,

1973), *Jesus and the World of Judaism* (Philadelphia: Fortress Press, 1983), and *The Religion of Jesus the Jew* (Minneapolis: Fortress Press, 1993).

30. For more detailed discussions of these, and other criteria, see: Mitchell G. Reddish, *An Introduction to the Gospels* (Nashville: Abingdon Press, 1997), 236-40; Meier, *Marginal Jew*, 1:167-95; and Norman Perrin, *Rediscovering the Teaching of Jesus* (New York: Harper & Row, 1967), 15-39.

31. Joachim Jeremias, *The Parables of Jesus*, rev. ed., trans. S. H. Hooke (New York: Charles Scribner's Sons, 1963); *The Lord's Prayer*, trans. John Reumann, Facet Books (Philadelphia: Fortress Press, 1964); and *The Eucharistic Words of Jesus*, trans. Norman Perrin (New York: Charles Scribner's Sons, 1966).

Chapter 6: Historical Portrayals

1. For a discussion of historical reason, its nature, mode of argumentation, and challenge to Christian faith, consult Van A. Harvey, *The Historian and the Believer: The Morality of Historical Knowledge and Christian Belief* (New York: Macmillan, 1966); also see I. Howard Marshall, *I Believe in the Historical Jesus* (Grand Rapids: Eerdmans, 1977).

2. Fulton Oursler, *The Greatest Story Ever Told* (Garden City, N.Y.: Doubleday, 1949).

3. Ian Wilson, *Jesus the Evidence* (San Francisco: HarperSanFrancisco, 1984).

4. David Smith, *The Days of His Flesh: The Earthly Life of Our Lord and Saviour Jesus Christ* (1905; reprint, Grand Rapids: Baker Book House, 1976).

5. Ibid., preface.

6. Hugh J. Schonfield, *The Passover Plot: New Light on the History of Jesus* (New York: Bernard Geis, 1965).

7. Ibid., 17.

8. Archibald M. Hunter, *The Work and Words of Jesus* (Philadelphia: Westminster Press, 1950; rev. ed., 1973).

9. T. W. Manson, *The Servant Messiah* (1953; Grand Rapids: Baker Book House, 1977).

10. Vincent Taylor, *The Life and Ministry of Jesus* (Nashville: Abingdon Press, 1955).

11. C. H. Dodd, *The Founder of Christianity* (New York: Macmillan, 1970).

12. Shirley Jackson Case, *Jesus: A New Biography* (Chicago: University of Chicago Press, 1927), preface.

13. For example: Morton Enslin, *The Prophet from Nazareth* (New York: McGraw-Hill, 1961); and, more recently, R. David Kaylor, *Jesus the Prophet: His Vision of the Kingdom on Earth* (Louisville: Westminster/John Knox Press, 1994).

14. Günther Bornkamm, *Jesus of Nazareth*, trans. Irene McLuskey and Fraser McLuskey with James M. Robinson (New York: Harper and Brothers, 1960), 21.

15. Ibid., 53, 55.

16. Ibid., 55, 154.

17. Ibid., 62, 64, 96.

18. Ibid., 172.

19. S. G. F. Brandon, *Jesus and the Zealots: A Study of the Political Factor in Primitive Christianity* (New York: Charles Scribner's Sons, 1967). For a response to Brandon and the debate over Jesus and the zealots, see Richard A. Horsley, *Jesus and the Spiral of*

Violence: Popular Jewish Resistance in Roman Palestine (1987; Minneapolis: Fortress Press, 1993); and Richard A. Horsley and John S. Hanson, *Bandits, Prophets, and Messiahs: Popular Movements in the Time of Jesus* (1985; reprint, San Francisco: Harper & Row, 1988).

20. Morton Smith, *Jesus the Magician* (New York: Harper and Row, 1978).

21. Brandon, *Jesus and the Zealots*, 350.

22. Ibid., 283-321.

23. E. P. Sanders, *The Historical Figure of Jesus* (London: Allen Lane, The Penguin Press, 1993).

24. E. P. Sanders, *Jesus and Judaism* (Philadelphia: Fortress Press, 1985), 11; *Historical Figure*, 10.

25. Sanders, *Historical Figure*, 73, 1.

26. Ibid., 183.

27. Ibid., 164, 168.

28. Ibid., 196-204.

29. Ibid., 215-17.

30. Ibid., 246-47, 261, 239-48.

31. Ibid., 274.

32. Ibid., 276-81.

33. John Dominic Crossan, *Jesus: A Revolutionary Biography* (San Francisco: HarperSanFrancisco, 1994).

34. John Dominic Crossan, *The Historical Jesus: The Life of a Mediterranean Jewish Peasant* (San Francisco: HarperSanFrancisco, 1991), xiii.

35. Ibid., xxviii.

36. Ibid., 266-69.

37. Crossan, *Revolutionary Biography*, 198.

38. Ibid., 44.

39. Ibid., 71, 66, 101.

40. Ibid., 99, 108, 80-82, 107.

41. Ibid., 127, 133.

42. Ibid., 197.

43. Marcus J. Borg, *Jesus: A New Vision: Spirit, Culture, and the Life of Discipleship* (San Francisco: Harper & Row, 1987).

44. Marcus J. Borg, *Meeting Jesus Again for the First Time* (San Francisco: HarperSanFrancisco, 1994).

45. Borg, *New Vision*, 1-21.

46. Ibid., 41.

47. Ibid., 131.

48. Ibid., 176, 179.

49. Ibid., 39, 184, 185, 191.

50. Ibid., 198, 202-3.

51. Ibid., 41, 49-51.

52. N. T. Wright, *The New Testament and the People of God* (Minneapolis: Fortress Press, 1992).

53. N. T. Wright, *Jesus and the Victory of God* (Minneapolis: Fortress Press, 1996).

54. Ibid., 87-88.

55. Ibid., 131-33, 149, 400-402.

56. Ibid., 126-27, 201.

57. Ibid., 150, 208.

58. Ibid., 198-474.

59. Ibid., 276.

60. Ibid., 320-68.

61. Ibid., 369-442; 473. Wright sometimes uses "god," as here, with the lower case to indicate the generic nature of the word.

62. Ibid., 610.

63. Ibid., 544.

64. Ibid., 657-62.

65. Elisabeth Schüssler Fiorenza, *In Memory of Her: A Feminist Theological Reconstruction of Christian Origins* (1983; New York: Crossroad, 1986).

66. Elisabeth Schüssler Fiorenza, *Jesus: Miriam's Child, Sophia's Prophet: Critical Issues in Feminist Christology* (New York: Continuum, 1994).

67. Schüssler Fiorenza, *In Memory*, 68-92.

68. Schüssler Fiorenza, *Jesus: Miriam's Child*, 82-88.

69. Ibid., 89.

70. Schüssler Fiorenza, *In Memory*, 106, 107.

71. Ibid., 110, 112, 115-18.

72. Ibid., 105-59; *Jesus: Miriam's Child*, 88-96.

73. Schüssler Fiorenza, *In Memory*, 118-30.

74. Ibid., 130, 132, 134.

75. Schüssler Fiorenza, *Jesus: Miriam's Child*, 108-9.

76. Ibid., 122ff.

77. Ibid., 127. In this book Schüssler Fiorenza uses G*d as a way of indicating the inadequacy of language about God. Her earlier adoption of the Orthodox Jewish spelling G-d had led to objections from Jewish feminists, who considered that spelling as presupposing a too conservative, or reactionary, frame of reference.

Chapter 7: Resurrection and Virgin Birth

1. Norman Perrin, *The Resurrection According to Matthew, Mark, and Luke* (Philadelphia: Fortress Press, 1977); Reginald H. Fuller, *The Formation of the Resurrection Narratives*, 2nd ed. (Philadelphia: Fortress Press, 1980); Pheme Perkins, *Resurrection: New Testament Witness and Contemporary Reflection* (Garden City, N.Y.: Doubleday, 1984); Gerd Luedemann, *The Resurrection of Jesus: History, Experience, Theology*, trans. John Bowden (Minneapolis: Fortress Press, 1994).

2. *New Testament Apocrypha*, ed. Edgar Hennecke and Wilhelm Schneemelcher, English translation ed. R. McL. Wilson (Philadelphia: Westminster Press, 1963–1964), 1:185-86.

3. Stephen J. Patterson, *The God of Jesus: The Historical Jesus and the Search for Meaning* (Harrisburg, Pa: Trinity Press International, 1998), 218-23.

4. Schüssler Fiorenza, *Jesus: Miriam's Child, Sophia's Prophet: Critical Issues in Feminist Christology* (New York: Continuum, 1994), 111-19, 125.

5. Gary R. Habermas and Antony G. N. Flew, *Did Jesus Rise from the Dead? The Resurrection Debate*, ed. Terry L. Miethe (San Francisco: Harper & Row, 1987); John Shelby Spong, *Resurrection: Myth or Reality? A Bishop's Search for the Origins of Christianity* (San Francisco:

HarperSanFrancisco, 1994); Gerd Luedemann, *What Really Happened to Jesus: A Historical Approach to the Resurrection*, trans. John Bowden (Westminster/John Knox Press, 1995).

6. Rudolf Bultmann, *New Testament & Mythology and Other Basic Writings*, trans. and ed. Schubert M. Ogden (Philadelphia: Fortress Press, 1984).

7. Wolfhart Pannenberg, *Jesus—God and Man*, trans. Lewis L. Wilkins and Duane A. Priebe, 2nd ed. (Philadelphia: Westminster Press, 1977).

8. Ronald F. Hock, *The Infancy Gospels of James and Thomas* (Santa Rosa, Calif.: Polebridge Press, 1995), 15.

9. Raymond E. Brown, *The Birth of the Messiah: A Commentary on the Infancy Narratives in the Gospels of Matthew and Luke*, rev. ed. The Anchor Bible Reference Library (New York: Doubleday, 1993); Richard A. Horsley, *The Liberation of Christmas: The Infancy Narratives in Social Context* (New York: Crossroad, 1989).

10. M. Eugene Boring, "The 'Third Quest' and the Apostolic Faith," in *Gospel Interpretation: Narrative-Critical and Social-Scientific Approaches*, ed. Jack Dean Kingsbury (Harrisburg, Pa.: Trinity International Press, 1997), 239.

11. Geza Vermes, *Jesus the Jew: A Historian's Reading of the Gospels* (London: William Collins Sons, 1973), 213-22.

12. Jane Schaberg, *The Illegitimacy of Jesus: A Feminist Theological Interpretation of the Infancy Narratives* (New York: Crossroad, 1990); and John Shelby Spong, *Born of a Woman: A Bishop Rethinks the Birth of Jesus* (San Francisco: HarperSanFrancisco, 1992).

Chapter 8: Titles of Honor

1. For a recent overview of ancient Jewish messianism and how expected eschatological figures were referred to, especially in the Dead Sea Scrolls, see John J. Collins, *The Scepter and the Star: The Messiahs of the Dead Sea Scrolls and Other Ancient Literature*, The Anchor Bible Reference Library (New York: Doubleday, 1995); and *Judaisms and Their Messiahs at the Turn of the Christian Era*, ed. Jacob Neusner, William S. Green, and Ernest Frerichs (Cambridge: Cambridge University Press, 1987). Older studies that approach the subject of honorific titles from the standpoint of New Testament Christology include: Ferdinand Hahn, *The Titles of Jesus in Christology: Their History in Early Christianity*, trans. Harold Knight and George Ogg (Cleveland: World Publishing Company, 1969); and Reginald H. Fuller, *The Foundations of New Testament Christology* (New York: Charles Scribner's Sons, 1965).

2. Hans Conzelmann, *Jesus*, trans. J. Raymond Lord (Philadelphia: Fortress Press, 1973).

3. Geza Vermes, *Jesus the Jew: A Historian's Reading of the Gospels* (London: William Collins Sons, 1973), 177-91.

4. Douglas R. A. Hare, *The Son of Man Tradition* (Minneapolis: Fortress Press, 1990), 280-82.

5. N. T. Wright, *Jesus and the Victory of God* (Minneapolis: Fortress Press, 1996), especially 360-7; 512-19; 574-76.

Chapter 9: Kingdom Preaching (Eschatology)

1. For additional reading on the topic of the kingdom of God that involves a survey of the many interpretations over the past century, see Norman Perrin, *The*

Kingdom of God in the Teaching of Jesus, New Testament Library (Philadelphia: Westminster Press, 1963); George Eldon Ladd, *Jesus and the Kingdom* (New York: Harper & Row, 1964).

2. Norman Perrin, *Jesus and the Language of the Kingdom: Symbol and Metaphor in New Testament Interpretation* (Philadelphia: Fortress Press, 1976).

3. For example: Stephen J. Patterson, *The God of Jesus: The Historical Jesus and the Search for Meaning* (Harrisburg, Pa: Trinity Press International, 1998).

4. See the discussion about the adoption of this phrase for the Scholars Version (SV), in *The Complete Gospels: Annotated Scholars Version*, rev. ed., ed. Robert J. Miller (Santa Rosa, Calif.: Polebridge Press, 1994), 12.

5. Elisabeth Schüssler Fiorenza, *Jesus: Miriam's Child, Sophia's Prophet: Critical Issues in Feminist Christology* (New York: Continuum, 1994), 93.

6. Shirley Jackson Case, *Jesus: A New Biography* (Chicago: University of Chicago Press, 1927), 244, n. 1.

7. For example: Edgar J. Goodspeed, *A Life of Jesus* (New York: Harper & Brothers, 1950).

8. An important forerunner of Schweitzer was Johannes Weiss, whose work on Jesus first appeared in German in 1892: *Jesus' Proclamation of the Kingdom of God*, trans. and ed. Richard H. Hiers and D. Larrimore Holland, Lives of Jesus Series (Philadelphia: Fortress Press, 1971). Hiers himself interpreted Jesus' kingdom message in terms of a futuristic eschatology: *The Historical Jesus and the Kingdom of God: Present and Future in the Message and Ministry of Jesus* (Gainesville: University of Florida Press, 1973), and *Jesus and the Future: Unresolved Questions for Eschatology* (Atlanta: John Knox Press, 1981).

9. In his 1985 monograph, *Jesus and Judaism* (Philadelphia: Fortress Press), Sanders repeatedly acknowledged his appreciation for the earlier work of Ben F. Meyer, *The Aims of Jesus* (London: SCM Press, 1979).

10. Marcus J. Borg, "A Temperate Case for a Non-Eschatological Jesus," *Foundations & Facets Forum* 2 (September 1986): 81-102. Reprinted in his *Jesus in Contemporary Scholarship* (Valley Forge, Pa.: Trinity Press International, 1994), 47-68.

11. For Crossan's discussion of the difference between apocalyptic and sapiential eschatology, see his *Historical Jesus: The Life of a Mediterranean Jewish Peasant* (San Francisco: HarperSanFrancisco, 1991), 287-92.

12. For this interpretation of the parable of the mustard seed, Crossan (*Historical Jesus*, 277) acknowledges agreement with Bernard Brandon Scott, *Hear Then the Parable: A Commentary on the Parables of Jesus* (Minneapolis: Fortress Press, 1989), 386-87.

13. Robert W. Funk, *Honest to Jesus: Jesus for a New Millennium* (San Francisco: HarperSanFrancisco, 1996), 168.

14. Dennis C. Duling uses the phrase "atemporal kingdom" in his article "Kingdom of God, Kingdom of Heaven," in *The Anchor Bible Dictionary*, 4:64.

Chapter 10: Torah Teaching (Ethics)

1. Pheme Perkins, *Love Commands in the New Testament* (New York: Paulist Press, 1982); and Victor Paul Furnish, *The Love Command in the New Testament* (Nashville: Abingdon Press, 1972).

2. A. E. Harvey, *Strenuous Commands: The Ethic of Jesus* (Philadelphia: Trinity Press International, 1990).

3. For additional reading on the topic of the ethics of Jesus as interpreted by Albrecht Ritschl and Johannes Weiss, Adolf von Harnack and Albert Schweitzer, C. H. Dodd, Rudolf Bultmann, and Amos Wilder, see Richard H. Hiers, *Jesus and Ethics: Four Interpretations* (Philadelphia: Westminster Press, 1968); and Ben Wiebe, *Messianic Ethics: Jesus' Proclamation of the Kingdom of God and the Church in Response* (Waterloo, Ontario: Herald Press, 1992), 25-54.

4. Geza Vermes, *The Religion of Jesus the Jew* (Minneapolis: Fortress Press, 1993), 11-45.

5. Marcus J. Borg, *Jesus: A New Vision* (San Francisco: HarperSanFrancisco, 1987), 97-116.

Chapter 11: Parables

1. See, for example: Robert H. Stein, *The Method and Message of Jesus' Teachings*, rev. ed. (Philadelphia: Westminster Press, 1994), 45-47.

2. Adolf Jülicher, *Die Gleichnisreden Jesus [The Parables of Jesus]*, 2 vols. (Tübingen: J. C. B. Mohr, 1888, 1899). Not available in English translation.

3. Ibid., 2:596.

4. C. H. Dodd, *The Parables of the Kingdom*, rev. ed. (London: James Nisbet, 1961).

5. Joachim Jeremias, *The Parables of Jesus*, rev. ed., trans. S. H. Hooke (New York: Charles Scribner's Sons, 1963).

6. Ibid., 21.

7. Ibid., 205.

8. Dan O. Via, *The Parables: Their Literary and Existential Dimension* (Philadelphia: Fortress Press, 1967).

9. John Dominic Crossan, *In Parables: The Challenge of the Historical Jesus* (New York: Harper & Row, 1973).

10. Ibid., 64.

11. Ibid., 66.

12. Robert W. Funk, *Parables and Presence: Forms of the New Testament Tradition* (Philadelphia: Fortress Press, 1982), 29-34.

13. Robert W. Funk, *Honest to Jesus: Jesus for a New Millennium* (San Francisco: HarperSanFrancisco, 1996), 170.

14. Including Mary Ann Tolbert, *Perspectives on the Parables: An Approach to Multiple Interpretations* (Philadelphia: Fortress Press, 1979); Charles W. Hedrick, *Parables as Poetic Fictions: The Creative Voice of Jesus* (Peabody, Mass.: Hendrickson Publishers, 1994); and Bernard Brandon Scott, *Hear Then the Parable* (Minneapolis: Fortress Press, 1989).

15. John Dominic Crossan, *In Fragments: The Aphorisms of Jesus* (San Francisco: Harper & Row, 1983).

Chapter 12: Miracles

1. For a historical overview of the issue of miracles that relies heavily on excerpts from the writings of representative interpreters, see Ernst Keller and Marie-Luise Keller, *Miracles in Dispute: A Continuing Debate*, trans. Margaret Kohl (Philadelphia: Fortress Press, 1969).

2. The texts of most non-Christian miracle stories commented on here may be found in *Documents for the Study of the Gospels*, rev. ed., ed. David R. Cartlidge and David L. Dungan (Minneapolis: Fortress Press, 1994).

3. Thomas Jefferson, *The Jefferson Bible: The Life and Morals of Jesus of Nazareth* (Boston: Beacon Press, 1989).

4. David Smith, *The Days of His Flesh: The Earthly Life of Our Lord and Saviour Jesus Christ* (1905; reprint, Grand Rapids: Baker Book House, 1976), 105-9.

5. David Friedrich Strauss, *Life of Jesus Critically Examined*, ed. Peter C. Hodgson, trans. George Eliot, Lives of Jesus Series (Philadelphia: Fortress Press, 1972), 507-19.

6. Rudolf Bultmann, *Jesus and the Word*, trans. Louise Pettibone Smith and Erminie Huntress Lantero (New York: Charles Scribner's Sons, 1934, 1958), 172-79.

7. See Bultmann's essay "New Testament Mythology," in *New Testament & Mythology and Other Basic Writings*, trans. and ed. Schubert M. Ogden (Philadelphia: Fortress Press, 1984), 1-43.

8. Rudolf Bultmann, *This World and the Beyond: Marburg Sermons*, trans. Harold Knight (New York: Charles Scribner's Sons, 1960), 155-66.

9. Graham H. Twelftree, *Jesus the Exorcist: A Contribution to the Study of the Historical Jesus* (Peabody, Mass.: Hendrickson Publisher, 1993).

10. Stevan L. Davies, *Jesus the Healer: Possession, Trance, and the Origins of Christianity* (New York: Continuum, 1995).

11. Reginald H. Fuller, *Interpreting the Miracles* (Philadelphia: Westminster Press, 1963).

12. John P. Meier, *A Marginal Jew: Rethinking the Historical Jesus*, 2 vols. (New York: Doubleday, 1991, 1994), 2:509-1038 passim.

13. Robert W. Funk and The Jesus Seminar, *The Acts of Jesus: The Search for the Authentic Deeds of Jesus* (San Francisco: HarperSanFrancisco, 1998), passim.

Chapter 13: Arrest, Trial, and Crucifixion

1. Marion L. Soards, "The Question of a PreMarcan Passion Narrative," appendix to *The Death of the Messiah: From Gethsemane to the Grave*, by Raymond E. Brown, 2 vols., The Anchor Bible Reference Library (New York: Doubleday, 1994), 2:1492-524.

2. Brown, *Death of the Messiah*, 1:4-35.

3. John Dominic Crossan, *The Cross That Spoke: The Origins of the Passion Narrative* (San Francisco: Harper & Row, 1988), 16-30.

4. John Dominic Crossan, *Who Killed Jesus? Exposing the Roots of Anti-Semitism in the Gospel Story of the Death of Jesus* (San Francisco: HarperSanFrancisco, 1995), 1-13.

5. Brown, *Death of the Messiah*, 1:13-24.

6. Josephus, *Antiquities of the Jews*, XVIII. iii. 1-2; iv. 1-2; and *The Jewish War*, II. ix. 2-3. The works of Josephus are available in the Loeb Classical Library (Cambridge: Harvard University Press).

7. See: W. Barnes Tatum, "The Christian Origins of Anti-Semitism," *The Fourth R* 8 (May-August 1995): 15-17; *Anti-Semitism and Early Christianity: Issues of Polemic and Faith*, ed. Craig A. Evans and Donald A. Hagner (Minneapolis: Fortress Press, 1993); and John G. Gager, *The Origins of Anti-Semitism: Attitudes Toward Judaism in Pagan and Christian Antiquity* (New York-Oxford: Oxford University Press, 1985).

8. Joachim Jeremias, *The Eucharistic Words of Jesus*, trans. Norman Perrin (New York: Charles Scribner's Sons, 1966), 14-37.

9. Shirley Jackson Case, *Jesus: A New Biography* (Chicago: University of Chicago Press, 1927), 282-86.

10. Brown, *Death of the Messiah*, 2:1373.

11. Crossan, *Who Killed Jesus?* 100.

12. C. H. Dodd, *Founder of Christianity* (New York: Macmillan, 1970), 153.

13. Eugen Ruckstuhl, *Chronology of the Last Days of Jesus: A Critical Study*, trans. Victor J. Drapela (New York: Desclee, 1965), 135-40.

14. Günther Bornkamm, *Jesus of Nazareth*, trans. Irene McLuskey and Fraser McLuskey with James M. Robinson (New York: Harper & Brothers, 1960), 160.

15. Haim Cohn, *The Trial and Death of Jesus* (New York: Harper & Row, 1971), especially 114-38.

16. Brown, *Death of the Messiah*, 1:557-60, 858-61.

17. N. T. Wright, *Jesus and the Victory of God* (Minneapolis: Fortress Press, 1996), 547-52.

18. Paul Winter, *On the Trial of Jesus* (Berlin: Walter de Gruyter, 1961).

19. William R. Wilson, *The Execution of Jesus: A Judicial, Literary, and Historical Investigation* (New York: Charles Scribner's Sons, 1970).

20. Crossan, *Who Killed Jesus?* 117.

21. Bornkamm, *Jesus of Nazareth*, 160.

22. Eduard Schweizer, *The Lord's Supper According to the New Testament*, trans. James M. Davis, Facet Books (Philadelphia: Fortress Press, 1967), 10-17.

23. *The United Methodist Hymnal* (Nashville: The United Methodist Publishing House, 1989), 10.

Selected Bibliography

In addition to the works listed in the footnotes and in this selected bibliography, students should consult the many articles on topics related to the Gospels and Jesus in the six-volume *Anchor Bible Dictionary*. This bibliography does not contain the titles of those historical reconstructions of Jesus summarized and analyzed in chapter 6 of this book.

Introduction: Who Is Jesus?

Pelikan, Jaroslav. *Jesus Through the Centuries: His Place in the History of Culture.* New Haven: Yale University Press, 1985.

Tatum, W. Barnes. *Jesus at the Movies: A Guide to the First Hundred Years.* Santa Rosa, Calif.: Polebridge Press, 1997.

Chapter 1: Gospel Origins

Burridge, R. A. *What Are the Gospels? A Comparison with Graeco-Roman Biography.* Cambridge: Cambridge University Press, 1992.

Kloppenborg, John S. *The Formation of Q: Trajectories in Ancient Wisdom Collections.* Philadelphia: Fortress Press, 1987.

Koester, Helmut. *Ancient Christian Gospels: Their History and Development.* Philadelphia: Trinity Press International, 1990.

Mack, Burton L. *Who Wrote the New Testament? The Making of the Christian Myth.* San Francisco: HarperSanFrancisco, 1989.

Talbert, Charles H. *What Is a Gospel? The Genre of the Canonical Gospels.* Philadelphia: Fortress Press, 1977.

Chapter 2: Gospel Criticism

Elliott, John H. *What Is Social-Scientific Criticism?* Guides to Biblical Scholarship. Minneapolis: Fortress Press, 1993.

Kingsbury, Jack Dean, ed. *Gospel Interpretation: Narrative-Critical & Social-Scientific Approaches.* Harrisburg, Pa.: Trinity International Press, 1997.

Malina, Bruce J., and Richard L. Rohrbaugh. *Social-Science Commentary on the Synoptic Gospels.* Minneapolis: Fortress Press, 1992.

Perrin, Norman. *What Is Redaction Criticism?* Guides to Biblical Scholarship. Philadelphia: Fortress Press, 1969.

Powell, Mark Allan. *What Is Narrative Criticism?* Guides to Biblical Scholarship. Minneapolis: Fortress Press, 1990.

Sanders, E. P., and Margaret Davies. *Studying the Synoptic Gospels.* Philadelphia: Trinity Press International, 1989.

Smith, D. Moody. *John Among the Gospels: The Relationship in Twentieth-Century Research.* Minneapolis: Fortress Press, 1992.

Chapter 3: Gospel Portrayals

Cameron, Ron, ed. *The Other Gospels: Non-Canonical Gospel Texts.* Philadelphia: Westminster Press, 1982.

Ehrman, Bart D. *The New Testament and Other Early Christian Literature.* New York-Oxford: Oxford University Press, 1998.

Fredriksen, Paula. *From Jesus to Christ: The Origins of the New Testament Images of Jesus.* New Haven: Yale University Press, 1988.

Kloppenborg, John S., et al. *Q Thomas Reader.* Sonoma, Calif.: Polebridge Press, 1990.

Miller, Robert J., ed. *The Complete Gospels: Annotated Scholars Version.* Rev. ed. Santa Rosa, Calif.: Polebridge Press, 1994.

Reddish, Mitchell G. *An Introduction to the Gospels.* Nashville: Abingdon Press, 1997.

Robinson, James M., ed. *The Nag Hammadi Library in English.* 4th ed. New York: E. J. Brill, 1996.

Chapter 4: Historical Problem

Funk, Robert W. *Honest to Jesus: Jesus for a New Millennium.* San Francisco: HarperSanFrancisco, 1996.

Johnson, Luke Timothy. *The Real Jesus: The Misguided Quest for the Historical Jesus and the Truth of the Traditional Gospels.* San Francisco: HarperSanFrancisco, 1996.

Käsemann, Ernst. "The Problem of the Historical Jesus." In *Essays on New Testament Themes.* Translated by W. J. Montague. Studies in Biblical Theology. London: SCM Press, 1964.

Meier, John P. *A Marginal Jew: Rethinking the Historical Jesus.* 2 vols. New York: Doubleday, 1991, 1994.

Chapter 5: Historical Search

Funk, Robert W. and The Jesus Seminar. *The Acts of Jesus.* San Francisco: HarperSanFrancisco, 1998.

Funk, Robert W., Roy W. Hoover, and The Jesus Seminar. *The Five Gospels: The Search for the Authentic Words of Jesus.* New York: Macmillan, 1993.

Robinson, James M. *A New Quest of the Historical Jesus.* Studies in Biblical Theology. London: SCM Press, 1959.

Rousseau, John J., and Rami Arav. *Jesus and His World: An Archaeological and Cultural Dictionary.* Minneapolis: Fortress Press, 1995.

Schweitzer, Albert. *The Quest of the Historical Jesus.* Translated by W. Montgomery. New York: Macmillan, 1968.

Theissen, Gerd, and Annette Merz. *The Historical Jesus: A Comprehensive Guide.* Translated by John Bowden. Minneapolis: Fortress Press, 1998.

Chapter 6: Historical Portrayals

Borg, Marcus J. *Jesus in Contemporary Scholarship*. Valley Forge, Pa.: Trinity Press International, 1994.

—————, ed. *Jesus at 2000*. Boulder, Colo.: Westview Press, 1997.

Charlesworth, James H., and Walter P. Weaver, eds. *Images of Jesus Today*. Faith and Scholarship Colloquies 3. Florida Southern College. Valley Forge, Pa.: Trinity Press International, 1994.

Witherington III, Ben. *The Jesus Quest: The Third Search for the Jew of Nazareth*. Downers Grove, Ill.: InterVarsity Press, 1995.

Wright, N. T. *Who Was Jesus?* Grand Rapids: Eerdmans, 1992.

Chapter 7: Resurrection and Virgin Birth

Brown, Raymond E. *The Birth of the Messiah: A Commentary on the Infancy Narratives in the Gospels of Matthew and Luke*. Rev. ed. The Anchor Bible Reference Library. New York: Doubleday, 1993.

Luedemann, Gerd. *The Resurrection of Jesus: History, Experience, Theology*. Minneapolis: Fortress Press, 1994.

Perkins, Pheme. *Resurrection: New Testament Witness and Contemporary Reflection*. Garden City, N.Y.: Doubleday, 1984.

Jane Schaberg, *The Illegitimacy of Jesus: A Feminist Theological Interpretation of the Infancy Narratives*. New York: Crossroad, 1990.

Chapter 8: Titles of Honor

Collins, John J. *The Scepter and the Star: The Messiahs of the Dead Sea Scrolls and Other Ancient Literature*. The Anchor Bible Reference Library. New York: Doubleday, 1995.

Fuller, Reginald H. *The Foundations of New Testament Christology*. New York: Charles Scribner's Sons, 1965.

Hahn, Ferdinand. *The Titles of Jesus in Christology: Their History in Early Christianity*. Translated by Harold Knight and George Ogg. Cleveland: World Publishing Company, 1969.

Hare, Douglas R. A. *The Son of Man Tradition*. Minneapolis: Fortress Press, 1990.

Chapter 9: Kingdom Preaching (Eschatology)

Chilton, Bruce D., ed. *The Kingdom of God in the Teaching of Jesus*. Philadelphia: Fortress Press, 1984.

Perrin, Norman. *The Kingdom of God in the Teaching of Jesus*. New Testament Library. Philadelphia: Westminster Press, 1963.

—————. *Jesus and the Language of the Kingdom: Symbol and Metaphor in New Testament Interpretation*. Philadelphia: Fortress Press, 1976.

Ladd, George Eldon. *Jesus and the Kingdom*. New York: Harper & Row, 1964.

Chapter 10: Torah Teaching (Ethics)

Chilton, Bruce D., and J. I. H. McDonald. *Jesus and the Ethics of the Kingdom.* Grand Rapids: Eerdmans, 1987.

Harvey, A. E. *Strenuous Commands: The Ethic of Jesus.* Philadelphia: Trinity Press International, 1990.

Hiers, Richard H. *Jesus and Ethics: Four Interpretations.* Philadelphia: Westminster Press, 1968.

Perkins, Pheme. *Love Commands in the New Testament.* New York: Paulist Press, 1982.

Wiebe, Ben. *Messianic Ethics: Jesus' Proclamation of the Kingdom of God and the Church in Response.* Waterloo, Ontario: Herald Press, 1992.

Chapter 11: Parables

Crossan, John Dominic. *In Fragments: The Aphorisms of Jesus.* San Francisco: Harper and Row, 1983.

————. *In Parables: The Challenge of the Historical Jesus.* New York: Harper and Row, 1973.

Funk, Robert W., et al. *The Parables of Jesus: A Report of the Jesus Seminar.* Sonoma, Calif.: Polebridge Press, 1988.

Hedrick, Charles W. *Parables as Poetic Fictions: The Creative Voice of Jesus.* Peabody, Mass.: Hendrickson Publishers, 1994.

Scott, Bernard Brandon. *Hear Then the Parable: A Commentary on the Parables of Jesus.* Minneapolis: Fortress Press, 1989.

Chapter 12: Miracles

Davies, Stevan L. *Jesus the Healer: Possession, Trance, and the Origins of Christianity.* New York: Continuum, 1995.

Fuller, Reginald H. *Interpreting the Miracles.* Philadelphia: Westminster Press, 1963.

Twelftree, Graham, H. *Jesus the Exorcist: A Contribution to the Study of the Historical Jesus.* Peabody, Mass.: Hendrickson Publisher, 1993.

Chapter 13: Arrest, Trial, and Crucifixion

Brown, Raymond E. *The Death of the Messiah: From Gethsemane to the Grave.* 2 vols. The Anchor Bible Reference Library. New York: Doubleday, 1994.

Crossan, John Dominic. *Who Killed Jesus? Exposing the Roots of Anti-Semitism in the Gospel Story of the Death of Jesus.* San Francisco: HarperSanFrancisco, 1995.

Rivkin, Ellis. *What Crucified Jesus? Messianism, Pharisaism, and the Development of Christianity.* New York: UAHC Press, 1997.

Index